Stolen from
library of
"The John Stewarts"

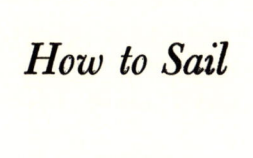

How to Sail

Books by Carl D. Lane

Nonfiction
HOW TO SAIL
THE BOATMAN'S MANUAL
BOATOWNER'S SHEET ANCHOR
AMERICAN PADDLE STEAMBOATS
WHAT YOU SHOULD KNOW ABOUT THE MERCHANT MARINE

Fiction
THE FLEET IN THE FOREST

How to Sail

A COMPLETE HANDBOOK OF THE ART
OF SAILING FOR THE NOVICE AND
THE OLD HAND *by Carl D. Lane*

ILLUSTRATED BY THE AUTHOR

NEW YORK
W · W · Norton & COMPANY · INC ·

COPYRIGHT 1947
BY CARL D. LANE

Book Design by John Woodlock

PRINTED IN THE UNITED STATES OF AMERICA
FOR THE PUBLISHERS BY THE VAIL-BALLOU PRESS

TO
MARIAN K.
Princess of the Blue

Contents

ONE	*The Boat*	13
TWO	*The Salty Vocabulary*	26
THREE	*Commissioning the Boat*	56
FOUR	*The Physical Phenomenon of Sailing*	79
FIVE	*The Sailing Positions*	86
SIX	*On the Wind*	94
SEVEN	*Off the Wind*	108
EIGHT	*Before the Wind*	115
NINE	*Making Sail*	133
TEN	*Carrying Sail*	152
ELEVEN	*Too Much Wind*	170
TWELVE	*Too Little Wind*	188
THIRTEEN	*Setting the Course*	199
FOURTEEN	*Mooring, Docking and Maneuvering*	226
FIFTEEN	*For Better or for Worse*	240
INDEX		263

Foreword

SINCE the publication and generous acceptance of *The Boatman's Manual* as a standard handbook and guide to small-boat seamanship, navigation, and operation, I have received many letters suggesting that I expand the material on sailing to meet the needs of the pure novice and the raw beginner. Of necessity that book assumed that the reader *could* sail. But seemingly there are many of us who love little ships but are completely at sea (or, rather, *not at sea*) in our knowledge and experience of their basic handling.

The writer with sufficient sailing experience to write about sailing for others sometimes assumes a knowledge of the fundamentals by the tyro which does not exist. It is so easy to forget that thrilling, terrifying moment when our first boat gathered the unseen power of the wind in her white sails and charged off to a freedom henceforth to know no curb but the trembling hand on tiller and sheet. Yes, they are long-ago days for many of us who sail and write. Yet each year thousands of young men and young women heed the call of blue water and must face that awful moment —the first sail.

It is my earnest wish that this book, which I promise shall start at the very beginning, will make that first moment the successful commencement of a long and lusty lifetime of sailing. We shall face the plain fact that many of us do not understand plain sailing. So the utter novice shall have his simplest question answered and explained and diagrammed to his full satisfaction. Old hands will find many hints and guides to perfect their own sailing habits and techniques. Even those auxiliary skippers who never hoist their nylon sails on their chromium tracks may find here the challenge to shut down their noisy bang-bang engines and join the ocean queens which move under free wind alone.

I have known of would-be sailors who sailed but once because their first attempt resulted in the disaster and shame of wrecking or dismasting or in damage to surrounding property. If this book keeps such beginners in the sport and launches them upon a happy voyage toward capable boat ownership and command, its presentation will have been justified. But there are many others—the first boatowners, the young skipper graduating to his next dream ship, the crew-guest of other skippers, the auxiliary owner, the charterer and day renter—who, I hope, will find this book of benefit and inspiration.

We shall remain strictly upon the subject of *How to Sail*. We shall touch upon the elementals of seamanship, piloting, boat maintenance, and the myriad allied arts of the owner-skipper, of course—but only enough to enable the reader to care for and protect his craft upon initial ownership. For full and detailed treatment of the complicated subjects of navigation, boat operation, handling and maintenance, marlin-spike seamanship, signalling, cruising, safety at sea, nautical etiquette and many related subjects, reference should be made to *The Boatman's Manual*. Indeed, that guide, plus this book, should enable the rankest amateur to master the subject of sailing sufficiently well to embark upon any inland or coastwise voyage without further inquiry into the mere academics of the art of wind sailing.

Our slope-headed forebears managed, with eminent success, to navigate their crude assemblies of log hulls and hide

Foreword

sails without benefit of the printed word or the drawn line. That they often met with disaster and discouragement must be admitted. That they also met with adventure and romance and the thrill of discovery is attested by the part the sailing vessel has played in the history of human civilization. That the application of the principles and practices of the ancient art of sailing, as presented in this book, will spare the reader disaster and discouragement and speedily qualify him as master of this strange beast of wood and canvas and mysterious parts so that he, too, may find adventure and romance and those pleasant far places in the blue, is the sincere wish of the author.

CARL D. LANE

Friendship, Maine, 1947

> In the diagrams appearing in this book, the symbol ⟵――――― is used to mean wind and its direction.

CHAPTER ONE

The Boat

A SAILBOAT is a boat with sails.

But a sailboat is also a cat, sloop, cutter, yawl, ketch, schooner or, as with some salty enthusiasts on the Chesapeake, a diminutive square-rigged brig or bark. A cat may be a cat-schooner and a schooner may be a schooner-cat as well as stays'l schooner, bald-headed, fisherman, tops'l, Marconi, wish-bone or bug-eye!

There are complications, you see, in this matter of blithely calling a sailboat simply a sailboat. A sailboat to a Maine man is a schooner, to a Cape Codder a cat, and to a Boulder Dam sailor a sloop. So the experienced skipper never says he owns or sails a sailboat—invariably he names it by rig, calling his boat a sloop, yawl, ketch, etc.

Now I assume that you are a newcomer to the ancient and honorable sport of taking free rides on the wind. Should you be asked about *your* boat, I hope that your answer will be:

"Yes, I have a sloop."

That's the correct and best answer, and this is why.

A sloop is the best possible type of boat in which to study and learn the art of sailing. When you can sail a sloop well, be it in calm or dirty weather, you can, with a little further experimenting, sail anything that's rigged fore-and-aft. The sloop rig, which is a simple two-sail rig, can alone give you that all-important sense of balance which is the basis of good sailing. The cat rig, or one-sail rig, does not do this. In the small-sized cat rig, like the dinghies and so-called "Frost-bites," you have a tender and sometimes treacherous little boat that challenges the talents of even experts. In the large catboat, you have an enormous single sail with a very long boom, an outfit which often requires unusual seamanship to keep it from rolling the boom into adjacent billows and from jibing. A single sail does not necessarily denote simplicity in handling. Single-sailed boats have their legitimate places in the sport, and in racing and cruising—but do your "learning" in a sloop-rigged boat.

I think that your first boat should definitely be of such size that you experience the "feel" of a large craft. Length is not the sole factor making up size; beam, model, rig and ballasting methods also contribute to size. For a centerboard boat, having only inside trimming ballast or none at all, I should recommend something of moderate beam, say a beam about one-third of the length, between the over-all lengths of 18 and 25 feet. For a boat with a ballasted fixed keel, the length can be somewhat less, say 17 to 21 feet. In such sizes you will not be buffeted around or stopped by the seas kicked up by an August breeze nor will you have a boat so large that it requires more than yourself to handle it under all conditions.

The question of centerboard or keelboat must be determined by local conditions. Shoal-water conditions indicate the centerboard craft, of course. In her you can sail with safety even over shallows; your centerboard will always tick bottom first and warn you and, being simply a blade in a sheath, it will slide into the sheath without damage to itself or the hull. In general shoal waters such as rivers, lakes, and salt bays call for centerboarders. Boats with fixed keels require generally deep waters. To strike bottom with a keel boat can be awkward and may even mean disaster by dis-

The Boat

masting or stoving in the hull or, in tidal waters, capsizing and filling. An excellent design is becoming more and more popular—this, known as keel-CB, has a fairly shallow ballasted keel through which a centerboard passes for use in windward sailing.

KEELS

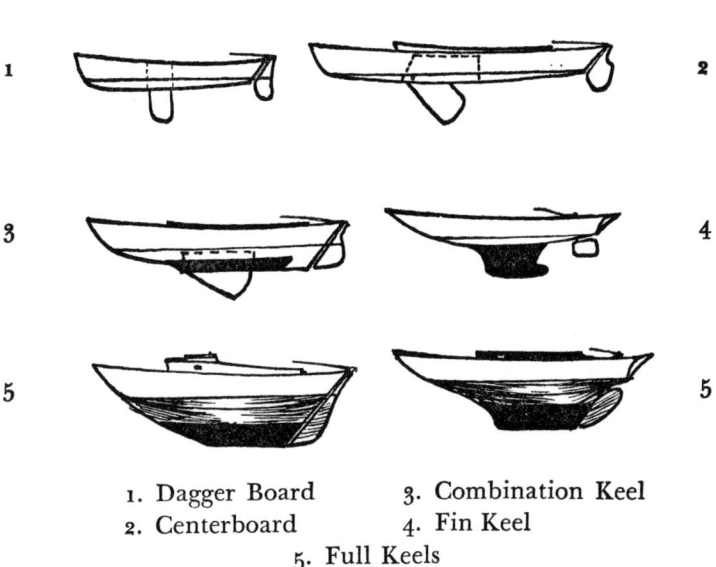

1. Dagger Board
2. Centerboard
3. Combination Keel
4. Fin Keel
5. Full Keels

While safety is an important consideration in selecting the ideal type of hull, there is also another factor to be considered. *Your sailing waters are always limited to those deeper than your own draft.* That sometimes closes many miles of pleasant waters to you, or keeps you from entering into a bay, inlet or cove protected by a shallow bar, if you carry a keel of fixed depth. I strongly recommend that you try to forecast the major uses of your boat. If you like to afternoon sail alongshore, or picnic on islands and beaches, take your family with you and *for the most part* avoid open waters, by all means get yourself a centerboard boat. Otherwise you will be like the motorist who remains on concrete highways, missing all the pleasant little shun-pikes that lead off to pleasant rural places. If you like to cruise, take long offshore slants from cape to cape, or if you are sure that you will never want to land for a beach roast or to clam or to camp, get a keelboat. If you like to race, the hull type will be dictated by the class you race in and the matter taken out of your hands.

SLOOPS

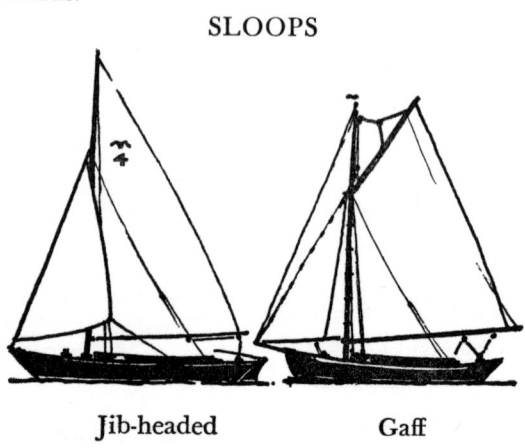

Jib-headed   Gaff

If you are not familiar with the waters you intend to sail, try this. On a Coast and Geodetic chart of the area, encircle with a red crayon all the areas, large and small, which show a depth less than two feet greater than the extreme fixed draft of your boat. The areas remaining are those which you can safely use; all else is closed to you. Only *you* know if this is sufficient "sea room" for your proposed life afloat. Then buy, build, or find the boat with the extreme fixed draft that will permit you to sail in the areas you wish to. I know that Gloucestermen depend upon the heel of the vessel to lighten draft in crossing certain shoals. Also I am aware that dinghies can be carried, but we shall discuss these advanced matters later.

The Boat

The sloop rig is of two types, gaff-headed or jib-headed. Before the days of modern flexible steel staying wire and light hollow masts, sloops universally carried a short heavy solid mast. To this were hung a boom and a gaff, also heavy, between which the designers tried to stretch the amount of canvas necessary to give the boat the speed desired. Forward was a jib, often very large. This was the traditional gaff-headed or bald rig. It is still correctly in use on certain ocean-going vessels and yachts. However, it is far from an efficient rig, especially on small boats, and has been almost universally supplanted by the jib-headed rig. Tradition says that this rig came to us by way of Bermuda, to which it probably came from the Mediterranean. It is sometimes called the Bermuda rig, but more often the jib-headed rig because the mainsail is pointed at the head like a common jib. By all means, try to make your first boat one with a modern jib-headed sail rig. She will not only sail and handle better and faster but she will retain her value for much longer than the old-fashioned gaff-headed rig.

As I look through boating journals depicting the post-war yachting scene, I do not see offered a single new small stock boat in the 20-foot class that has the gaff rig. In Chapter X we shall present the scientific advantages of the jib-headed rig. I assure you that they are convincing.

The type of boat—open, decked cabin, wide, narrow, clinker-built or carvel, keel or centerboard—is fairly indicated by observing the classes in use in the sailing waters about you. These are undoubtedly the best types for you to consider. They are in use for sound reasons—the chief one is that they are safe and ideally suitable for the waters they sail in, which should be reason enough for you to follow suit. Another reason is that your boat investment will be somewhat guaranteed by having your dollars in what your locale accepts as an ideal boat. A used Star boat is worth more in a Star boat area than in a region which races six-meters or Comets. Perhaps this means nothing to you. It always has to me—and, I suspect to most of us who sail little ships instead of paring down the mortgage.

In selecting this first boat you will need to exercise more care than necessary for any subsequent boat. All sailors advance through the yachting scene in a fairly regular pattern —they eventually want a bigger boat. Soon your own experience and matured judgment will be able to appraise a boat correctly on its apparent merits and potentialities. But for now, you will have to rely upon the advice of others and upon demonstrations—which, after all, won't mean very much to you since an experienced skipper is probably doing the advising and demonstrating. Beyond recommending size and rig, I would be foolish indeed to attempt to define your first boat. However, here are some thoughts to keep in mind as you study the beautiful folders of the builders or tramp the yacht storage yards in search of a used boat.

1. Avoid extreme racing machines, like the Star boats. Safety factors have been omitted in the design to achieve speed; they are strictly for experienced sailors and, in their hands, perfectly safe.

2. Class boats, especially if the class is popular and large, may be considered safe; the speed factors have been given secondary place. Such a class boat may race, of course, but it races like a saddle horse, not like Man-o'-War.

3. A boatbuilder, who shows evidence of having built and *sold* small stock or custom boats, especially if the boats have been designed by known naval architects, may be trusted to give you the boat he and his advertising says he will. The stock boat is more than wood and canvas. In it is a great deal of experience, of trial and error; all the bugs have been eliminated from the design. Beware, however, of the boat

The Boat

dealer who tries to sell you a boat of a type which you have decided is too large, too small or too deep. If you want a new 20-foot boat, consider only builders who offer this size or very close to it; turn a stony heart to the nice salesman who tries to sell you a 14-footer or a 26-footer. His firm probably does not make a 20-footer!

4. Beware of used boat bargains. Often they are bargains, but seldom to the novice owner. Usually they require repairs, refinishing, rerigging and/or recanvasing. Boatyards can do this work for you, of course, or possibly you can do it yourself, but you will always be surprised that the total cost is not very far from a brand new boat. Above all, do not be tempted by the obvious "wreck"—the nail-sick, rot-gutted, basket that, aided by shores, pitch, low price and that powerful springtime urge to get afloat, seems to be an ideal boat for you. Never, never, buy her! There is no quicker way to become discouraged in this game of sailing than to risk your life, your money and your precious vacation time in one of these antique craft. I hope that we shall someday have condemnation laws to control the sale and purchase of these criminally unsafe boats. Unfortunately, the inexperienced new sailor is often the purchaser, and, should he by chance survive the perils he has bought, will often quit yachting in complete disgust.

Of course, economic reasons sometimes permit only the purchase of a used boat. Insist that such a boat has a known history, good parentage and youth within reason and, by all means, even if you have read my *Boatowner's Sheet Anchor*,[1] which has material on the subject of used boats, their restoration, care and maintenance, have the boat passed upon by a professional marine surveyor, a naval architect, a disinterested boatbuilder or a nautical friend of long ex-

[1] Published by W. W. Norton & Company, New York, N.Y., 1941.

perience. The cost of such a survey, even if you have to give your nautical pal a half-case of rye, is cheap insurance on your investment.

5. Look with favor upon modern innovations of tried and true worth. Sheet and halyard winches, light modern patent anchors, wood preservative treatment, plywood correctly used, stainless steel standing rigging, linen or Nylon running rigging, streamlined and handy cleats, turnbuckles and chandlery—all these contribute toward the factors of safety, seaworthiness and handiness and leave your mind and your body free to concentrate on the important first consideration of learning to sail.

6. Do not, at this stage of the game, consent to try out boats representing new or radical design, construction methods, or materials. Stick to what has been proved a safe, popular type of boat, rig and design. You must have, if you are to learn plain sailing, a boat without kinks, hitches or special handling problems.

This boat will cost you a pretty penny, plus a few more pretty pennies. She will probably come to you "bare." Depending upon the uses to which you will put her, she will undoubtedly require some extras. For day sailing and racing, you will have to procure life preservers, charts, compass, foghorn, dock lines, fenders, bilge pump, deck mop, anchor and anchor warp, mooring gear, possibly lights, oars or outboard engine, a dinghy or tender, storm clothing, flags, sail covers, boat hook, name and port of hail. For cruising you will need in addition, mattresses, stove, cabin lights, and icebox, fresh-water storage facilities, a john, simple or complicated, possibly an engine and its auxiliary equipment, much of which is included in the stock cruising boat, of course. I remind you of these things only so that you realize that there will probably be costs beyond that of the boat it-

The Boat

self. If you have $1000 in the budget don't spend more than 90 per cent of it for the boat itself. The rest will be required to make the boat completely useful, safe, and secure while afloat.

Another cost to be reckoned is marine insurance, which, while not compulsory, is certainly advisable. Insurance firms and their agents, who are often yacht brokers or yacht yards, offer protection from loss by fire, theft, storm, collision and stranding, damage to rigging, spars or the boat itself, or to, or by, other boats. The cost for the few months the boat is in commission is not excessive. While in winter storage, only fire and possibly theft insurance (called Port Risk) are desirable. The storage yard *does not* carry insurance on your boat during storage unless so instructed by you.

There are no charges of any kind for anchorages and mooring places in public waters. However, there may be a charge for use of another's mooring gear, or for lying in a berth at a public or private wharf. Costs of mooring are about $2.00 to $5.00 a month, somewhat more if anchor-light service is included. Pier berths vary; for a 20-footer it should be not more than $5.00 to $8.00 a month. If you anchor off and use a tender, there may be a small charge for use of the dinghy float and storage of the tender itself. If available, launch service to and from your boat is at a fixed rate per trip, usually 10¢ to 25¢.

Hauling, winter storage and launching costs vary greatly. In rural areas, the small creek-side boatyard will take your boat on for these three services for about $1.00 a foot, overall length. This is for open storage, not in a shed. Double it for undercover storage and triple it for the charges of a city yacht yard. The foot charge does not include such items as scrubbing the bottom upon hauling, laying up the boat for winter, or covering it, pulling the spars, storing the equipment, sails or the dinghy and, of course, no spring painting.

Fire or other insurance is not included. Sometimes the yard insists that it do spring painting of the exterior, or at least the outside from keel to rail, and it expects you to buy paint, supplies and services from it. This is only fair; boatyards cannot make profits by storage alone. Of course, you may do work on the boat yourself; and your friends may, but the yard owner has a just gripe if you import hired labor to do work which the yard is equipped to do for you. Incidentally, the yard cannot be expected to provide free brokerage service. If your boat is for sale, and the yard operator sells it for you, you owe him a fee. Ten per cent is standard unless you have agreed upon another commission rate beforehand.

Here is a sample yard bill for a 22-foot keel sloop which was stored in a small yard in a small Long Island Sound village.

To BLANK YACHT YARD, Dr.

BLANKBURY, CONN.

Storage	Paints & Varnishes
Commissioning	Marine Supplies—rope
Fitting Out	American Engines
Repairs	Gas and Oil

June 1st, 1946

Winter storage, sloop Gull, 22 ft. @ 1.50 per ft.		$33.00
To Scrubbing bottom	4.00	
Pulling and storing spars	4.50	
Storing cushions, cabin equipment, sails	4.00	
Laying up boat for winter Labor & material	8.65	
Port Risk insurance ($800—9 mos.)	21.00	42.15

The Boat

To stepping spars & rigging, 1 new turnbuckle, 8 hand splices, marlin	12.30	
Painting—bottom, 2 cts. gr. anti-foul Topsides, 1 ct. semi-gloss Boottop, red Labor & material	27.75	
Dinghy storage, 9 mos. @ 50¢ per mo.	4.50	44.55
		$119.70

This probably represents the average yard bill of the owner who likes to tinker on his boat in the spring. Note that this owner evidently does his own painting above the rail, varnishes his spars and dinghy and commissions the boat himself. It amounts to about $5.00 a foot. This is a fair figure to use in forecasting the probable basic yearly cost of owning a small sailboat. An auxiliary or a cruising boat will run higher. It will double at least, if you have the yard do *all* the work, turning your boat over in June with canvas bent and ready to sail. About every third year you will need new running rigging, say (if you can turn in a splice yourself) at a cost of about $10.00 for a 20-footer, the wooding down and refinishing of bright work and possibly an extra fine job on the hull, including heavy sanding or scraping and minor caulking. *Every year* you will need to renew your mooring warp. Sometime, also, you will want new sails costing from 50 to 75 cents a square foot. Add it all together and a small sloop will cost you a yearly average of $7.50 a foot over a five-year period.

Of course, it is perfectly possible to haul the boat yourself if space is available, to buy $8.00 worth of paint and forget about insurance and bring these figures down to silver money. That's just what I'd do (and I have done it!) if high ownership costs threatened to keep me land-bound for the summer. However, if I could not afford to make my boat *safe,* I'd stay ashore. A boat painted with house paint and sails patched with the seat of junior's ski pants can give you a good deal of enjoyment, but if she needs a new plank that you can't afford—leave her!

Any yard will cheerfully give you an approximate estimate of costs before buying. If you must watch the dollars closely, I recommend that you seriously go into the question of costs. I'm sure that more sailors founder on the reef of financing than on those gentler ones inside the channel buoys.

I cannot recommend too strongly that the novice commence his sailing life under the burgee of a well-organized, active yacht or boat club. Essentially, and behind the smoke screen of country, dancing and social club atmosphere often so distressingly prominent, most yacht clubs are a strong group of boat-minded men. They have combined for fellowship and for community objectives of anchorages, harbor improvement, locker and storage space, launch, steward and boat services, etc., too expensive for the individual. The novice, especially the one who wishes to go in for racing, can greatly increase the challenge and adventure of boat ownership by becoming identified with a club. He will learn sailing more quickly and will take greater pride in learning it well. Boating will become a true hobby and pastime, even during the long winter when many clubs sponsor seamanship and navigation courses, fellowship affairs, winter dinghy racing and the like. Costs vary greatly. The best club that I belong to is in Maine and costs $10.00 a year; another, to which I seldom go, since I am only an associate member and cruise near it perhaps once a season, costs active members $100.00 a year.

The combined voices of American yacht and boat clubs, the U.S. Power Squadrons, class sailing clubs such as the

The Boat

Snipe, Star, Moth and dinghy clubs, each with its local chapters, the yacht racing associations, the Off Soundings and other cruising clubs, and the boating journals, are lusty and powerful. While yachting will always be a minority interest, by means of ready organization and the free interchange of information and ideals, it has in the past been responsible for much constructive legislation, for beneficial local and group actions and for a general improvement in all phases of the sport. Organized yachting can serve you well in many ways, and at times needs you. By all means, give serious consideration to becoming identified with a worthy club.

So much for "background stuff!" You want to talk and learn about *your* boat and how to sail her. Fair enough, skipper. Soon, in logical steps (there's a good deal of logic to sailing, you know) we'll get down to the dockside and take the tiller. But first we've got to become acquainted with our boat and that almost incomprehensible jargon used to describe her mysterious parts.

CHAPTER TWO

The Salty Vocabulary

I ASSURE you that this chapter is not included to obfuscate the simple art of sailing a boat. It is absolutely necessary to know the language of the sailorman; there is no way for author and reader to get together in this business of describing your boat and its parts or of teaching the maneuvers of sailing unless we converse in the jargon of the sea. I know of no substitute for the salty vocabulary.

The square-rigger seaman of long ago had to know what amounted to a foreign language to the landsman. Fortunately, we in yachting can communicate with each other with a comparatively small nautical vocabulary; no more than a hundred terms and expressions will serve us. Glossaries of old-time sea terms required a hundred printed pages! Ship terms with the flavor of Stockholm tar and the spice islands, like martingale, gluts, topgallant (which the sailorman made even more confusing by pronouncing it "t'garn"), brail, croj'k, vang, swifter, thrum and Davy Jones' Locker, are romantic and colorful. But they are not required as part of your vocabulary.

All small-boat sailors are not nautical linguists, of course. But those who make no attempt to learn the language are not only almost inarticulate among more seasoned skippers but are sometimes quite ridiculous. A tiller, we must remember, can never be a steering stick nor can a sheet be a sail or a cleat be a thingamajig or below be downstairs.

The Salty Vocabulary 27

Let's take a sailorman's look at your boat first.

Technically, a "boat" is a vessel capable of being carried on a ship, in davits or on skids. Practically, for you and me, a boat is a non-commercial vessel of any size or design permitted by our purses. We might place limits by defining a sailboat as any vessel moved by sails which is not square-rigged. If she is square-rigged, she is a ship, or so nearly so that nobody cares. Practically, also, as we have learned in Chapter I, your boat is also a catboat, sloop, cutter, yawl, ketch or schooner, or possibly one of a few archaic variations.

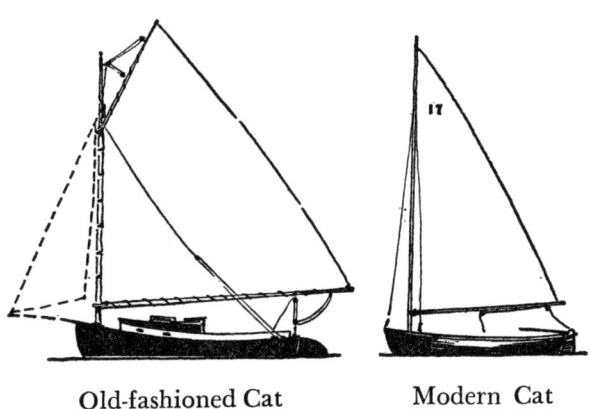

Old-fashioned Cat   Modern Cat

A cat-rigged boat is any boat, of any size and used for any purpose, which has one main or working sail. She is characterized by extreme beam and by having the mast set almost in the bows. Many dinghies are cat-rigged; but not many boats over 25 feet over-all length are so rigged. The addition of a temporary light-weather jib on a bowsprit does not make a catboat into a sloop. She's still a catboat—or, a better designation, is cat-rigged.

A sloop has two main or working sails—a mainsail (pronounced mains'l) and, forward of it, a smaller triangular sail called a jib. *Her mast is stepped about one-third of her total length aft of the stemhead.* No matter how these sails are flown—whether the mainsail is jib-headed or gaff-headed, whether the jib tack secured to the fore-deck, stemhead or a bowsprit, whether the jib overlaps the mainsail or not—she is still a sloop. She may even at times fly a jib topsail or a maintopsail if she is gaff-rigged or a spinnaker—she's still a sloop! A sloop is sometimes called a knockabout, a derivation from "knockabout sloop," and refers to a handy sail rig which is all inboard.

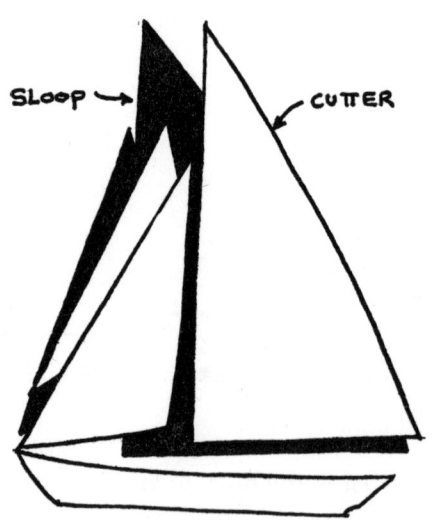

Relative Sail Plans of the Sloop and Cutter Rigs

A cutter is almost like a sloop. The difference is strictly in the sail rig, not the hull. *The mast of the cutter is somewhat more than one-third the length aft the stemhead;* seeming rather to be just slightly forward of the very fore-and-aft center of the hull, and she normally flies at least two headsails or jibs. In reality it is a *divided* sloop rig; the divisions

The Salty Vocabulary

of the total canvas spread being designed to afford various combinations of sails for varying wind and sea forces. Cutters sometimes fly three jibs, sometimes a maintopsail, often a spinnaker or overlapping reaching jib. But the mast location alone distinguishes her from a sloop.

For all practical purposes (you will be correct 90 per cent of the time if you so call them), the catboat has one sail, the sloop a jib and mainsail, and the cutter a mainsail and two or more jibs. You are unlikely to meet a genuine old-time cutter or sloop, nor will you see many lug, leg-o'-mutton or sprit rigs in American ports.

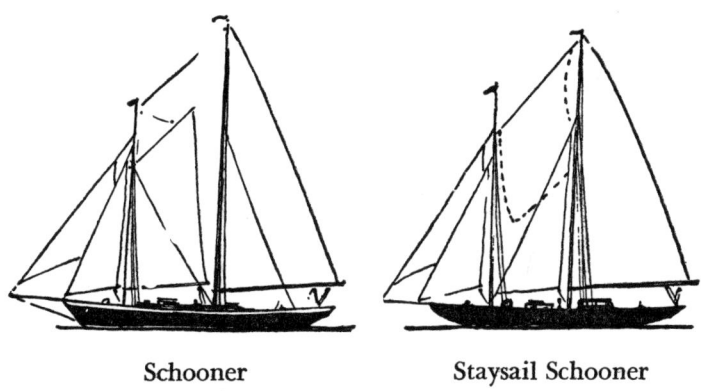

Schooner   Staysail Schooner

Two-masted fore-and-aft rigged boats represent an effort to reduce the individual sail areas to proportions which afford easy and safe handling for all sea and wind conditions. In general, the two-masted rig is able to combat strong wind by reducing sail or changing sail combinations instead of reefing. Another advantage is that the rig does not require excessively lofty masts with complicated staying systems.

The schooner is the basic two-masted rig. In yacht sizes she has two masts, the forward one or foremast *never* taller than the after one or mainmast. From these sticks she may fly the simplest schooner rig consisting of jib, foresail and mainsail or be "full-sailed" and fly up to four jibs, foresail and mainsail, foretopsail and maintopsail and a "fisherman" or staysail between the masts. No matter, she's always a schooner unless she's a ketch or yawl.

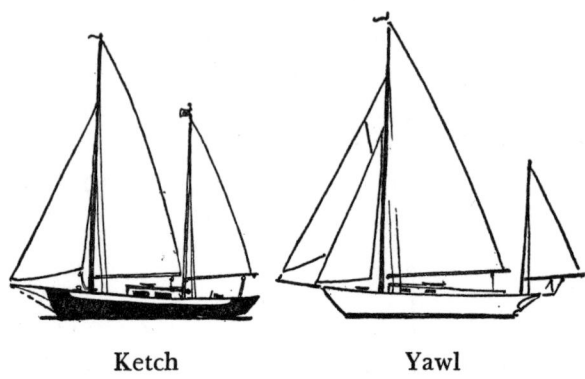

Ketch   Yawl

If she's a ketch, her foresail will be larger than the mainsail, and of course her foremast taller than her mainmast. Incidentally and to make it seem harder, the foremast and foresail will now be called the mainmast and mainsail and the former mainmast and mainsail will be called the mizzenmast and the sail the mizzen. The mizzenmast will be stepped *forward of the rudder head*. Positively! If not, she's a yawl!

A yawl is almost like a ketch in rig, although you will, if your eyes are keen, notice that the mizzen is smaller and the mainsail larger than these sails would be if the same boat was ketch-rigged. Positive identification is made by noting the location of the mizzenmast. In the yawl it is *always aft of the rudderhead,* sometimes indeed perched on the very after edge of the taffrail.

You are unlikely to move in boating circles comprising other types than these and it is pleasant, even if not necessary, to be able to identify the various types of rigs. Nautical

The Salty Vocabulary 31

language will require you to name these boats by rig; "sailboat" is not sufficient. For this reason alone have we wandered so far from your boat—that little craft which I sincerely hope is a sloop.

The years ahead will be challenging adventurous years; it will not require many seasons afloat and among sailormen to learn the nautical language as it applies to the more complicated types and rigs. As I promised, I shall use the simple sloop as the exemplar and demonstrator. Here she is—

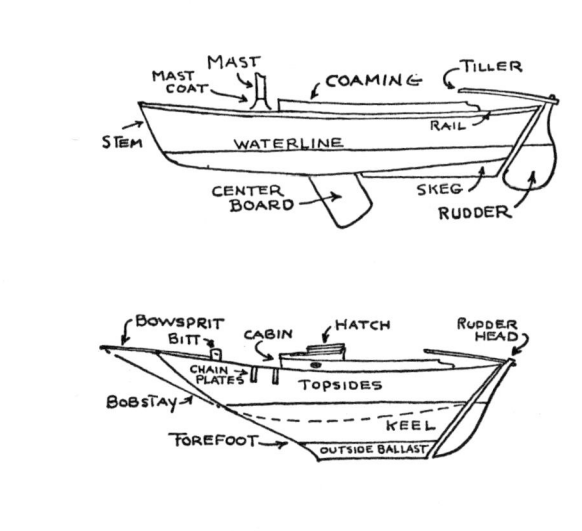

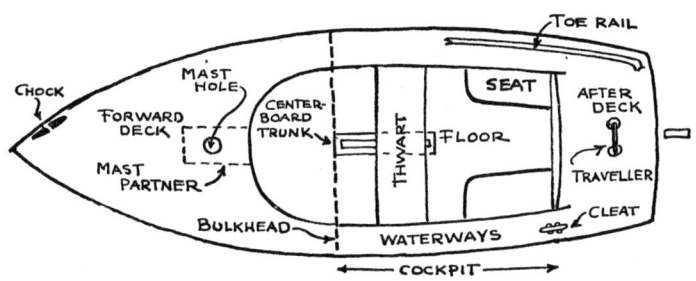

How to Sail

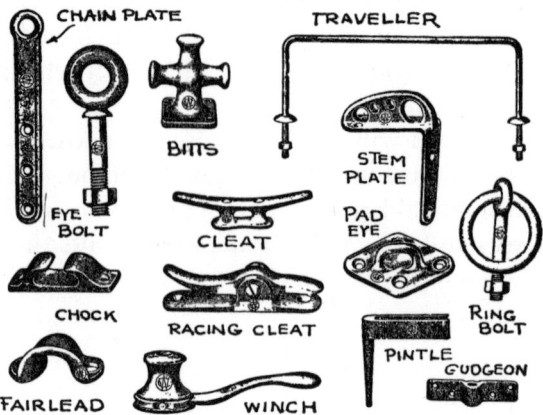

The drawings on pages 31 to 51, seem to do the job of getting acquainted with her parts better than might any words here. As you see, she is essentially hull, spars, rigging and sails, and a great many gadgets. Where the name of the part does not explain itself, I have made notes so that these drawings should give you not only the correct nautical nomenclature but the uses of the parts as well. The glossary of sea terms, which forms an appendix to this chapter, will further clarify the matter for you.

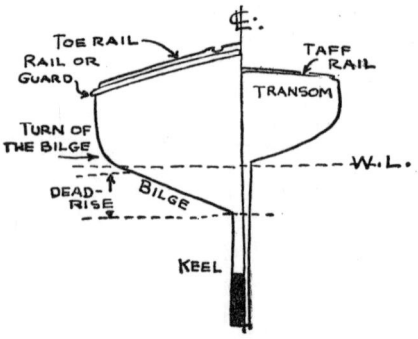

Conceivably, you can sail singlehanded and make a perfect job of it without knowing the correct name of one part,

The Salty Vocabulary

place or maneuver. However, when you sail with others, or direct your crew as commander, or order work done by the boatyard or go to buy ship chandlery, it behooves you to talk in the accepted tongue. And here's another reason—it's going to be a lot easier for me and a lot more fun for you if from now on we talk the same language. So I urge you to read, several times, the glossaries which follow.

GLOSSARY OF SELECTED SEA AND BOAT TERMS
PERTAINING TO BOAT PARTS

Apron.—A timber fitted abaft the stem to reinforce the stem and to give a sufficient surface on which to land the hood ends of the planks.

Awning.—A covering of canvas over a vessel's deck, or over a boat, to keep off sun and rain.

Ballast.—Heavy material, as iron, lead or stone, placed in the bottom of the hold to keep a vessel steady.

Beams.—Transverse supports running from side to side to support the deck.

Belaying pins.—Movable pins placed in pinrails on which to belay running gear.

Bilge.—The part of the bottom, on each side of the keel, on which the boat would rest if aground.

Bitts.—Upright timbers running through the deck on which hawsers and other lines are secured.

Blade, oar.—The broad flattened part of an oar as distinguished from the loom.

Boat falls.—Blocks and tackle with which the boats are hoisted aboard at davits.

Boat hook.—A pole with a blunt hook on the end to aid in landing operations or hauling alongside.

Boat plug.—A wooden or screwed metal plug fitted in the bottom planking of the boat at the lowest point to drain the bilges when boat is out of the water.

Bollard.—Upright post, half sunk in ground, used for mooring lines.

Booby hatch.—Small, raised hatchway.

Boom.—Spar used to extend foot of a fore-and-aft sail.

Bottom boards.—The fore-and-aft planks secured to the frames, or to floor beams, forming the floor of the boat, frequently removable.

Bowsprit.—Heavy spar rigged from bow of vessel carrying the headsails.

Breasthook.—A wood or metal knee fitted behind the stem structure.

Bull's-eye.—A small piece of stout wood with a hole in the center for a stay or rope to reeve through, without a sheave, and with a groove round it for the strap, which is usually of iron. Also a piece of thick glass inserted in the deck to let in light.

Bulwarks.—Woodwork around a vessel above decks.

Butt.—The end of a plank where it unites with the end of another.

Cable.—A large, strong rope, made fast to the anchor, by which the vessel is secured.

Capping.—The fore-and-aft finishing piece on top of the clamp and sheer strake, at the frame heads, in an open boat.

Carling.—A fore-and-aft beam at hatches.

Chock.—A metal casting used as a fair-lead for a mooring line or anchor chain.

Clamp.—A main longitudinal strengthening member under the deck in decked-over boats and at the gunwale in open boats.

Cleat.—A device on which to belay ropes.

Coamings.—Raised work around the hatches to prevent water from going into the hold, also used around cockpits.

The Salty Vocabulary

Coat.—Mast coat is a piece of canvas, tarred or painted, placed around a mast or bowsprit where it enters the deck, to keep out water.

Cockpit.—A compartment, usually for passengers, in an open boat.

Companion.—A wooden covering over the staircase to a cabin. *Companion ladder*, leading from the deck to below. *Companionway*, the staircase to the cabin.

Counter.—That part of a vessel between the bottom of the stern and the wing transom and buttock.

Deadeyes.—Bits of hardwood through which are rove lanyards to set up rigging.

Deadwood.—Timber built on top of the keel or shaft log at either end of the boat to afford a firm fastening for the frames and to connect the keel to the end timbers.

Dogvane.—A small vane, usually made of bunting, to show the direction of the wind.

Drag.—A sea anchor to keep the head of the vessel to the wind.

Eyebolt.—Bar with circular hole at end projecting from ship's deck on side.

Eyes of ship.—Extreme forepart of bows.

Fenders.—Portable wooden or rope sennit bumpers hung over the side during landings to protect the hull.

Fid.—Wooden block at heel of mast holding it in place. Wooden marlinspike.

Floors.—The transverse timbers which reinforce the frames and carry the strength athwartships across the keel.

Forefoot.—A piece of timber at the forward extremity of the keel, upon which the lower end of the stem rests.

Foremast.—The forward mast of a schooner.

Foresheets.—The portion of the boat forward of the foremost thwart.

Frames.—The ribs of the boat; curved timbers, frequently

steam-bent, secured to the keel and extending upward to the gunwale or deck.

Freeboard.—Part of vessel out of water.

Gaff.—Spar to which head of fore-and-aft sail is bent.

Garboard.—The lowest strake of outside planking next to the keel.

Grapnel.—A small multiple-fluked anchor used in dragging or grappling operations.

Gudgeons.—Small metal fittings, similar to eyebolts, secured to the sternpost of very small boats on which the rudder hangs. Used in place of the rudder hanger of larger boats.

Gunwale.—The upper rail of a boat or vessel.

Hanger, rudder.—A vertical strip of metal, secured to the sternpost, forming the traveler upon which the rudder braces are secured.

Hatch or *Hatchway.*—An opening in the deck to afford a passage up and down. The coverings over these openings are called hatches.

Hawsehole.—The hole in the bows through which the anchor cable runs.

Head.—Prow of a vessel. Also the upper end of a mast, called the masthead.

Heel.—The after part of the keel. The lower end of the mast or boom. Also, the lower end of the sternpost.

Helm.—The machinery by which a vessel is steered, including the rudder, tiller, wheel, etc. The tiller itself.

Helm port.—The hole in the counter through which the rudderhead passes.

Hoisting pads.—Metal fittings inside the boat often attached to the keel to take the hoisting slings or hoisting pads.

Horn timber.—The after deadwood (often called *counter timber*) fastening the shaft log and transom knee together.

Hounds.—Projections near the masthead serving as shoulders for rigging splices to rest upon.

The Salty Vocabulary

Jaws.—Inner ends of gaffs and booms partly encircling the mast.

Jib boom.—Boom rigged to bowsprit to which tack of jib is secured.

Jigger.—After mast on a ketch or yawl; small tackle used for tautening sheets, halliards, etc.

Jury mast.—Temporary mast rigged to replace one lost.

Keel.—Lowest and chief timber in a vessel, running its entire length.

Keel stop.—A small metal fitting on the keel, at the after end, to act as a stop in locating the boat in a fore-and-aft position on the keel rest when stowing the boat in the cradle.

Keelsons.—Fore-and-aft structural timbers either above or outboard of the keel.

Knee.—A shaped timber for connecting construction members installed at an angle to each other. Some knees are sawn from straight-grained wood, while in other cases the grain follows the natural bend of the tree at a limb or root.

Leather.—The portion of an oar which rests in the rowlock. This is sometimes covered with canvas, but is usually covered with leather.

Leeboard.—A board fitted to the side of a flat-bottomed craft, to prevent its drifting to leeward.

Loom.—Rounded portion of an oar between the blade and handle.

Life lines.—Ropes carried along yards, booms, etc., or at any part of the vessel to hold on by.

Locker.—Chest or box for stowing things. *Chain locker,* place for anchor chain; *bosun's locker,* storage place for small stuff used in ship's work.

Marlinspike.—Pointed instrument used in splicing rope.

Mast.—A spar set upright from the deck, to support rigging, yards, and sails.

Mizzenmast.—The aftermost mast of a ketch or yawl; the jigger.

Peak.—Forepeak is extreme forward part of the ship; afterpeak, extreme afterpart of ship; both below deck. Peak of a sail is the upper, outer edge.

Pillow.—Block supporting inboard end of bowsprit.

Pin.—Center axis of a block. *Belaying pin,* iron or wooden bar used for making lines fast. Belaying pins are set in pinrails.

Pinrail.—Oak ledges bolted inside the ship's rail to hold belaying pins.

Pintles.—Small straight pieces of metal secured to the rudder and fitting in the gudgeons on the sternpost of very small boats, thus supporting the rudder. Pintles and gudgeons are used in place of the rudder braces of larger boats.

Plank-sheer.—The outermost deck plank at the side.

Quarter-deck.—That part of the deck aft of the mainmast.

Ring.—The iron ring at the upper end of an anchor to which the cable is bent.

Ringbolt.—An eyebolt with a ring through the eye.

Risings.—The fore-and-aft stringers inside a boat, secured to the frames, on which the thwarts rest.

Rowlocks.—Forked pieces of metal in which the leathers of oars rest while pulling. *Sunken rowlocks* are those which are set down in the gunwale of the boat. *Swivel rowlocks* rotate, the shank of the rowlock fitting in a socket in the gunwale.

Rudder.—That by which a vessel or boat is steered, attached to the sternpost.

Scuppers.—Holes cut in the waterways for the water to run from the decks.

The Salty Vocabulary

Scuttle.—A hole cut in a vessel's deck as a hatchway. Also a hole cut in any part of a vessel. *To scuttle* is to cut or bore holes in a vessel to make her sink.

Scuttle butt.—Cask on deck containing drinking water.

Shank.—The main piece of an anchor; the stock is made fast at one end, and the arms at the other.

Sheer.—Sometimes called *sheer strake*. Top line of planking running fore and aft along a vessel's gunwale.

Sheer strake.—The uppermost strake of planking at the side following the line of sheer.

Sheet anchor.—The ship's largest anchor.

Spars.—General term for masts, yards, gaffs, booms.

Staff.—A pole or mast used to hoist flags upon.

Stanchions.—Upright pieces of timber placed along the sides of a vessel to support the bulwarks and rail. Also, any fixed, upright support.

Stem.—Extreme forward timber in a vessel.

Stem band.—A metal facing or cutwater fitted on the stempost.

Stern fast.—A stern painter for use in securing the stern of a boat.

Stern hook.—Same as breasthook, for stern on a double-ended boat.

Sternpost.—The principal vertical piece of timber at the after end of a boat, its lower end fastened to the keel or shaft log by a stern knee.

Stern sheets.—The space in the boat abaft the thwarts.

Step.—Block of wood at base of mast that holds its heel.

Strakes.—Continuous lines of fore-and-aft planking. Each line of planking is known as a strake.

Stretchers.—Athwartship, movable pieces against which the oarsmen brace their feet in pulling.

Stringers, bilge.—Longitudinal strengthening timbers inside the hull.

Swivel.—A long link of iron, used in chain cables, made so as to turn upon an axis intended to keep the turns out of a chain, also used in halyards, etc.

Taffrail.—The rail around a ship's stern.

Tholepin.—A pin fitted in the gunwale plank for use in place of a rowlock. Used with manila ring about five inches in diameter, called a *tholepin grommet*.

Throat.—The inner end of a gaff, where it widens and hollows in to fit the mast. Also, the hollow part of a knee. The throat brails, halyards, etc., are those that hoist or haul up the gaff or sail near the throat. Also, the angle where the arm of an anchor is joined to the shank.

Tiller.—A bar of wood or iron put into the head of the rudder, by which it is moved; the helm.

Timberheads.—The ends of the timbers that come above the deck. Used for belaying hawsers and large ropes.

Towing bitts (often called *towing posts*).—A vertical timber securely fastened for use in towing or mooring.

Transom.—The planking across the stern in a transomed boat.

Traveler.—A transverse rod on dials with a ring to which is fastened the sheet of a fore-and-aft sail.

Truck.—Uppermost end of the mast.

Vane.—Light bunting at masthead used as weather vane.

Washboard.—Light pieces of board placed above the gunwale of the boat.

Waterways.—Long pieces of timber running fore and aft on both sides, connecting the deck with the vessel's side. The scuppers run through them.

Yard.—A spar, tapering slightly toward the ends, and hung by the center to a mast, upon which to spread a square sail.

Yardarm.—The extremities of a yard.

Yawl.—A vessel with two masts, the small one aft of the rudderhead.

The Salty Vocabulary

Yoke.—Athwartship piece fitting over the rudderhead, by which the rudder is moved by yoke ropes when the tiller is not shipped.

PERTAINING TO RIGGING PARTS

Backstays.—Rigging running from the masthead to the vessel's side, slanting a little aft.

Bight.—The double part of a rope.

Block.—Land term is pulley. Round, boxlike, wooden or metal frame with a wheel within, through which ropes run.

Bobstays.—Standing rigging running from bowsprit to cutwater or stem.

Bush.—The centerpiece of a wooden sheave in a block.

Collar.—An eye in the end or bight of a shroud or stay, to go over the masthead.

Downhaul.—A line attached to the head of sails and used for hauling them down along mast or stay.

Eye.—Shroud or stay where it goes over mast.

Eye splice.—A splice to form loop at end of a rope or wire.

Fake.—One of the layers of a coil of rope.

Fall.—Ropes running through blocks by which a boat is hoisted.

Gooseneck.—A metal fitting at the end of a yard or boom, attaching it to the mast.

Grommet.—A ring formed of rope, by laying around a single strand. A hole, such as in a sail, with a metal ring inserted.

Gun-tackle purchase.—A purchase made by two single blocks.

Guy.—A rope attached to anything to steady it, and bear it one way or another in hoisting.

Halyards or *Halliards.*—Ropes or tackle used for hoisting and lowering yards, gaffs, and sails.

Hawser.—A large rope used for various purposes, as warping, for a spring, etc.

Lanyards.—Ropes rove through deadeyes for setting up rigging. Also a rope made fast to anything to secure it.

Luff tackle.—Purchase composed of a double and a single block.

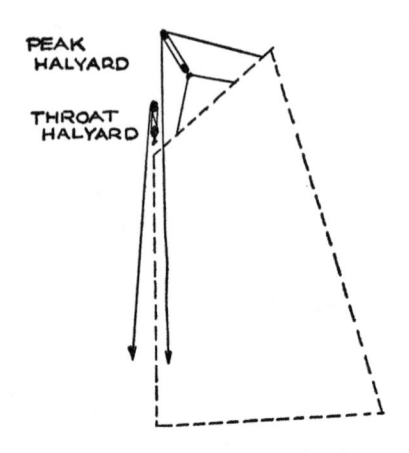

Marlin.—Fine two-stranded small stuff, usually tarred.

Monkey block.—A small single block strapped with a swivel.

Mouse.—To put a turn of rope yarn or spun yarn around the end of a hook and its standing part when it is hooked to anything, so as to prevent it from slipping out.

Nip.—A short turn in a rope.

Outhaul.—A rope used for hauling out the clew of a sail.

Painter.—Rope at bows of a small boat to make her fast.

Part.—To break. Also a section of rope when rove through a block, as the standing part and the running part.

Pennant or *Pendant.*—Narrow strip of bunting triangular in shape. Rope on which is hooked a purchase.

Preventer.—Additional stay or spar used to support one already in place.

The Salty Vocabulary

Purchase.—Extra power applied, usually by means of a block and tackle.

Ratlines.—Light lines running across the shrouds, thus forming a rope ladder.

Rigging.—The general term for all the ropes of a vessel. Also, the common term for the shrouds with their ratlines; as, the main rigging, mizzen rigging, etc.

Rope yarn.—A thread of hemp, or other stuff, of which a rope is made.

Runner.—A rope to increase the power of a tackle. It is rove through a single block, and a tackle is hooked to each end, or to one end, the other being fast.

Running rigging.—The ropes that reeve through blocks and are pulled and hauled, such as braces, halyards, etc.; in contrast to the standing rigging, the ends of which are securely seized; such as stays, shrouds, etc.

Seizings.—The fastenings of ropes that are seized together.

Sennit or *Sinnit.*—A braid, formed by plaiting rope yarns or spun yarns together.

Shackles.—Links in a chain cable fitted with a movable bolt so that the chain can be separated.

Shears.—Two or more spars, raised at angles or lashed together near their upper ends, used for lowering or hoisting heavy objects.

Sheave.—Wheel within a block.

Sheepshank.—Hitch used to shorten a rope without cutting it.

Shell.—Outside casing of a block.

Shrouds.—Standing rigging running from masthead to channel plates to support masts.

Sister block.—Block with two single sheaves, one above the other.

Small stuff.—Spun yarn, marlin, and other light rope.

Snatch block.—Single block made so that the sheave can be opened and the bight of a rope led through.

Spun yarn.—A rope formed by twisting together two or three rope yarns.

Standing rigging.—That part of a vessel's rigging which is made fast to the sides.

Stays.—Wire or ropes used to support masts, and leading from the head of one mast down to another, or to some part of the vessel. Those which lead forward are called *fore-and-aft stays,* and those which lead down to the vessel's sides, *backstays. In stays,* or *hove in stays,* a vessel when she is staying or going from one tack to another.

Strand.—Part of a rope composed of smaller bits.

Strap.—Rope or metal binding around a block.

Tackle.—A purchase; formed by a rope rove through one or more blocks.

Tail.—A rope spliced into the end of a block and used for making it fast to rigging or spars is called a tail block.

Tail tackle.—A watch tackle.

Toggle.—A pin placed through the bight or eye of a rope, block strap, or bolt to keep it in its place, or to put the bight or eye of another rope upon, securing them together.

Topping lift.—A lift used for topping up the end of a boom.

Triatic stay.—A stay of wire or rope secured to heads of the fore-and-aft mainmasts.

Vang.—Rope leading from a gaff to ship's side to steady the gaff.

Warp.—A warp is a rope used for warping. If the warp is bent to a kedge which is let go, and the vessel is hove ahead by the capstan or windlass, it is called kedging.

Watch tackle.—A small luff purchase with a short fall, the double block having a tail to it, and the single one a hook. Used about deck.

The Salty Vocabulary

Whip.—A purchase formed by a rope rove through a single block. To whip is to hoist by a whip. Also, to secure the end of a rope from fagging by seizing of twine.

PERTAINING TO SAILS

Battens.—Put upon rigging to keep it from chafing. Battens are often used on yachts on the leech of a mainsail or jib to make it set flat.

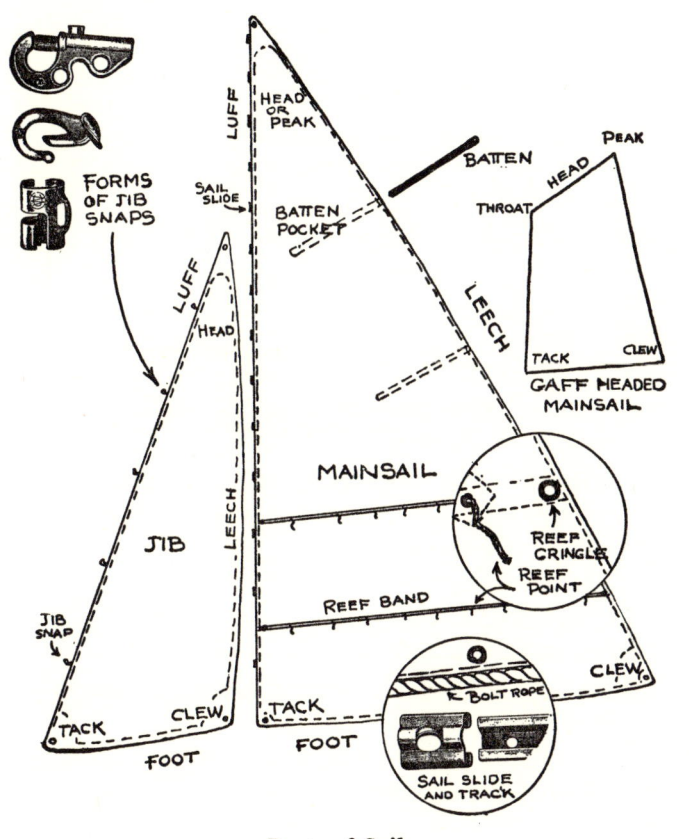

Parts of Sails

Boltrope.—Outer edge of sail to which canvas proper is sewed.

Bunting.—Thin woolen stuff of which flags are made.

Canvas.—Sailcloth; strength indicated by numbers 0 to 9.

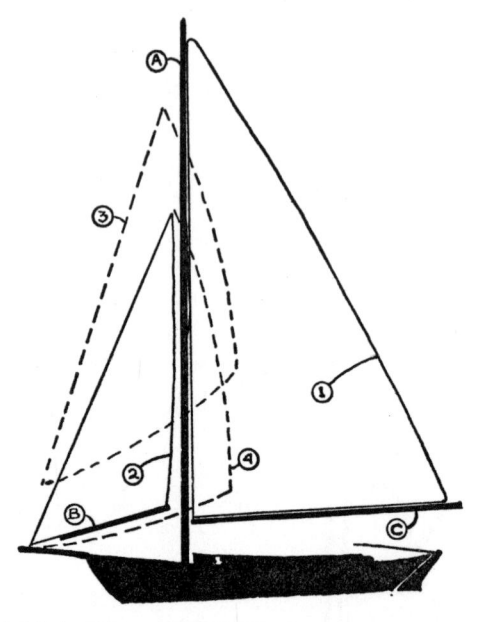

(A) Main Mast; (B) Jib Club; (C) Main Boom

(1) Mainsail; (2) Jib; (3) Jib Topsail; (4) Overlapping Jib

Clew.—The after corner of fore-and-aft sails or the lower corners of square sails.

Cringle.—Rope spliced into the boltrope of a sail to enclose iron ring or thimble.

Drop.—The depth of a sail, from head to foot, amidships.

Duck.—A kind of cloth, lighter than canvas, used for small sails.

The Salty Vocabulary

Earing.—A rope attached to the cringle, by which it is bent or reefed.

Foot.—The lower end of a mast or sail.

Gaff topsail.—Light fore-and-aft sail rigged to gaff.

Headsails.—All sails that set forward of the foremast.

Jib.—Chief headsail running on a stay to bowsprit or stemhead. Flying jib and outer jib run on other stays.

Lacing.—Rope used to lash a sail to a spar.

Leech or *Leach.*—The after edge of a fore-and-aft sail.

Leech line.—A rope used for hauling up the leech of a sail.

Main.—Principal mast or sail.

Point.—Reefpoints are small lines sewn in a sail with which to make it shorter or for shortening.

Reef band.—Extra width of canvas sewed in sail to support strain of reef points.

Reef tackle.—Small tackle used to stretch a reefed sail tightly to the boom.

Roach.—The curve of the leach in a fore-and-aft sail.

Sails.—Are of two kinds: *square sails,* which hang from yards, their foot lying across the line of the keel, as the course, topsail, etc.; and *fore-and-aft sails,* which set upon gaffs, booms, etc., their foot running with the line of the keel.

Sheet.—Lines used to keep the lower parts of sails spread. In fore-and-afters, to hold booms from swinging too far.

PERTAINING TO POSITION, SITUATION AND MANEUVERS

Aback.—The position of the sails when the wind presses their surface toward the mast, tending to force the vessel astern.

About.—To go on the opposite tack.

Adrift.—Broken from moorings or fasts.

Afloat.—Resting on the surface of the water.

Aground.—Touching the bottom.

Alee.—When the helm is in the opposite direction from that in which the wind blows.

All in the wind.—When all the sails are shaking.

Apeak.—When the vessel is hove taut so as to bring the vessel over her anchor.

Back.—To back a sail is to throw it aback. *To back and fill* is to alternately back and fill the sails.

Bare poles.—The condition of a vessel when she has no sail set.

Beams.—On the weather or lee beam, is in a direction to windward or leeward, at right angles with the keel. *On beam end,* the situation of a vessel when turned over so that her beams are inclined toward the vertical.

Bear.—To bear down upon a vessel is to approach her from the windward.

Beating.—Going toward the direction of the wind, by tacks.

Becalm.—To intercept the wind. A vessel to windward is said to becalm another. So one sail becalms another to leeward of it.

Board.—Course of a vessel on one tack. Sternboard, when a vessel is going astern. By the board, when a ship's masts fall over side.

Bring to.—Throwing a vessel up into the wind.

Broach to.—To swing a vessel running before the wind broadside to wind or at right angles to course. A most dangerous thing if the sea is heavy.

By the head.—When the head of a vessel is lower in the water than her stern. If her stern is lower, she is by the stern.

Chockablock.—When the lower block of a tackle is run close to the upper one, so that you can hoist no higher.

Clawing off.—To work off close-hauled from lee shore.

Close-hauled.—When a vessel is sailing as close to the wind as she will go.

The Salty Vocabulary

Close-reefed.—When all the reefs are taken in.

Cranky.—Vessel that rolls a great deal and cannot carry much sail.

Draw.—A sail draws when it is filled by the wind.

Drive.—To scud before a gale, or to drift in a current.

Even keel.—The position of a vessel when she is so trimmed that she rests evenly upon the water.

Flare.—Temporary blaze made, usually by sailing vessels being overtaken, to indicate ship's position. Also used in small boats to attract attention.

Flowing sheet.—When a vessel has the wind free, and the sheets are eased off.

Flush.—Level.

Forge.—To forge ahead, to shoot ahead, as, in coming to anchor, or when going in stays.

Foul.—The opposite of clear.

Founder.—When a vessel fills with water and sinks.

Free.—Running before the wind. *Free of water,* clear of water.

Full and by.—Sailing order meaning to keep the sails full yet to steer a course as close to the wind as possible.

Gybe or *Jibe.*—To change the position of the sails of a fore-and-aft vessel from one side to the other without going in stays (by the stern).

Haul.—Haul her wind, when a vessel comes up close upon the wind.

Heave to.—To put a vessel in the position of lying to.

Home.—The sheets of a sail are said to be home when the clews are hauled chock out to the sheave holes. An anchor comes home when it is loosened from the ground and hove in.

Irons.—When a ship misses stays in tacking and hangs in the wind she is in irons.

Labor.—A vessel is said to labor when she rolls or pitches heavily.

Leeway.—What a vessel loses by drifting to leeward.

Lie to or *Lay to.*—To stop progress of a vessel at sea either by counter-bracing the yards or by reducing sail so that she will make little or no headway, but will merely come to and fall off by the counteraction of the sails and helm.

List.—Inclination of a vessel to one side; heavy list to starboard means much tilted over to the right.

Luff.—To bring the ship closer to the wind.

Lurch.—Sudden rolling of a vessel.

Misstay.—To fail of going about from one tack to another.

Scud.—To drive before a gale with no sail or only enough to steady the vessel. Also, low, thin clouds that fly swiftly before the wind.

Sternboard.—Motion of vessel backward. Also called *sternway.*

Tack.—To put a ship about, so that from having the wind on one side it is brought around on the other by way of her head. The opposite of wearing. A vessel is on the starboard tack, or has her starboard tack on board, when she has the wind on her starboard side.

Trim.—The way a vessel floats. *Trimmed by the head* means with bows lower than they should be.

Weather roll.—The roll which a ship makes to windward.

Wing and wing.—The situation of a fore-and-aft vessel when she is going dead before the wind, with her foresail on one side and her mainsail on the other.

Yaw.—The motion of a vessel when she goes off her course.

The Salty Vocabulary

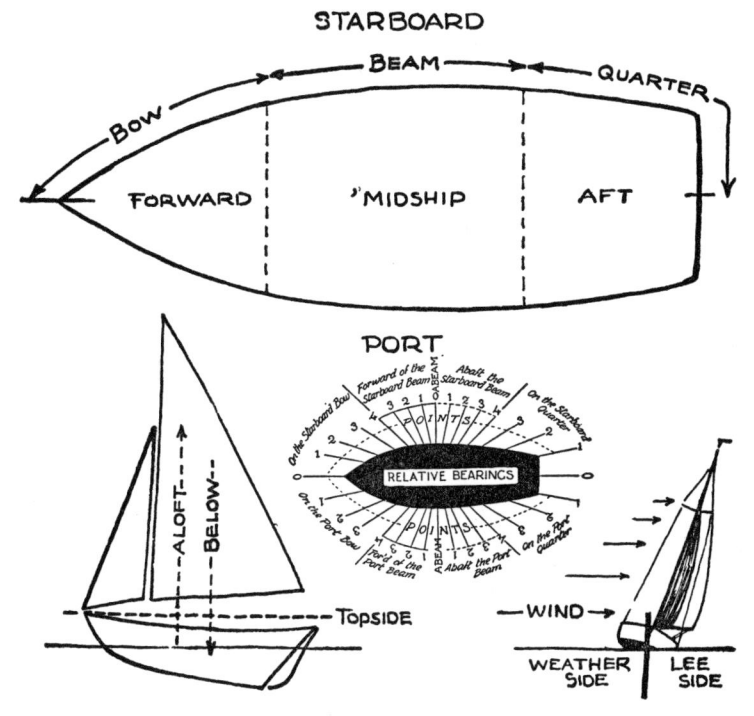

Place and Direction on Shipboard

PERTAINING TO DIRECTION

Abaft.—Toward the stern.
Abeam.—On the side of the vessel, amidships, or at right angles.
Aboard.—Within, on board the vessel.
Abreast.—Alongside of. Side by side.
Aft.—Near the stern.
Ahead.—In the direction of the vessel's bow. *Wind ahead* is from the direction toward which the vessel's head points.
Aloft.—Above the deck.

Amidships.—In the center of the vessel; either with reference to her length or to her breadth.

Astern.—In the direction of the stern. The opposite of ahead.

Athwart.—Across.

Athwartships.—Across the length of a vessel. The opposite to fore and aft.

Bearing.—The direction of an object from the person looking.

Bow.—Rounded part of a vessel forward.

Broadside.—Side of a vessel.

Fore.—Used to distinguish the forward part of a vessel, or things forward of amidships; as, foremast, forehatch. The opposite to aft or after.

Fore and aft.—Lengthwise with the vessel. The opposite of athwartships.

Forward.—In front of.

Landfall.—Making land.

Leading wind.—A fair wind. Applied to a wind abeam or quartering.

Lee.—The side opposite to that from which the wind blows; if a vessel has the wind on her starboard, that will be the weather side, and the port will be the lee side. A *lee shore* is the shore upon which the wind is blowing. Under the lee of anything is when you have that between you and the wind.

Leeward.—The lee side. In a direction opposite to that from which the wind blows, which is called windward. The opposite of lee is weather, and of leeward is windward.

Midships.—The timbers at the broadest part of the vessel.

Offing.—Distance from the shore.

Port.—Left side of vessel looking forward. A harbor. Also

The Salty Vocabulary

holes in vessel's side through which cargo is worked. *Bunkerport,* holes leading to the coal bunkers.

Quarter.—Side of vessel toward the stern; opposite of bow.

Sag.—To sag to leeward is to drift off bodily to leeward.

Starboard.—The right side of a vessel looking forward.

Stern.—After end of vessel. (Never say rear, back, or behind.)

Weather.—In the direction from which the wind blows. A ship carries a *weather helm* when she tends to come up into the wind. A *weather ship* is one that works well to windward, making but little leeway.

PERTAINING TO ORDERS AND ACTION
(NAUTICAL VERBS)

Avast.—To stop. "Avast heaving!"

Belay.—To make a rope fast; but not to hitch or tie it.

Bend.—To make fast. *Bend a sail* is to put it on a yard, gaff, or boom; *bend a cable,* make it fast to anchor.

Broach.—To open a cask or box.

Capsize.—Upset; overturn.

Careen.—Heave a vessel on her side.

Carry on.—To crack on all sail possible.

Coil.—To lay a rope up in a circle, with one turn or fake over another. A coil is a quantity of rope laid up in this manner.

Conning or *Cunning.*—Directing the helmsman in steering a vessel.

Douse.—To lower suddenly.

Fast.—Secured. All fast, make fast are common sea terms.

Flat.—A sail is said to be hauled flat when it is hauled down close.

Freshen.—When referring to ballast it means altering its

position; when referring to a rope it means to ease it so it cannot chafe.

Furl.—To roll a sail snugly on boom or yard.

Hail.—To speak or call to another vessel or to men in a different part of the ship.

Hand.—To hand a sail is to furl it. *Bear-a-hand,* make haste; *lend-a-hand,* assist; *hand-over-hand,* hauling rapidly on a rope, by putting one hand before the other, alternately.

Heave in stays.—To go about, tacking.

Luff.—To bring the ship closer to the wind.

Off and on.—To stand on different tacks toward and from the land.

Overhaul.—Applied to rigging it means to examine and repair. Applied to rope it means to keep it clear from running through the blocks. To overhaul a ship is to catch up with or overtake it.

Pay.—To pay off is to let vessel go away from the wind. To pay out a line is to let it run.

Ready about.—Order to stand by for tacking.

Reef.—To shorten sail.

Reeve.—To pass the end of a rope through a block.

Right.—To right the helm, is to put it amidships.

Round in.—To haul in on a rope.

Round up.—To haul up on a tackle.

Run.—By the run, to let go by the run is to let go altogether, instead of gradually.

Seize.—To fasten ropes together by turns of small stuff, to secure hooks, etc.

Serve.—To wind small stuff, or rope yarns, spun yarns, etc., around a rope to keep it from chafing. It is wound and hove around taut by a serving mallet.

Set.—To set up rigging is to tighten it.

Shore.—Prop.

Slack.—To slack away means to loosen gradually.

The Salty Vocabulary

Snub.—To check a rope suddenly.

Spill.—To shake wind out of sail by luffing.

Stay.—To tack a vessel, or to put her about, so that the wind, from being on one side, is brought upon the other, around the vessel's head. To stay a mast is to incline it forward or aft or to one side or the other, by the stays and backstays.

Steady.—To keep the helm as it is.

Strip.—Dismantle.

Surge.—To surge a rope or cable is to slack it up suddenly where it renders around a pin, or around the windlass or capstan.

Sway.—To hoist up.

Sweep.—To drag the bottom. Also, large oars used in small vessels.

Tail on.—To take hold of a rope and pull.

Trice.—To haul up by a rope.

Turn.—Half turn, round turn applied to rope means passing it about a pin. *Turn in,* stop work or go to bed; *turn out,* get up or get on the job.

Unbend.—To cast off, most frequently applied to sails.

Veer.—To pay out chain; also the wind veers when it changes against the compass (from westward to eastward); it shifts when it changes from eastward to westward.

Warp.—To move a vessel from one place to another by means of a rope made fast to some fixed object, or to a kedge.

Wear.—To turn a vessel around so that from having the wind on one side, the wind will be on the other side, carrying her stern around by the wind. In tacking the same result is produced by carrying a vessel's head around by the wind.

CHAPTER THREE

Commissioning the Boat

YOUR introduction to sailing will prosper best if your first boat is handed to you on a silver platter, completely and correctly rigged and equipped, sails bent, wind and tide just right, ready to sail away. It will prosper least (though I know of plenty of new skippers who have given the lie to this!) if you find yourself the owner of an old, perhaps battered, craft that needs repairs from keel to truck—and you must make these repairs yourself. But the ends emphatically justify the means in this case!

If you buy a new boat she will be delivered to you by railroad car or motor truck, unless, of course, you happen to live near the building yard. Her mast and boom will be unstepped, running and standing rigging neatly coiled and tagged and her sails stowed in a canvas bag ready to bend. There might even be a book of assembling instructions. Now, if you have bought this boat through a local agent of the builder, he will probably consider it his job to see your boat rigged and launched (at your cost, of course) and ready for you to take over. This is also true if you buy direct from the builder and take delivery at his yard. He'll usually swap the cost of loading your boat for shipment for launching cost and make no extra charge for rigging since he has to do it anyway.

However, if you are taking remote delivery direct and have no one to assist in putting this strange creature to-

Commissioning the Boat

gether, you have a few problems, fortunately none very serious.

First, you must transport the boat from the delivery point to the waterfront. A light centerboard boat can usually be handled by four to six men, a few rollers and a platform truck. A keelboat will require heavy hauling and rigging equipment. Let the boat remain in the cradle in which it arrives. By a series of rollers, numbering at least three, and made up of 2 or 2½-inch iron pipe and a tackle, you should have no trouble moving the boat onto a truck and later from truck to beach or launching ways. The sketches below suggest some rigs to handle boats of from 1 to 3 tons in the situations which might arise.

Remember *always* to maintain control over the load. Do

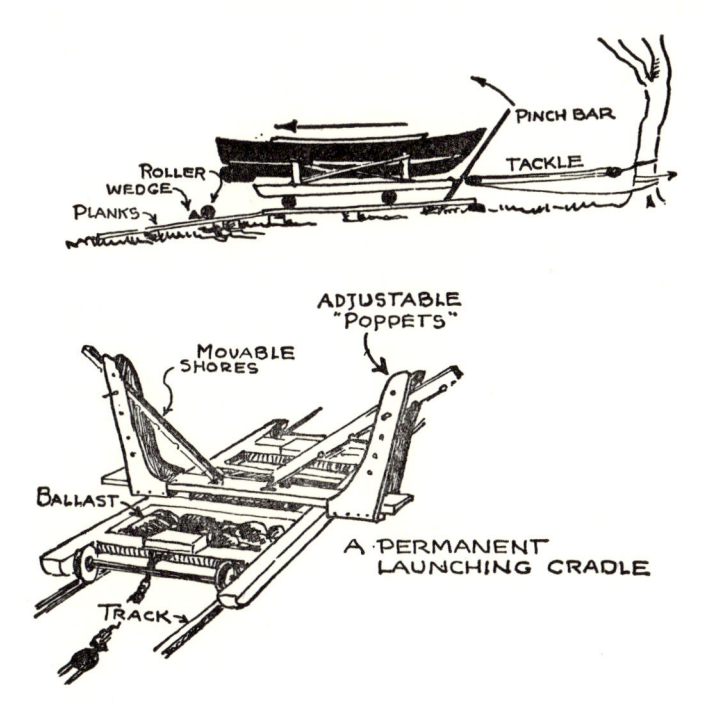

not attempt down-hill flying launches. Unless you have a very strong set of ways or track, you run the risk of capsizing your boat on dry land. Boats which capsize on land do not bounce; they stove in. Rather, set plank runners ahead on which the rollers run, and let the boat slowly, always under control, creep toward the water. Whether going up or down grade, secure the load by a good tackle. You can *haul up* by manpower or by a car or truck with considerable live or other weight over the rear wheels. You can *let down* by pinching the load forward with pinch or crow bars, always pushing against the preventer tackle which, of course, is tended by a man ready to snub the fall should gravity take charge.

While I do not recommend the practice, I have seen small boats launched by means of a stone boat and tractor. If the shore is reasonably smooth and the boat will not become subject to undue racking or jouncing, the method is probably practical. It is especially useful for launching in nontidal waters.

The reason we do not want our boats racked or jounced is simple enough. The new boat, having never been in the water, hasn't begun to attain her eventual structural strength. She attains this only after water has swelled the planks and they are gripped firmly, edge to edge. Unswelled, your boat can easily loose the cotton and compounds which now fill the seams. In fact, she may already have lost some of it on her way to you and you should make a careful check of all seams to see that they are filled and smooth. This applies to a planked boat only, of course. Plywood boats are built with watertight glue joints and plywood does not swell in the same sense that solid wood plank does. Metal and plastic boats, understandably, need no swelling to make them watertight.

If your boat is planked, she will leak, probably quite

Commissioning the Boat

badly, for several hours after she is afloat. Warm summer water, fresh or salt, will quickly swell the planks and so close the seams. It will require a longer time in the cold water of early spring. You can speed up the swelling process by, before launching, sloshing gallons of fairly hot fresh water into the bilges. If a seam appears to be quite widely opened because of dryness, smear ordinary brown soap into it before launching. It will squeeze out and soon wash away. Be wary of caulking and puttying. This seam was closed once and it will close again—but not if you have jammed it full of caulking. I once saw a boat which had been "caulked dead." An open garboard seam had been tamped full of oakum and when, in the water, this strake swelled it exerted such expansive pressure that it sheared off the bronze bolts which held the lead keel in place. In Maine, our quarrymen crack marble and granite by drilling a line of holes, driving wooden wedges into them and then wetting the wood. The mere swelling of the wood cracks the stone. Few boat fastenings can take that kind of swelling.

Under no circumstances attempt to sail your boat until she is completely tight. She simply is not strong enough to take the strains and stresses of carrying sail. Once tight, she's good for all season and probably will never again be as "dry" as when first launched.

If your boat does not tighten up in a reasonable time, say within a day, look for something that has brought blushes of shame to many men more experienced than you. Look for a small round hole, way down in the garboard near the keelson or inside plank keel. This is the drain scupper. It should have, driven in from the *outside,* a snug wooden plug.

The next job is to step the mast. Since they are often hollow and very light, you can handle many small-boat masts by hand from a wharf or dock. Heavier masts require a shear legs or the assistance of a fisherman equipped with a net or

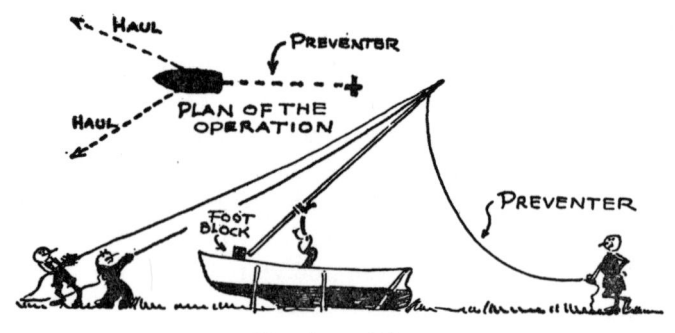

Footing a Mast

cargo boom. Most yacht and boatyards and many boat clubs have a standing shear legs available. Make the sling fast, using a timber, pipe or spar hitch, a trifle above the middle of the mast, stand the mast up and lower away. Guide the foot into the mast hole, through the partners and into the step in the keel or floors. Now, tap home the wooden mast wedges and set up the shrouds lightly. You are ready to rig.

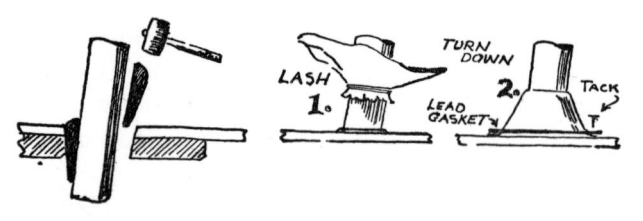

Wedging in the Mast   The Mast Coat

Of course, *before stepping the mast,* you rove the running rigging through the proper blocks, set and lightly seized the standing rigging on and to the hounds and the spreader arms and slipped the hawk in place. Perhaps you remembered, if you plan to race, to lash a small block and signal halyard aloft.

You now have a mast and a bundle of rigging looking quite like a wind-blown Maypole. The standing rigging is all

Commissioning the Boat

of wire. It should fit into place without any more effort than setting up the turnbuckles after you have secured the lower clevis to the proper chain plate or fitting. One or possibly two stays lead from the forward side of the mast to the stem fitting; the topmast stay forward and the lower stay (called the jibstay because the jib will later hank to it) directly aft of it. Probably these stays have no turnbuckles fitted. That's okay. Setting up on the shrouds will also set up the fore and jibstays. The shrouds (or side stays) secure to the fittings port and starboard of the mast, the upper shroud leading, by way of the spreader arm if you have one, to the forward fitting and the lower shroud leading directly to the after fitting. If you find an extra stay, it's probably the Swedestay or permanent backstay and leads to a fitting at the taffrail or on a short bumpkin aft. Jumper stays, which you might have, are rigged before setting the mast. As a rule these do not reach the deck.

Set this standing rigging up only hand-tight. Unless you race in the more delicate classes which use piano tuners to get the correct tension on their stays, be satisfied when your stays *look* straight and tight and are somewhat past the tension best described as sloppy. Too much tension can—and will!—warp your mast, set up an unpleasant vibration and, by a downward tension on the mast, open seams in the way of the mast step. Equalize tensions by sighting upward along the mast. It should be straight.

You may find two more wire stays, port and starboard, terminating in blocks or rope pennants. These are backstays, or runners. Their rope ends form a tackle, one end of which secures to a fitting in the waterways or thereabout, near amidships, and lead to a cleat near by. These are extra stays, used when sailing in strong breezes or jumpy seas and we shall learn more about them in later chapters.

Running rigging is of rope or of flexible wire and rope.

It is made up of both sheets and halyards. Halyards hoist and lower, giving vertical movement. Sheets pull in and out, giving horizontal movement. All halyards will lead from the deck to a block on the mast and down again to the deck.

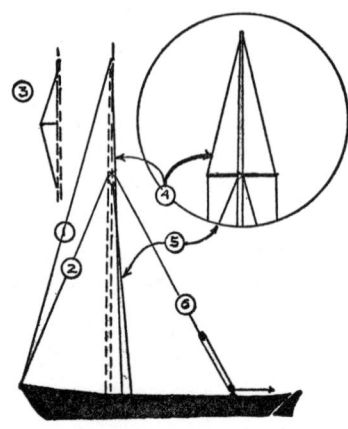

Standing Rigging

(1) Headstay; (2) Jibstay; (3) Jack Stay; (4) Upper Shroud; (5) Lower Shroud; (6) Backstay

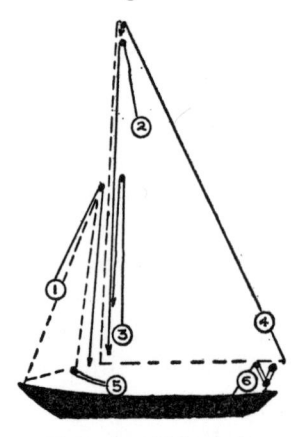

Running Rigging

(1) Jib Halyard; (2) Main Halyard; (3) Spinnaker Halyard; (4) Topping Lift; (5) Jibsheet; (6) Mainsheet

The forward halyard will be used to hoist the jib. There may also be halyards to hoist various light air sails such as a spinnaker, genoa and parachute. The after halyard will hoist the mainsail. If the rig is gaff-headed, the lower halyard will hoist the throat of the gaff and the upper halyard the peak of the gaff. You may find an odd rope leading downward from the masthead or near it. This is the topping lift, a semi-halyard, used to lift the boom under certain sailing conditions. There are several ways of belaying the topping lift, the most common being to a cleat on the boom. Halyards may be a single rope part or be tackles. They belay to cleats provided in the vicinity of the mast or at forward end of the cockpit.

Commissioning the Boat

There are permanent sheets for each of the two working sails, jib and mainsail. The jibsheet (which you may find rigged as two separate sheets, one serving the port side and the other the starboard) leads aft and belays near the helmsman's position. The mainsheet controls the "swing" of the main boom and, through a tackle, belays handy to the helm. Types of tackles, leads and methods of belaying are legion. The arrangement of blocks on boom and deck will give you the clue as to the builder's method of rigging the sheet tackles of your particular boat. Spinnaker sheets are not standing; they are attached to the spinnaker itself or coiled and stowed separately.

This is about the rigging of the average small sailor. If it is a centerboarder the boat will come with the centerboard pennant rigged. This is usually a wire and rope tackle, belaying to a cleat on the centerboard case. You might find the boat equipped with sheet or halyard winches. Nothing can set up running rigging better and with less man-hauling than a proper winch in the proper place. See that winches run freely, that the handles are firmly attached or securely racked nearby, and have a spare handle in the bosun's stores.

In rigging even the brand new boat, you will probably have to use a few knots, hitches, splices and rope endings. This is as good a place as any to present knots for the beginner. There is a book on the market which shows 15,000 knots, bends, hitches and splices. Fortunately, we can get along on our little hooker with about a dozen all told. Since I was eight, I have sailed Skidoo boats to Bangor River schooners, and have gotten along with about twenty knots and hitches. Not many compared to the clipper sailor who had to know a hundred or more. But, like him, I try to know *all* my knots well, where and when to use them, how to cast them, blow high blow low, in freezing weather, with my teeth, behind my back, in darkness and under water.

Learn those which you need to serve you; learn them well and I doubt that you ever miss the other 14,980!

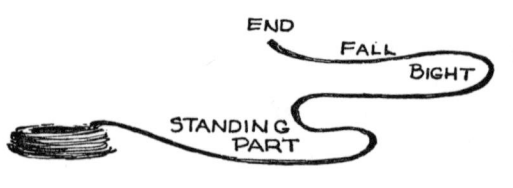

Parts of a Rope

I recommend these as basic for the beginner:

KNOTS

The Square Knot.—For joining two ropes *of the same diameter*, the square knot takes first place. Not the least of its good features is that it casts off very easily by merely backing the two bights away from each other. If you seize the two ends to their standing parts, you have an absolutely

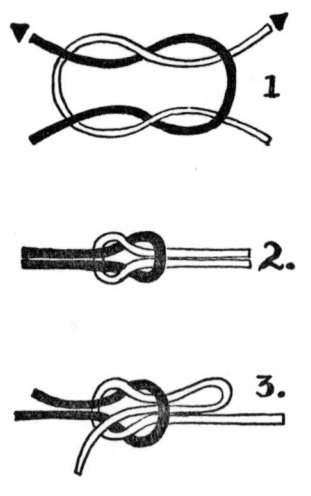

1. Forming the Square Knot 2. The Square Knot Set
3. The Slippery Square

Commissioning the Boat 65

trustworthy knot. The rule for casting is simple; right over left, then left over right, and pull taut. This is also the reef knot, which you will need often for stopping down your furled sails and for shortening sail by reefing. For these uses practice tying the knot "slippery," that is, with one fall tucked as a bight. By pulling on this bight, the knot quickly falls apart—and that's a particular blessing in wet or icy weather and at night. Beware that your knot is neither a granny nor a false reef knot. Both are guilty of the greatest sins known to the marlinspike seaman; they jam and slip. Follow the sketches *exactly*.

The Bowline

The Bowline.—This is the knot to use wherever you need an eye or loop in the end of a line, such as you might want in securing to a ring bolt, an anchor ring, a pile, or a rope of different diameter. It's non-slip, easy to cast off, and the knot you will probably use most. There are several ways of casting this knot but only one correct way for the sailor. Follow the sketches. These show the quickest way and seconds will many times count in your life afloat.

Figure of Eight.—This is a stopper knot. Its chief use on the small boat is to prevent a line from running through a block or fairlead.

Figure of Eight

HITCHES AND BENDS

The Clove Hitch.—This hitch is the basis of several useful knots. Sometimes it is cast about an object; sometimes, as in the round turn and two half-hitches, about its own standing part.

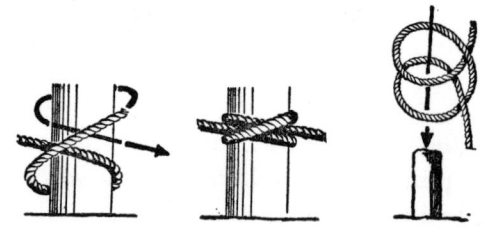

The Clove Hitch

This is the way to cast it: Hold the line in both hands, palms up. The left end will be the fall, the right end the standing part. Now, twist both hands clockwise half over, pass the right end (standing part) under the left end (fall) forming a bight or loop with the standing part underneath. Throw this over the pile or spar or, for practice, over your shoe or a broomstick held vertical between the knees. Then

Commissioning the Boat

do exactly the same thing again, i.e., throw another bight atop the first with the standing part (right) underneath. Pull taut and you have the completed hitch.

It will hold well providing the tension or strain on either part is steady, not surging, as it might be if used to secure a bow line from boat to a pile. It will hold only if the strain is at approximately right angles to the spar or pile. This is *not* the hitch to use for towing a spar or stepping a mast by means of a sheer legs and tackle.

The useful and well-known combinations of two half hitches is simply the clove hitch cast around its own standing part. Two or three round turns and a clove hitch as above serves as an anchor hitch, mooring hitch, small-boat painter knot and in many other places. If the hitch is to be left unattended and always when used as an anchor hitch, seize down the fall to the standing part with a length of small stuff. Then you have a completely reliable foolproof hitch.

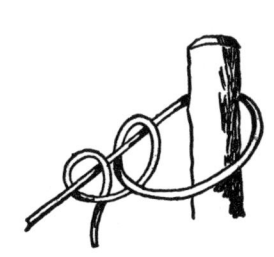

Round Turn and
Two Half Hitches

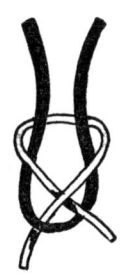

Sheet Bend

Sheet Bend.—This is an old-time hitch used for tying together two ropes of different diameter. The smaller rope should be woven around the bight made by the larger rope as shown in the sketches. Seize the falls to the standing part if there is any question of it not holding.

SPLICES

The art of splicing is something like the art of skiing—you can or you can't. Probably your start has a good deal to do with your finish. In order to get the right start, I suggest that you do not read this chapter any further until you have equipped yourself with a fathom of three strand rope about one-half inch in diameter. Only then will "you see what I mean."

You can get by for years with two splices—the short splice and the eye splice. The long splice, which will run through a block, costs more in time than a new line for the average small boat; forget it, along with the flemish splice, the grommet splice, and the chain splice. These have been nothing but parlor tricks ever since square-rigger days, as far as the amateur rigger is concerned.

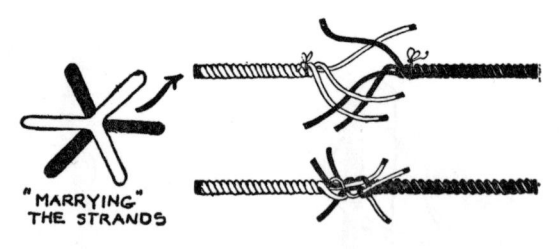

Steps in Forming the Short Splice

Short Splice.—The short splice is for joining two lines together permanently. It will *not* pass through a block or fairlead. I have made the sketch above as clear as I possibly could and I think it explains itself. The first step, after each end has been unlayed for a few inches is to "marry" the strands. From there on, starting with any strand that you wish on either side, just tuck the strand over, under and out. Then, follow around—over, under and out—pulling each tuck snugly into place. You can't fail to recognize the pattern after the first three tucks. Go around three times. Then do the same thing on the other end. The short splice is then structurally completed.

It will help to roll the splice underfoot or, if very heavy rope, to pound the strands into place with a wooden mallet. Then start tapering, which is simply the process of cutting out half the rope yarns of each strand and continuing for one tuck of each strand as you did before. Then halve the halved strands and go around again. This ought to be enough for rope up to three-quarters of an inch in diameter. For heavier rope, halve the remaining strand once for each additional half inch of diameter.

A marlinspike or fid will help a good deal in prying apart the strands of new or large rope. But you can easily open the strands of small line up to half an inch in diameter by twisting it *against* the lay of the rope. It helps very much, especially while you're learning, to whip the ends of each strand to prevent them from becoming frayed and unravelled as you do the tucking. Incidentally, the heart, which is the small center strand on which the three rope strands are layed should be cut away before you start. The heart is not for rope strength; it is for lubrication and is necessary to the rope maker in forming the rope.

The Eye Splice.—This splice is for forming a permanent loop or bight in a line. It is often formed over a metal thimble; the thimble being merely a protection against wear and chafing. You will find thimbles in use in many places on your boat, at the beckets of blocks, at pad eyes and at sister or snatch hooks.

You form the eye splice exactly as you formed the short splice. However, since you are working with but one end or fall, you unlay this for several inches longer than the splice you propose. Better whip the strand ends. Then form the bight of the size you require laying the fall where it begins to unlay against the standing part. If you are forming the splice over a thimble, tuck the thimble into the bight and snug up so that the rope lies completely in the channel of the thimble. The three unlayed strands will now lay flat and in

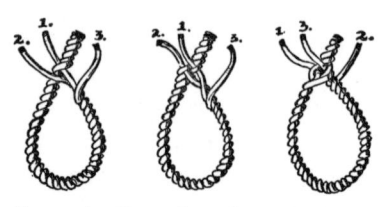

Steps in Forming the Eye Splice

a line—left strand, middle strand and right strand. Start with the middle strand—over, under and out, as with the short splice. Do the same with the left or right strand, and then the same with the remaining strand. The secret of success is in the start. Each strand should emerge from the rope at exactly the same point, with a strand of the standing part between them.

Continue as with the short splice, four times tucked for a good plain solid job; three times tucked and three times tapered and tucked for a fancy but solid job. Some folks might call it lubberly but I think it's perfectly good practice to varnish an eye splice. The little yarns will stay put better and you won't soon have cowtails surrounding the splice as the tucked strands back out under the stretch of work.

Knot and rope splicing are fascinating subjects. As time goes on, learn all you can about them. You might, when you own that schooner, find need for more than these few. But, I am sure, that except during complete rerigging, these few will serve you well in working and sailing your little ship.

Commissioning the Boat

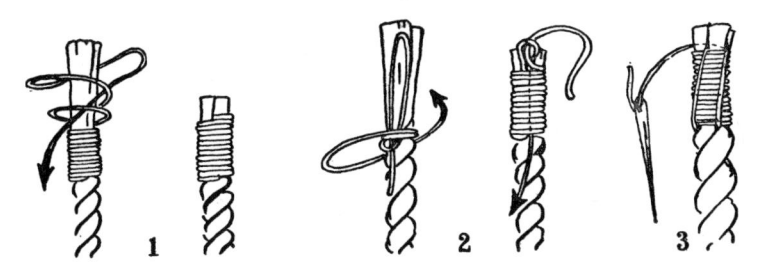

Methods of Whipping

WHIPPING

Rope ends have an annoying habit of unravelling and unlaying unless stopped from doing so by a stopper knot, backsplicing or serving. Serving in this instance is called whipping. The sketches above show several methods of whipping so that your rope ends won't become Irish pennants, or cowtails or, as we call them in Maine, masthead kelp.

Use ordinary cotton sail thread and a triangular section sail needle. Here again, a dab of varnish or white paint, will assure a permanent job.

Two more slight, but I hope helpful matters, and we're finished with the subject of rope.

There is only one correct way to belay to a cleat. It is shown in the sketch. Avoid the practice, too often seen 'longshore, of tucking the last turn under itself. This is called jamming and it's dangerous, as you might find out if you ever have to let a sheet or halyard run in a hurry. The only tuck permitted in belaying is the slippery hitch which, as you see by the drawing on page 72, is a neat wrinkle, especially for the mainsheet in gusty weather.

There is only one correct place for unused rope on your boat—out of the way. To get rope ends out of the way (rope ends or falls like those of halyards after you have hoisted your sails), always coil the rope. Coil it with the lay, which means right-handed, left to right, the same direction of rotation taken by the hands of your watch. Begin with the stand-

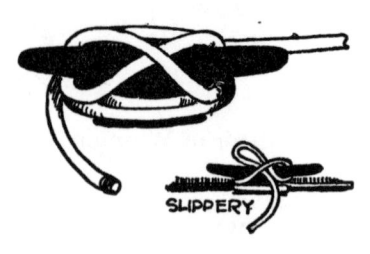

How to Belay to a Cleat

ing part and coil toward the free end. If it is a large coil, like that made by an anchor cable or the peak halyards of a gaff-rigger, lay the coil flat on the deck in some place where you know you won't need to be or stow anything else. Be sure to capsize (which simply means "turn over") the coil so that it will run off the top of the coil when you need it.

Hanging the coil on a cleat or pin is even better than leaving it on deck. This is the way to hang a coil: Reach through it, draw out a bight of the line between the coil and the cleat, twist this several times and hook it over the top horn of the cleat.

My last picture of us, skipper, was unravelling this maypole of rigging which fell about our ears after we had stepped the mast. But everything is triced up and snug now. We're almost ready for canvas.

But first there's the boom to rig. It attaches to the mast by a hinged device permitting it the same action as a ball-and-socket joint. This is called the gooseneck. There is nothing complicated about it. The after end of the boom rests on a removable crotch or a boom shears. The track of the boom

Commissioning the Boat

should be on top and the mainsheet, through a tackle, secures to it.

You might have a jib boom, which is simply a light boom to which the foot of the jib laces. Its forward end is also

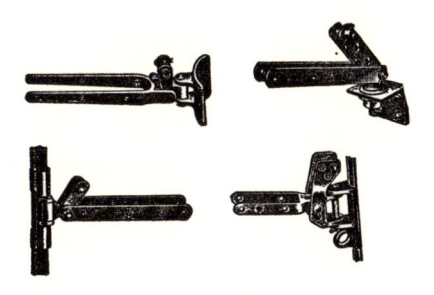

Goosenecks

hinged, usually to the same fitting which holds the jibstay and the jibsheets lead to a block or a pad eye near the after end. Or you might have a jib club, which serves the same purpose as a jib boom but is not attached to the boat at its forward end. Usually you leave this laced to the jib and it is not a standing spar. Or you might have no jib spar at all, which is perfectly all right. Many modern rigs do not use a club or boom but fly the jib loose-footed. This must be the case if the jib is overlapping.

The following paragraphs will concern themselves with sails only to that extent required to put canvas on your boat and get her sailing. Later, we shall go into the intricacies of bending and flying sails from the efficiency viewpoint. That's very important; just as important as tuning up the engine of a power boat. For your sails, like the engine, are your motive power.

The jib-headed rig always provides a track-like arrangement on the after side of the mast to which the luff, or forward edge of the mainsail, is attached. The usual mechanism is a metal track, with a gate at the lower end, on which ride small staple-like plates, called sail slides, which have been sewn to the sail luff. Open up your sail and thread these slides onto the track, starting with the top, or head, slide. Be sure that you thread them right end up and in correct order. Close the gate to keep the slides from falling off the track, and attach the main halyard. To do this, snap the hook at the end of the halyard into the hole in the headboard which is nearest the mast.

Now, if the boom has a track also, thread the foot slides onto it, working toward the stern, starting with the after or clew slide. At the clew of the mainsail, you will find a grommet of rugged size. This you bring to the heavy slide, called the clew outhaul slide, already threaded on the track and insert it in the clevis of this slide, locking it in with a pin or some similar device. A similar grommet at the tack, attaches in a similar manner to a clevis which is usually part of the gooseneck.

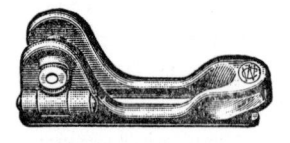

Two Forms of the Clew Outhaul Slide

There are also other methods of attaching sail to mast and boom. Sometimes both mast and boom are pear-shaped and have a routed channel in which the luff rope and foot rope slide. Sometimes, too, the foot of the sail laces to the boom instead of attaching by slides. To lace such a sail foot, take a light cotton line, twice as long as the boom and secure it, by a bowline, to the boom at the tack. Now, passing it spiral-

Commissioning the Boat

wise around the boom, lead it aft, through a grommet in the sail at each turn. Temporarily belay this line at the clew. Then, starting at the tack, pull out and aft all the slack line until the foot sets fair and snug on the boom and, finally taut, permanently belay it in such a manner as to maintain tightness, which we will take up in the next paragraph.

Your sails are your motive power; the wind your fuel. You can adjust your sails to use the fuel most efficiently. This is a fine art; you can feel the results of careful sail bending and trimming in the lift and jubilant behavior of the boat, in the tiller, and by better speed and performance. If you race, you will *have* to understand this art; if you just sail for pleasure, you will *want* to understand it. But not now; let's take that up later when we take up the matter of making sailing a fine art. For now, bend your sail like this: Pull out the foot of the sail *hand-tight only,* making certain that there are no wrinkles or puckers between slides or lacing grommets.

The jib hanks to the jibstay (the innermost headstay) by means of snap hooks, or small dog-eared staples, sewn to its forward edge. Hank these in careful order, attach the jib halyard to the grommet or eye in the head; then, sail still unhoisted, secure the foot if there is a jib club. Usually this is done with lacing line, just as it is done for the mainsail without track. Pull it *hand-tight only*. After a while—just before we are ready to sail—we shall hoist the jib. When you do, get the jib halyard tight, but I don't know how tight. The best tension is that tension which does not bend the mast forward and slack off the headstays. It is never as tight as the main halyard; seldom will you need to sway it, except in large boats. Never take it up by a winch.

Your jib may be loose-footed or overlapping. You will then need no club or boom. Both jib and mainsail may be fitted with battens. These are flat staves of wood or plastic designed to help keep the leech of the sail from curling and thus hindering the free flow of air over the surface of the sail. Mainsail battens are removed between sails; jib battens, because they are short, may be left in the pockets. Insert the batten in its proper pocket, which is usually keyed to a corresponding mark on the batten itself. Tie it by passing a length of the cotton line, sewn to the sail near the end of the pocket, through the hole in the batten; then through the opposite pocket grommet, and finally tie the two batten cords together with a square knot. Be very careful to fit the correct batten to the correct pocket. There should always be an inch or two more pocket than batten, otherwise the sail will set badly and likely tear. Occasionally batten pockets are fitted with snap fasteners. Simply snap the pocket shut.

Check all your gear. Is the centerboard in operating condition? Can you reef if necessary? Is the boat in full commission?

Commission! That's what we started out to do in this chapter. To put the boat "in commission" is more than making sail and dashing off into the blue. Commissioning is placing the boat in service in such a manner that it is efficient, safe, and equipped to meet all the hazards and emergencies of going to sea. Everything that could happen to a sailing ship in mid-Atlantic could happen to you 100 yards off shore!

This equipment at least should be *part of the boat.* You should know how to use it, have it ready for use and never sail without it.

Life preservers.—One for every passenger on board and children's size preservers if you take children. Each pas-

Commissioning the Boat

senger should know where they are kept, how to get into them, and use them.

Pump.—Means pump, bailing cans, bailing scoops, sponges, etc., to clear the boat quickly of water.

Anchor.—Some form of an anchor and sufficient warp to hold in storm or tide in depths and character of bottoms likely to be under you at any time.

Charts.—Of local waters in which you sail. And this means U.S. government charts, not the kind distributed free by oil companies.

Compass.—If you are absolutely certain and positive that fog and thick weather will *never overtake you,* skip the compass. Even a wrist or pocket compass will do.

Foghorn.—See above. But don't forget that a foghorn, a bell, or a mouth whistle can also serve as a distress signal.

Lights.—If you sail at night, the law says you must show certain lights while under way. Have the required ones on board and with spare batteries or fuel.

Fire-extinguisher.—You must carry one or more if your boat is an auxiliary. You will *want* to carry at least one if you cook on board a straight wind boat, or even if you merely carry matches! The only fire I ever had at sea started from an overturned kerosene running light. This was on an engineless boat and we had no fire extinguisher. I learned the hard way, as I can prove by a certain scar, and now I always carry a fire extinguisher.

Spare rope, gear, battens, anchor key, simple tools, sail slides, twine, needle, lacing line for reefing—obviously!

The above things are *musts*. I think the following, also, even though they make primarily for comfort rather than safety, could be musts.

Fresh water, storm clothing, K-rations, cushions and sailing blankets, sunglasses, binoculars, sunburn lotion, canvas gloves, deck mop, flashlight—we could go right on to a chamber pot and a book of campfire songs! The idea is to have on hand the basic items which contribute to creature comfort. I'm not so sure but that a happy ship is a safe ship and a safe ship is the only ship we want to sail.

Your boat is ready to sail, if you bought your boat from a builder or from an owner who was a sailorman. I'm sorry that there is not the space in this book to go into the problems of the man who bought a boat which needs extensive repairs. I have written a book for him (*Boatowner's Sheet Anchor*) and there are others on the market. The yachting and boating journals often publish articles which explain ship repair, boatbuilding, rigging, sailmaking and such subjects in detail from the viewpoint of the novice. Bend every effort to make this boat, however antique, completely safe. There are plenty of 30- and 40-year-old boats afloat which can show their taffrails to the gleaming new craft. Their scars are honorable; their broken bones (mended I hope!) are proud badges.

And so we go on—while the sails await hoisting—to a brief examination of the force which is going to drive our boat into adventure and the best hours of our lives.

CHAPTER FOUR

The Physical Phenomenon of Sailing

You may, as did the great sailors of the past, sail a boat beautifully, efficiently, and joyfully without knowing or caring a good hoot about the physics involved in the theory of sailing. I'd suggest that you skip this chapter. On the other hand, some of you might be of a more inquiring mind as to what makes it go. But we will not go in very deep, or for very long.

Like most wind sailors, I sailed for years in blissful ignorance of the physical force which made sailing, especially windward sailing, possible. Far back in my mind, like a mental picture of heaven, was the equally dreamlike details of what the wind, considered as a force, was doing to move my boat against itself. How could this uncanny thing occur? But it did. And so I sailed on, happy and untroubled in a delightful "who cares" attitude. I even won some races.

Perhaps I could have won more of them had I troubled to delve into the phenomenon of sailing. I don't know. But I'm pretty sure that it would have been quite confusing to approach fly-casting from the viewpoint of the catenary curve of my line and leader and a graph of strains and stresses of my rod. So it might be for the novice sailor who approaches the art of sailing with that devilish pictograph, the parallelogram of force, constantly tugging at the bunt of his filled sails. Skip this, if you wish. But come back to it when you later begin to raise sailing from a mere art to a fine art.

The *fine art* of sailing requires considerable scientific knowledge plus considerable luck.

Until this century probably nobody, not even Nathaniel Palmer, Cap'n Dick Brown, Nat Herreshoff, Edward Burgess or Joshua Slocum, understood the physical theory of sailing. And they were the world's best sailors. They all knew what the wind did but they didn't know how or why. For the first inkling of the truth we must thank the early flying machine experimenters. They soon discovered that their planes were not supported in the air by air pressure underneath the wings but rather by negative pressure, or vacuum, exerted on the upper surfaces of the wings. This was a revolutionary theory in the early nineteen hundreds; now it is scientific fact, proved a million times over.

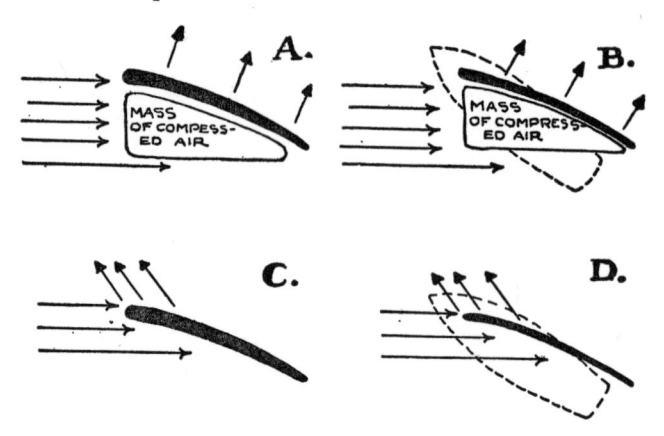

The sketch A above shows what airplane designers *thought* the wind did to their wings. The theory looked sound enough. Now, conceding that a sail is nothing but an airplane wing set vertically instead of horizontally, let's apply the airplane designer's theory to the sail in sketch B. No good; it doesn't work! Our boat would go backwards.

After a few dramatic experiments, some of them fatal, the

The Physical Phenomenon of Sailing

condition of wing coverings, of wing paint, and leading edges gave the designers a new theory. There seemed to be another force at work here. The upper surfaces upon which the wind did *not* blow, took a worse beating in flight than the under surfaces where the wind *did* blow. It was soon suspected and later proved in wind tunnels, that, in truth, it was the upper surfaces which supported the wing; that a negative force was created on these upper surfaces especially in the vicinity of the leading edges which acted exactly as a vacuum and, what was far more important, the direction of the original force was sharply changed.

Sketch C shows this theory applied to the plane wing. Wind blowing *at* the wing changed the direction of its force so that it actually drew the wing with it, by vacuum, in this new direction, which was upward. Now, in sketch D, we see the wing set vertically as a sail. We apply the wind force and show the change of direction of this force. No longer does our boat go backward. Now, obviously, this force which pulls a horizontal wing upward also pulls a vertical wing forward. Thus our boat moves not only across the wind but against it.

There are other and adverse forces at play during all this. These forces must be overcome or minimized so that we preserve that all-important force upward for the airplane, forward for the sailboat. The airplane solves its problems by applying power from an engine and a propeller. The sailboat solves its problems by a much quieter means.

The adverse forces of the wind's power tend to move the boat sideways and we don't want to go sideways. We want to go ahead, as fast as possible. So we "kill" side motion as much as we are able by designing our boats in such a manner as to go forward with the least possible resistance and sideways with the most possible resistance. That is the reason that your boat has a large underwater area in the form of a fixed keel or an adjustable centerboard, to which is added the resistance represented by the lateral plane of the hull itself and the rudder. That is the reason its bow is sharp, its underbody smooth and streamlined. That is why you can push a 30-footer forward with your little finger but have trouble pushing it sideways with your back muscles. You can do both, of course, but you can push the boat forward much easier and much quicker than sideways. And that is the ideal condition, within limits, that we want when we sail. In a given length of time, we want our boat to move very much further forward than it does sideways.

Modern hull design has so wonderfully utilized and combated the forces involved that we seem to move forward only. That is not true; we move both ways, forward and sideways; for the force of the wind is divided—the little finger of the wind is pushing forward and meeting little resistance and the back muscles of the wind is pushing sideways and meeting a great deal of resistance. Obviously, if the force is maintained for a minute (or an hour, or a day) the boat will move forward much further than sideways. For all practical purposes at the end of a minute we are definitely very far forward of our original position and only a very little to the side of it. "How much" depends upon the design of hull and sails, upon hull condition and upon the skipper at the helm.

The boat squeezes between these two forces, taking the course of least resistance. We diagram the situation in a figure called the Parallelogram of Forces. This is the invisible tugboat which goes to work for you whenever you sail. Its shape changes on different points of sailing, as we shall later see.

In the sketch on page 83, the line John–Bill represents the direction and force of a wind on this point of sailing, which is called sailing on the wind or sailing close-hauled. Part of the total force will be expended in forward move-

The Physical Phenomenon of Sailing 83

ment. This we see diagrammed in the line John–Tom, the length of this line being proportional to the forward drive in the line John–Bill.

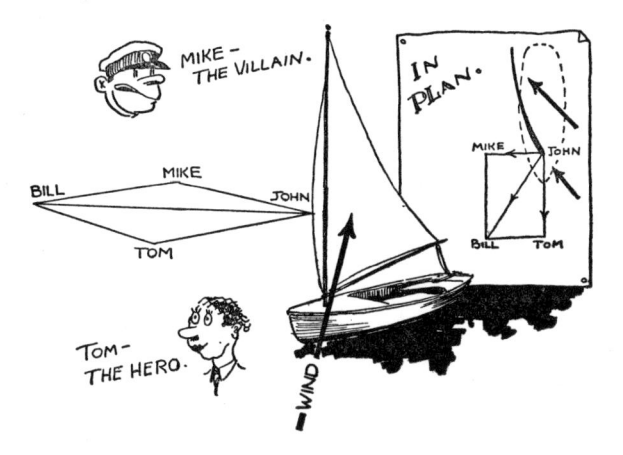

John–Tom is your friend.

The other part of the total force will be expended in side movement. This we see diagrammed in the line John–Mike, the length of this line being proportional to the sideways drive in the line John–Bill.

John–Mike is your enemy.

We cultivate John–Tom's friendship by designing a smooth, easily-driven underwater hull, by eliminating skin friction as much as possible, by streamlining deck and spars and by keeping sails properly set and trimmed. We make it easy for John–Tom to pull us forward.

We discourage John–Mike by designing broad underwater areas which resist side-push. We make it hard for John–Mike to pull us sideways.

John–Tom and John–Mike start to fight the moment we start to sail. But we've put horseshoes in John–Tom's gloves and given John–Mike a glass jaw. John–Tom always wins.

But John–Mike always gets in a few slugs. And he keeps slugging. For every powerful punch that John–Tom makes forward, John–Mike makes a weak one sideways. As a result, our boat moves forward along the approximate (never exact!) line John–Tom. Our boat stays on the line John–Tom to that extent that Mike gets in his slugs. If we could eliminate Mike entirely, the boat would move *forward* only. If we are careless in matters of trim, sail setting, centerboard positions, or have unduly high-sided boats or large deckhouses, Mike becomes quite powerful, and he pulls us hard from the straight, forward line John–Tom. Prove this sometime, when sailing off the wind, or on a reach, by hauling up the centerboard. The boat visibly moves sideways, or makes leeway—sometimes it makes as much leeway as forward motion. This is Mike at work; this is how Mike pulls us away from a straight, forward course when, by hauling up the centerboard and thus reducing the area of lateral resistance, we give Mike power.

I could have used the A–B, C–D designations of the engineer in explaining this matter to you, but that seemed so impersonal; so lifeless. As I sail, especially when I sail in a race, I always like to think of these three pals who man my mystic tugboat. I always want to see Bill as close to windward as possible. I want to see Tom way out ahead. I want to see Mike right hard aboard my beam! You thought I made a mistake in mentioning only three pals. I didn't. You see, I'm John—the boss! If I'm a good boss, I can keep Bill, Tom and Mike just where I want them. If I do, I'm probably a good skipper also.

It's interesting to see what happens to the parallelogram of forces on different points of sailing. We have seen how it appears when on the wind. In the sketches following, we see how it appears off the wind and before the wind. For one it approaches a square, for the other it becomes a straight line!

The Physical Phenomenon of Sailing 85

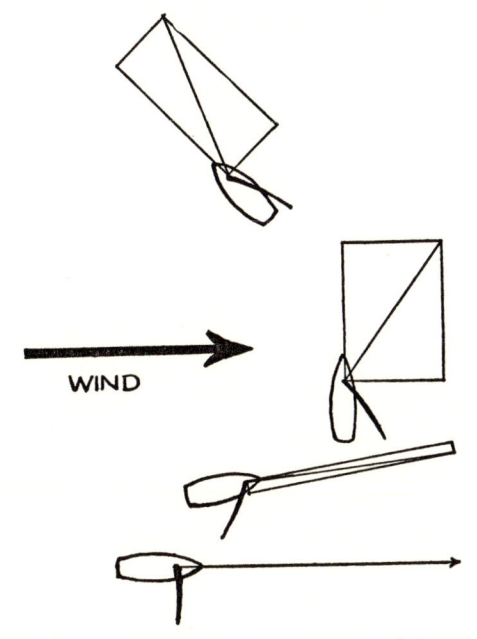

The Ever-changing Parallelogram of Forces

Please don't worry about all this. Beyond all this scientific theory there is one factor which counts for far more. That's the human mind and body which interprets and converts cold science into simple feels and hunches. In a dozen ways, many of which you do not even suspect you apply, *you know when your boat is doing its best.* There comes a time, like the time of marriage, when you and your boat become one. You have become the brain, the master of this joyful creature; she becomes your loving faithful slave; you *know* her. I'm sure you get the idea.

CHAPTER FIVE

The Sailing Positions

Your boat is a dead thing. It has no power of any kind. In order to move you must obtain power—from someplace. And, of course, it is from moving air—wind—that we take the power to make our boats go where we want them to go.

Let air begin to move, ever so gently, and immediately it presents us with the gift of power—unlimited power, free power—generously bestowed. There is only one joker. The power is presented from but one direction at one time. You must convert this direction into the direction in which you wish to proceed. You must serve as sort of human gearbox and transmission, doing for your boat what these mechanical devices do for your car in converting its power to the kind of power you require to move the car in the direction you want it to move.

It is perfectly possible to apply the power of the wind and obtain the same movements of direction possible to your car. Your sailboat has a forward gear and a reverse gear. It even has a neutral. It will go fast or slow. There is nothing that it will not do in the plane of horizontal motion, provided you understand the rudiments of the process of converting this fixed power of the wind into the type of power you require.

In spite of the light business about John, Tom, Bill and Mike in the preceding chapter, sailing by a formula of

The Sailing Positions

physics is a deadly, gruesome approach. So take my sincere advice and sail as 90 per cent of all sailors do, exactly the same way sailors sailed before we knew a blessed thing about the theory of sailing.

The first thing to remember is that there is only one fixed factor in any sailing situation. That factor is the wind. It blows, ideally, from a fixed direction and with a fixed velocity. (Of course, it doesn't always do this and we'll take that up under later chapters. But for now we are working with a fixed, steady wind in still water. There are no tides, no currents, no puffs, no calms. May the Lord furnish heaven with sailing conditions like these!) Whatever we wish to do, wherever we wish to make our boat go, we shall always have to remember that this fixed wind which is our power, is presented to us from one direction only.

If we wish to go in the same direction as the wind, it is obvious that we must merely permit the wind to "blow" us along. We become as a blown leaf, a thistledown, fortunately under control. Sailors call this "sailing before the wind." Sometimes it is called "scudding," "running," "sailing free," or "sailing downwind or downhill." It is one of the sailing positions and the correct name of the position is "before the wind."

As in all sailing positions, we do the following procedures in assuming the position: We steer or aim the boat toward the direction in which we wish to go with the rudder and then adjust the sails, by trimming or slacking them by means of their sheets, so that the power of the wind is used most efficiently.

Whenever this maneuver results in the wind reaching us from directly astern, or from very nearly astern, but definitely not from the beam, we are sailing *before the wind*.

Whenever this maneuver results in the wind reaching us from abeam, but definitely not from ahead, we are "reaching" and the correct term for the sailing position is *off the wind*.

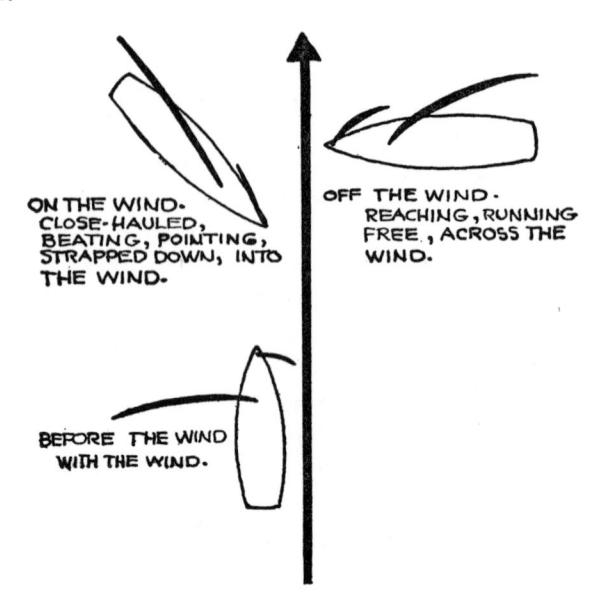

```
ON THE WIND.
CLOSE-HAULED,
BEATING, POINTING,
STRAPPED DOWN, INTO
THE WIND.

OFF THE WIND.
REACHING, RUNNING
FREE, ACROSS THE
WIND.

BEFORE THE WIND
WITH THE WIND.
```

Whenever this maneuver results in the wind reaching us from ahead and well forward of the beam we are sailing "close-hauled" or "strapped down" and the correct term for the sailing position is *on the wind*.

No matter how many sails we have, what type of rig, or from which side of the boat the wind blows, these are the terms used. They are chiefly important as language, as handles, for the ideas which we must present. And we shall need a language because you seldom sail on only one position of sailing. Every sail you take involves change from one position to another, and back again, and through them all and from first position to third position, skipping through the second without pause, etc., etc. We need a "language" to describe these maneuvers.

The Sailing Positions

So—You sail before the wind when you go *with* the wind.
You sail off the wind when you go *across* the wind.
You sail on the wind when you go *into* the wind.

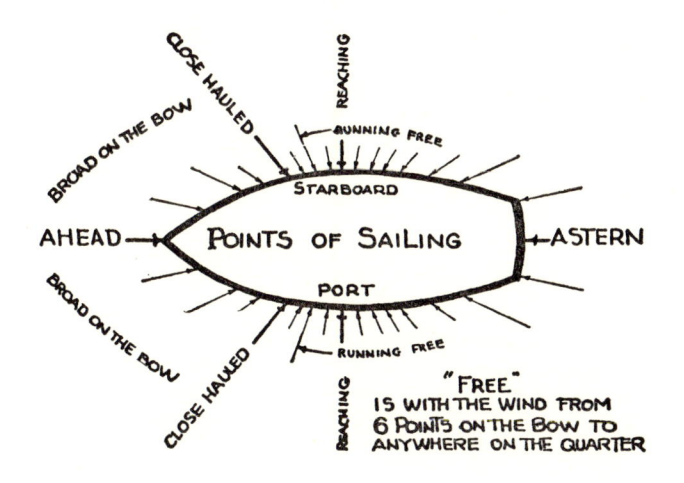

```
            CLOSE HAULED       REACHING
    BROAD ON THE BOW    RUNNING FREE
                    STARBOARD
    AHEAD →  POINTS OF SAILING  ← ASTERN
                      PORT
    BROAD ON THE BOW   RUNNING FREE
            CLOSE HAULED
                REACHING
                           "FREE"
                    IS WITH THE WIND FROM
                    6 POINTS ON THE BOW TO
                    ANYWHERE ON THE QUARTER
```

In each position we must present the sails to the wind at a different angle, trial-and-error angles, calculated to best utilize the power of the wind. When sailing on the wind or off the wind, we change the direction of the power in the wind.

Sailing before the wind requires that the sail be spread so as to present the greatest flat area to the blast of the wind. The boom will be almost broad off on either port or starboard side and the jib spread on the opposite side or, more likely, hanging quite lifeless. Since the wind blows both sail and hull in the direction we wish to go, there is no leeway and it matters not if we have a centerboard or keel.

When you sail on the wind, both mainsail and jib will be hauled into a position almost over and parallel to the keel. This is what is meant by the expression "close-hauled" or "strapped down." Since the force of the wind is now divided, part of it pulling ahead and part pushing to leeward, we need as much centerboard or keel as possible to resist side motion. (Remember that enemy, Mike!)

When you sail off the wind both mainsail and jib will be started, which means that they will not be close-hauled but neither will they be broad off. They will be somewhere midway between the positions for sailing on the wind and before the wind. You will need *some* centerboard and keel but not as much as for sailing on the wind.

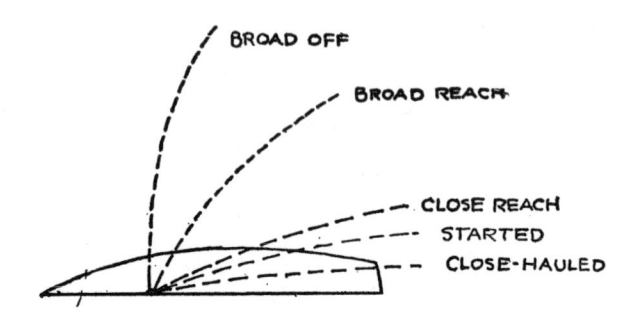

```
          / BROAD OFF
         /
        /   ,- BROAD REACH
       /  ,'
      / ,'         ,-- CLOSE REACH
     /,'      ,--'  --- STARTED
    /,'  ,--'   -------- CLOSE-HAULED
```

If the sails are started only a trifle from the position of close-hauled, you are sailing a "close reach." If they swing off at approximately a 45-degree angle from the keel, you are sailing a "broad reach." In either event you are still off the wind.

Sailing before the wind is the most dangerous sailing position.

Sailing on the wind is the safest.

Sailing off the wind is the fastest.

We might here discuss the evolution called "tacking" or "beating." It is evident that a boat cannot sail directly into the wind. The best course it can make is one of about 45 degrees left or right of a course directly into the wind. So, in order to make progress into the wind, we sail first a right-side course and then a left-side course, averaging them so that in

The Sailing Positions

a series of slants we actually move against the wind. This is tacking. A diagram of the maneuver looks somewhat like a stairway and a banister. The banister is the path of the wind. Your boat cannot sail directly up this path any more than you can go directly up the stair on the banister. So your boat takes a series of steps, left and right, just as you must to climb the stairs. Your boat tacks against the wind, it sails to windward, it moves against the force which is driving it.

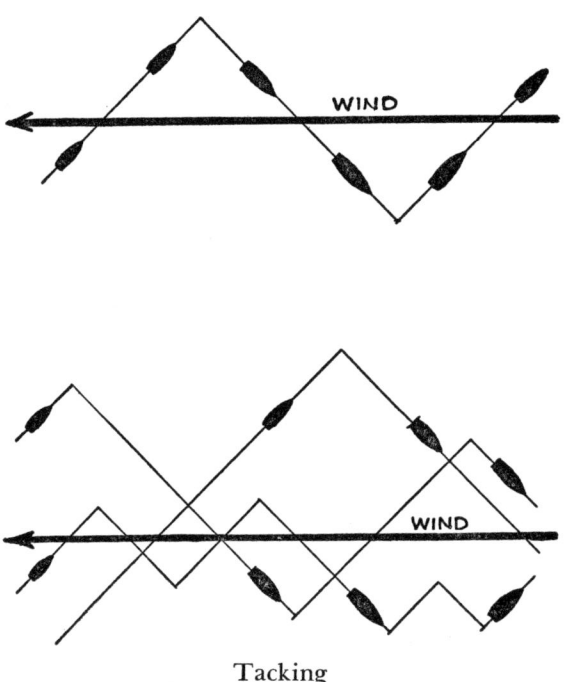

Tacking

If the wind blows from the starboard side of the boat, you are on the starboard tack. The boom and sails will be to port of the center line of the boat. If the wind blows from the port side of the boat and the boom and sails are to the starboard of the center line, you are on the port tack. Similarly, taking its name from the side from which the wind blows, we name reaches port and starboard reaches, or close port reach, broad starboard reach, etc.

Throughout all the combinations of change from position to position, from tack to tack, reach to tack, tack to reach, etc., the wind has remained the one fixed permanent component of the situation. Never for one moment forget the wind. To the skipper it is exactly what the road is to the autoist—it sets his path and his limits. Keep your eye on the road; keep your eye on the wind. You can't see the wind, but you can see its effects, and that's just as good.

Your boat should have a hawk. This is simply a weather vane set in a pivot on the masthead. At rest, it always points into the wind. Under motion, it will assume an angle between the force of the wind and the forward force of the moving boat. Practice will soon tell you the amount of its variation. Thereafter, sail with the hawk at a fixed and steady angle to your sails and it will become a true and reliable indicator of wind direction. If it is a good hawk and well clear of drafts off the head of your sails trust it more than you trust the "feel" of the wind on your body, or the direction of waves. The true wind does not reach you in your position in the cockpit. Sails, hull, cabins all set up eddies and backwinds which fool you. Waves very, very seldom move or roll directly with the wind. Tide, current and other factors divert them.

The best sailing hawk is one of metal, fitted with an adjustable counterbalance so that, no matter what the angle of heel, it registers approximately correct wind direction. If the vane is an angle, so much the better—you can see it much more easily, especially at night, than a flat plate like a metal flag. Cloth hawks are not as reliable as metal hawks. The best of these are in the form of a wind sock or a pennant, flown flat. A flag is of little use.

The Sailing Positions

An excellent dodge in light airs, or ghost breezes, is to attach short lengths of light silk ribbon, or cotton yarn, to port and starboard after shrouds. These will often flutter and stream when a sensitive hawk will not. Cigarette smoke or the flame of a match will also sometimes indicate movement in air which you will swear is completely dead.

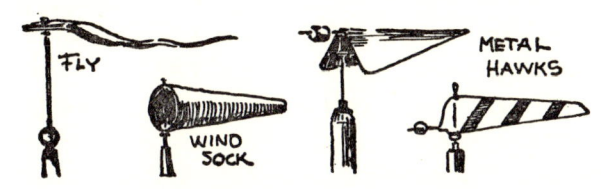

Masthead Wind Indicators

Please note that I have not suggested that you steer by a hawk, or a silk ribbon, or a match flame. Use these registers simply to ascertain wind direction. There is a "hawk" in your sails that is far more reliable for steering as we shall see in the next chapter.

CHAPTER SIX

On the Wind

Most books on sailing discuss sailing "on the wind" last. I don't know why, except possibly because their authors feel that this point of sailing is hard on both boat and skipper and therefore hard on reader interest also. But I have promised to be logical. And, logically, when you drop your mooring you are sailing on the wind. You might manage to get off the wind but, surely, unless you moor by the stern, you would not get under way before the wind!

It seems to me that normally you are likely to start sailing on the wind for several reasons. One is that, in the average small boat anchorage, your nearest safe practicing grounds, which are open waters, are offshore. And offshore, along both our American coasts especially of summer afternoons which is the time you are most likely to be sailing, is to windward in usual weather. Another reason is that your boat lies streamed to the wind at her mooring and, when you haul her ahead to cast off, she first falls into a position of sailing on the wind. And it behooves you, once you have cast off, to get moving at once. Sailboats are least dangerous when sailing. The quickest available sailing position to get you moving is on the wind.

We left our boat in commission at her mooring with mainsail and jib bent, ready to hoist. Everything is shipshape, I hope. That means no loose gear about, lines neatly coiled flat or hung, water bailed or pumped out, tiller secure on the rudderhead and centerboard (if you have one) all the way down. You get it down by simply slacking off on the centerboard pennant. The board is of metal or of weighted wood and will sink of itself. The length of the pennant is the correct distance down for windward sailing. If your board happens to be operated by a lever projecting from the trunk, shove this lever aft as far as it will go.

Hoist the mainsail first always. This practice will keep your boat streamlined to the wind and she will not start sailing. Haul the sail up by its halyard, hand-tight. Then take a turn around the halyard cleat and "sway" it taut by hauling on the halyard with one hand and gathering in the gain thus made with the other. The halyard should be quite taut; in all probability it will soon stretch and, generally, a tight luff is desirable. Belay the halyard, being careful to avoid a jam hitch on the cleat, coil the fall, capsize the coil (so that it will run off without fouling when lowering sail later), and stow it out of the way.

The jib-headed mainsail presents no complicated problem when hoisting. Sometimes sail slides stick, but you can free these easily by dropping sail slightly and rehoisting. Sometimes a gentle heave down on the luff rope will be necessary. The gaff-rigged boat is different. Take both peak and throat halyards in hand together. Hoist so that the gaff ascends *parallel* to the boom. Temporarily belay the peak halyard; then permanently belay the throat halyard, with the luff taut. Now hoist the gaff so that the sail is spread between the two spars. Be careful about wrinkles. Small ones, radiating from the sail lacing grommets and the head and foot, are harmless but deep creases from clew to throat or downward from the peak indicate that the gaff is set too high or too low. Adjust the peak halyard until the sail sets flat and you feel that the pressure of the wind when sailing will smooth out the remaining wrinkles. Of course, the sail will never set perfectly flat while luffing. Its fullness or draft makes that impossible. A sail, you see, is not a flat sheet but has a "bag" or bunt deliberately cut into it.

Mainsheet should be slack and not belayed; boom crotch should be taken in and stowed; topping lift should be slack, unless the wind is very strong (which it shouldn't be for your first sail!); backstays should be slack also.

Now be sure that jibsheets are also slack. Then smartly hoist the jib. Belay the halyard and coil it, remembering also to capsize it.

Every sail on her will be rattling and shivering; she'll be practically a flag waving in the breeze, with wind on *both* sides of the sails. She won't stay that way very long. Once the hull swings port or starboard and the wind remains on *one* side of the sails your boat will want to commence sailing. But you still have a little time, for your sheets are not belayed and so the sails will flutter flaglike and powerless at least to the limits of their sheets. During this time, get your mooring cast off and its buoy thrown clear of the boat. Then go aft, take tiller and sheets in hand—you are ready to sail.

Small boats, especially shallow centerboarders, usually fall off onto the wind without effort on your part. Wave and wind action on the hull do this. However, in this case it is the boat, not you, which decides the tack. You might wish to decide the tack or perhaps have a heavy or keelboat which sometimes requires a bit of encouragement to get sailing. You can do two things to get your boat out of this fluttery condition which, by the way, is called "in irons" or "in stays."

The first and the surest is to take the leech of the jib and swing it toward the side on which you wish the wind to blow. The bow of the boat will slowly turn the opposite way and soon be headed along the course of your first proposed tack. As the bow begins to fall off, release the jib, let it flutter, go aft to tiller and sheet.

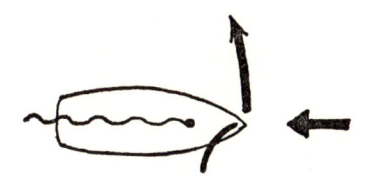

The second way to move the bow in the direction you wish is, after you have let go the mooring, to "scull" the boat around by pumping on the rudder. If you will jerk the tiller *hard* in the opposite direction from which you want the bow to pay off, then *gently* move it toward the center again and repeat this fanning motion several times, you will soon have the boat on her course.

Immediately, as she swings toward the starting course, close haul the mainsail; then close haul the jib. Two things will happen. You will heel, perhaps rather sharply, then begin to move forward through the water, gathering speed and life from the wind. Only now do you commence to steer. Until you have applied the magic of motion, the rudder has been dead. Only rank amateurs clutch the tiller for dear life before the sails are filled and drawing.

You will now notice (if your boat is properly designed) a phenomenon which astonishes many novices. Quite contrary to what many expect, we do not have to steer very much at all. There seems to be a subtle balance present in the boat, between hull and sails, that requires only an occasional touch of the fingers to the tiller to keep our boat going straight and true. And still another amazing matter—our boat does not seem to want to fall off in the direction that the wind seems to be forcing her at all! Quite the opposite, she seems inclined to veer *into* the wind. You will remember that only a moment ago, as the boat lay in this position of heading into the wind at the mooring, she was perfectly docile; she did not heel or sail and she was completely safe.

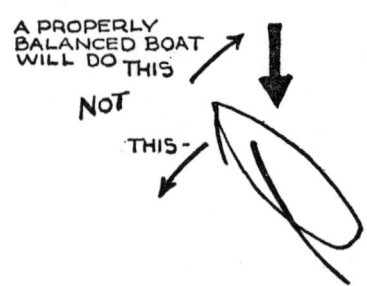

A PROPERLY BALANCED BOAT WILL DO THIS

NOT

THIS —

That is why, in the preceding chapter, we stated that the safest sailing position was on the wind. More than on any other point of sailing, a well-hung boat wants to creep into the wind and reach the position called "in irons." Sailors say that the boat wants to "luff," meaning that she wants the wind to blow on both sides of the luff of the sails. She wants to go into a *safe position* and if you let go the tiller she'll do just that.

So our job, normally, is to steer just enough to keep the boat from luffing or, to keep her "footing." A good steersman soon fixes his course as one which presents the luffs of the sails, especially that of the mainsail, to the wind so that it is always filled. The luff does not flutter or collapse; neither is it hard. You will note that nothing has been said about a landfall or reaching the place you wish to go. That has nothing to do with sailing on the wind unless your objective *happens* to be at the end of the best sailing course possible.

The best sailing course is that which uses the wind to the utmost and keeps the boat moving fast. Of course, it cannot be into the very eye of the wind but is about 45 degrees left or right of the wind. If your objective lies within this 90-

On the Wind

degree arc (45 degrees left of the wind and 45 degrees right of the wind) you must sail on the wind to reach it. If it is outside this arc, you can reach it by sailing off the wind, which we will later discuss.

Forty-five degrees is an approximate figure. Most modern boats with jib-headed sail plans, properly trimmed and sailed, can make good a 45-degree course or less without much effort. Some racing craft can reduce this to around 30 degrees. An interesting new experimental craft, using a rigid airplane wing for a sail, can sail as close as 16 degrees to the wind. Gaff-rigged boats generally cannot hold as close a course as a jib-headed rigged boat because of the sag of the head of the sail to leeward.

This art of pointing as closely as possible into the wind has the obvious name of "pointing." Sometimes the term "pointing" is used to describe the position of on the wind.

The correct position of the mainsail when pointing is strapped well inboard but never directly over the keel—usually the boom is about over the quarter. The correct position for the jib is about parallel to the mainsail, providing it does not shed the wind from its leech in such a manner that the luff of the mainsail collapses. To avoid this, it is often necessary to "start" the jib slightly, which means that its angle to the keel is slightly greater than that of the mainsail. At all costs, keep the luff of the mainsail full. This is where the real power of your sail dwells.

Once the two sails are set and properly drawing, it is the skipper's job to steer the boat in relation to the wind so that they remain so. For this, use the hawk on the masthead or steer by the luff. *Forget about a land objective.* It is the wind alone that sets your best course to windward. However, *after* you have determined the best *wind* course, a quite proper practice is to convert it (by sighting over some part or object on the boat) to a *visible* course by selecting some object on land and heading for it. Thus, if you are sailing well and your shrouds and a prominent landmark happen to line up, you may use this landmark in keeping on the course. Leeway and current must be allowed for if the course is of any length.

You do not have much latitude in sailing the best windward course. A few degrees deviation, toward or away from the wind, will soon "kill" the boat. If you head too far into the wind (shown by the collapse of the luff, the ripple of the sails, or less angle of heel) the boat moves slowly. If you fall away from the wind (shown by a hard luff and sails and increased heel) your boat may move faster but it will make excessive leeway. The ideal point of sailing is between these two extremes.

As skipper you always have a decision to make in windward sailing—that of sailing a short distance slowly or a longer distance quickly. There are no rules that can be applied. You can only gauge the individual situation for what it's worth and act accordingly. Close-hauled, most boats have a "bound" feeling. They fight bravely into the wind, gaining distance to windward always, but never really step out and sail. They take a long time to make good a short distance. With sheets slightly started, they become alive and joyous. They dash along, shucking rainbows, but they do not make the most possible windward gain. They take a short time to make good a long distance. Reduced to *time* there is often no difference between the two methods of sailing at all. What kind of a windward sail do you want?

I think that the spirit of the day, and also perhaps the tide, sea conditions and force of the wind, determines the answer. In a race or when maneuvering about an anchorage or running one of the Maine thoroughfares, I'm mighty glad that I know how to get the most out of my boat in close windward sailing. When I go afternoon sailing I have no trouble at all forgetting all about it and, with started sheets, just go sailin' to windward in my own, sweet time.

If your goal is within a 90-degree arc, the center of which is dead into the wind, your goal is said to be to windward, and you must sail to windward, or point, or sail on the wind to reach it. If you cannot do this in one tack, you must make several tacks; you must sail in a series of steps, first one tack then the other, each one taking you a little closer to where you want to go. Actually you will have to sail about double the air-line distance to the objective.

To tack, changing from step to step, you simply deliberately luff the boat, i.e., head it directly into the wind. However, since you are moving and the boat has momentum which will carry it for quite a distance without assistance from the sails, you use this power to swing the boat *past* the point of luffing and onto the opposite tack where the wind will take up and continue to drive you. You will be heading, roughly, 90 degrees from your original heading (See diagram below).

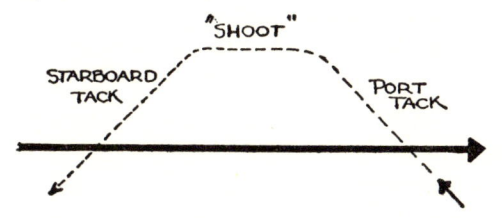

This maneuver is called "coming about."

You need not reset sails unless the jib happens to be of the loose-footed or overlapping variety. In which case, as you go about, the leeward jibsheet must be cast off and the opposite one trimmed. The common knockabout rig has self-trimming sheets on both jib and mainsail and once correctly trimmed they will continue to remain so on both tacks.

There is a danger in the maneuver which you should guard against. As the boat passes dead center of the wind, the sail will flutter and stream somewhat like a weather vane and the boom will pass from one side to the other, seemingly bent on braining the passengers. It is good practice to explain always to the novice guest what is going to happen and warn him to "duck" when you tack the boat. The correct nautical handling of the situation is to call, a few seconds before you are ready to make the maneuver, "Ready about!" or "Stand by to come about!" Passengers will be warned and sheet handlers, if you have them, alerted. As you make the steering motions to actually change tack, call "Hard a' lee!" signifying that you have put the helm down and the boat is about to swing and the boom pass over the heads of your people.

The secret of successful tacking is to understand and know thoroughly the "shoot" or momentum of your boat. A heavy boat will shoot much further than a light one. Heavy seas or adverse tides may substantially reduce the shoot. Every boat behaves differently in tacking and you should always try a few tacks to become acquainted with the habits of the boat you are handling. Good skippers make use of the shoot to carry them many extra yards to windward, sometimes tacking simply for the gains thus made. In general, avoid snapping the boat sharply from tack to tack. Bring her around by slow and deliberate tiller work, being careful to keep the boat always moving. Otherwise you will go into irons, just as you were while lying at the mooring, and will have to take one of the two steps mentioned to get the boat sailing once more.

I find that I have been holding out something on you. Perhaps I have been overly conscientious about my promise to try to keep this book simple. But, since I just had a horrible vision of the way some people try to get out of irons by pushing the main boom into the wind, I think I ought to tell you about another way to get sailing if an unsuccessful tack finds you in stays. Well, you simply cannot get out of your trouble by doing this obvious thing, pushing the boom into the wind. But, since your boat while in stays is actually moving backward and is not idle as you might think, we make use of this movement, however slight, to *steer* the boat onto the tack we wish. Here's the way to do it. Strap down both the jib and mainsail as hard as you can—get 'em both dead amidships. Then push nothing but the tiller. Push it to port if you want to get off on the starboard tack and to starboard if you want to get off on the port tack. As soon as you swing onto the wind again, slack off sheets and you will start sailing again. It's a good trick to know and I hope that I have not confused you by including it here.

Some boats do not tack freely because of great beam or hull windage, poor sail balance, or adverse tides and currents. They must be "driven" around. "Helped" would be a better term since you cannot drive any boat into the wind.

A common method is to get the boat sailing very fast just before tacking, thus giving her considerable additional momentum. This is done by falling off to a close reach, which is a faster point of sailing than close-hauled, and when the boat is really footing it, quickly swing her on the wind, then into it and off on the opposite tack.

Another method is to slack off the jib sheet just before starting the maneuver so that the bow will swing more freely against the wind. Immediately the boat is passed dead center, trim the jib sheet again.

The performance of many boats can be improved by careful use of the centerboard, the placing of both live and dead ballast, and scientific balancing of sails. We shall have a lot to say about these matters later. But for this sail, our first, let's just remember that the best probable position for the centerboard is all the way down or nearly so. Live ballast, which is yourself and your passengers, should be placed so that you require a minimum of rudder angle. It may be fore or aft of amidships, or amidships. It may be to windward in fresh breezes. It is *never* to windward in a calm light air. Boats simply do not sail if heeled to windward. When sailing alone in the very small classes, it often pays to have a tiller extension so that you can throw your weight around as needed. Tucked up on the stern thwart, the lone skipper often completely destroys the fore-and-aft trim essential to good sailing.

The proper angle of heel varies with different boats. In general, the boat that settles into a comfortable groove with her lee rail about awash should be allowed to get and stay there. It is not necessary to scramble to the high side at every tack in an effort to make the boat stand up. Very few boats capsize in plain sailing due to wind pressure. It's something else again in puffs or heavy seas.

Boat hulls are designed with a "hard spot" beyond which it takes a half gale to heel them. Keelboats especially have this pronounced hard spot. Boats of wide beam, to which class most of the centerboarders belong, reach a critical point when extremely and sharply heeled and it takes very little additional force to push them all the way over once it has been reached. But this point is far beyond ordinary heeling angles and it is some comfort to know that the more a boat heels the less becomes the pressure on her sails; the wind blows over the leech of the sail and is harmlessly "spilled." I think that, if a rule can be applied at all, this is one which might be found practical: *Trim your boat so that the lee rail is substantially out of water when sailing.* A dollop or the top of a white one on deck won't swamp you but, on the other hand, to sail with the seas swirling around the cabin trunk or coamings, chain plates and shrouds buried,

On the Wind

greatly cuts down your speed. The hull is the only part designed to be pushed through water—sail on it.

The fear of capsizing is great in the novice. But just analyze a capsizing; what can happen? Nothing very much, really. Centerboard boats float, ballasted boats often have air tanks or watertight compartments and also float. Watertight cockpits can flood but they very soon scupper off. After all, if you can swim (and every sailor should swim!) you are unlikely to get into much more trouble than a good ducking. Capsizing is a mild disgrace sometimes but not very often a tragedy. I strongly advise you to guard against it and know how to right a capsized boat, and then forget all about it. I know hundreds of amateur sailors; I know two who capsized. One was drunk and the other did it for the movies.

In windward sailing under fresh breezes, your backstays will come into use (unless your boat is fitted with one of those very grand shipmates, a permanent backstay). These are simply extra stays to support the mast under the conditions of heavy stresses and strains to the mast caused by great wind pressure on the sails. Backstays supplement the support given by the fixed shrouds. You always sail, when you need backstays at all, with the windward one set up and the leeward one hanging slack. The time to set up a backstay is in that moment of the maneuver of coming about when the sail is fluttering and the mast standing straight. It is largely a question of timing. Immediately the pressure is removed from the mast and as the boat swings from board to board (which means from tack to tack) slack off one backstay and quickly set up the other *before the mast is again under pressure*. Setting up is done by means of a tackle or a lever device of some kind. A very quick and handy belaying device is the so-called "racing cleat" from which the fall of the tackle is instantly cast off by a simple tripping mechanism.

So important is timing that racing boats sometimes carry

a man whose duty it is to tend the backstays and nothing else. A racing boat cannot always take a leisurely swing in coming about nor can she head up and luff while a backstay is being set or tightened. The pleasure boat can do both of these. It's just a matter of practice.

The leeward backstay should always be well slacked off and never be permitted to cut into the airfoiled form of the filled sail. Be very careful about this or your boat will become sluggish and dead.

Backstays are a nuisance and new boat designs show a marked inclination to abandon them in favor of the permanent backstay. This is all to the good. However, we cannot get away from them in gaff-rigged craft since the gaff must pass from side to side with freedom. Fortunately, the main sheet itself acts as a very effective backstay, especially in the gaff rig, and backstays become necessary only in fairly strong breezes or very jumpy seas. They are required least when sailing on the wind, most when before the wind.

There can be no hard and fast rules about when to use backstays. It depends upon the type of mast, hollow or solid, and rig, peak or gaff, and other factors. Your mast should set in a regular though very slight curve to leeward when under sail. If there is a kink or a waver that backstays could straighten out, use them by all means. If seas are confused and gear rattles and jumps, or the boat is hobby-horsing along in heavy weather, get the backstays set up. Certainly set them up when you add a reaching spinnaker or a big ballooner to the sail plan. If you want a rule, here's one: Set the backstays whenever, for any cause, you can expect an overload on the mast and shrouds. Use them to prevent accident caused by such overloads, which is just why backstays are often called "preventers."

Backstays are of two varieties, running and permanent. The permanent backstay, or Swedestay (since it is supposed to have been developed in the Swedish racing classes), is fixed between masthead and a fitting on the after rail or on a short boom, called a bumpkin, requires no adjusting as you tack. Only jib-headed rigs can be fitted with it. The permanent backstay is an excellent shipmate and is found on most modern boats.

But we don't want to sail on the wind all the time. We want freedom, range—and for that we must develop two more sailing techniques.

CHAPTER SEVEN

Off the Wind

THE FINEST point of sailing is that of sailing "across the wind" or "reaching." On no point is the boat livelier or faster; off the wind she steps out joyously, a thing free and alive.

You sail on a reach whenever the wind comes from approximately the beam. Another way to put it is that you sail on a reach whenever you are not sailing before the wind or on the wind. If the wind is from forward of the beam and sheets must be started, you are sailing a close reach. If the wind is aft of the beam and sheets are slacked well off, you are sailing a broad reach. The zenith of the position is when the wind is dead on the beam and the sails must be carried about 45 degrees off the keel line.

The correct position of the mainsail is at that point between a hard and fluttering luff. You can best reach that point, after setting a course, by slacking off sheets until the luffs flutter and then trimming them in slightly. As in sailing close-hauled, the jib is likely to remain filled and yet not backwind the mainsail at a slightly greater angle from the keel than the mainsail.

The centerboard should be partly sheathed. Three-quarters of its area or less will be sufficient to prevent undue leeway. The purpose of sailing with as little centerboard as possible is to reduce the skin friction of the hull which is considerable, especially at high speeds. The exact amount of

Off the Wind

centerboard necessary on various points of sailing can be determined only by experiment. The most reliable indicator of leeway (which sufficient lateral resistance in the form of

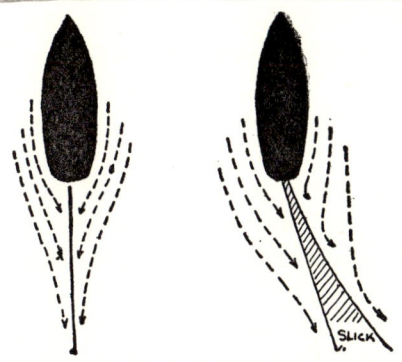

The Wake as a Leeway Telltale

keel or centerboard will reduce to an irreducible minimum) is the wake. It should trail straight astern and without the telltale slick of smooth water to windward which shows that the hull has slid sideways as well as forward through the water. This slick meets solid water to leeward and often curls against it like a miniature tide rip. So minimize slick and curling by presenting additional centerboard area.

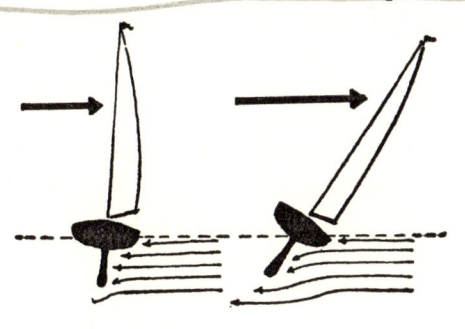

Excessive heel will cause some boats to make leeway. This is because the centerboard or keel is not plumb, but at a considerable angle off the vertical, and permits water to slide rather freely around and off the area. The cure is to shift live ballast to the windward side so that the boat sails more nearly upright.

As an experiment, sail on a broad reach; then suddenly haul up the centerboard. You will distinctly notice the slick and curl in the wake as well as sense a sudden sideways motion to leeward. Then drop the board until the wake clears and seems composed of two slip streams of water, one from port and one from starboard, which meet in a small cycloidal wave form seeming to trace a straight path through the water.

This question of the correct area of centerboard is an extremely tricky one. Centerboard positions often win races, especially in light airs. In general, you will have to experiment in finding the correct position, starting from a full board on a close reach and working from there toward a broad reach. The further aft the wind, the less centerboard is required. None is required before the wind!

Since wave force is approximately in the same direction as the wind force and the wind is on the beam, a reaching course will generally find the boat sailing "across the seas." Waves will be attacking from the beam, and this might cause considerable more roll on a reach than close-hauled. However, counteracting this roll is the strong pressure of a beam wind on the sails which steadies the boat enormously. The boat has a tendency to roll away from the wind and waves but not toward them. For this reason, and since the main boom is apt to be quite far over the water on the leeward side, it may be advisable to top the boom by means of the weather (or windward) topping lift. At all costs, the boom and clew of the sail must be kept out of the water. If it dips on steep rolls it will take charge of the boat, acting as a rudder—and a much more powerful rudder than the one with which you are steering! Of course, a cure is to ballast the windward side and thus make the boat sail "standing up."

Backstays will usually be required when reaching. Not only is there a strong forward thrust to the mast which the shrouds cannot completely control but roll puts additional pressures on the mast which, coinciding with strong wind pressures, may strain the mast to the point of breaking. In any beam wind that causes the boat to heel, rig your backstays. In light reaching airs, airs which barely fill the sails, and confused seas the whip of an unstayed mast can shake the air completely out of the sails and kill headway. Setting the backstay will greatly minimize this whipping.

I can remember few times that I trimmed sheets at the mooring and whisked off full-and-by for an afternoon on only one point of sailing. Sailing is a combination of sailing on all points, changing from on the wind to off the wind, to before it, back to on, etc. Indeed, that's the great fun of sailing. That's why I, for one, would rather work into a harbor every night than stay at sea when I sail coastwise. I get a big bang out of handling my little ship; very little out of sailing an offshore course with the wind steady for days at a time.

Just as life is not a series of neatly defined short stories, so sailing is not a series of neatly defined positions of sailing. Almost unconsciously, as you change step and stride over irregular ground, you shift back and forth between the various sailing positions as you get to where you want to go. So you must know how to change from sailing off the wind to on the wind and vice versa and later, how to swing before the wind and back again.

If you are sailing on the wind and want to get off the wind on the same tack, you head the bow *away* from the wind and *at the same time* slack off sheets to suit the new direction of the wind. You must do these things together. To fall off the wind with sails close-hauled will heel you sharply and, in heavy weather, cause a knockdown, which is the unfortunate position of being heeled without steerageway. The way to perform the maneuver is to take it easy. *Slowly* pay out the main sheet as the bow swings away from the wind. Settle on the course (which now is not confined to one about 45 degrees from the wind as when close-hauled but may be from 45 to about 135 degrees from it); then slack off the jib slightly; then test the luff of the mainsail by veering slightly to either side of the course. Trim or slack the mainsheet until the luff behaves—neither too hard nor on the verge of collapse. Then trim the jib so that it is full but does not backwind the mainsail by funneling wind against the leeward side of the luff. Haul the centerboard up part way. Set your backstays—you're off the wind.

To reverse this, going from off the wind to on the wind, first drop the centerboard. Then trim in the mainsheet and at the same time, taking it easy, head the bow into the wind. When the mainsail is in, flat and drawing, trim the jib in. It is better to trim both mainsail and jib at the same time if the boat is not short handed. You are sailing on the wind. The idea is to keep the boat moving throughout the change and to make the maneuver a smooth one. The course of the boat should describe a long gentle curve, not a dog leg.

Tacking from board to board while off the wind is the same idea carried to completion. You pass from off the wind, to on the wind, to dead center, to on the wind and then to off the wind quite deliberately. Few small boats carry enough momentum to shoot from a broad starboard tack to a broad port tack. Throughout the maneuver you must have motion to obtain steerageway. You can get this motion for all but 90 degrees of the maneuver. In that 90 degrees, while passing

Off the Wind

from port tack on the wind to starboard tack on the wind or vice versa, you must "shoot" as we have seen in the chapter on sailing "On the Wind." It is expecting too much of your boat and your luck to ask it to shoot 180 degrees from reach

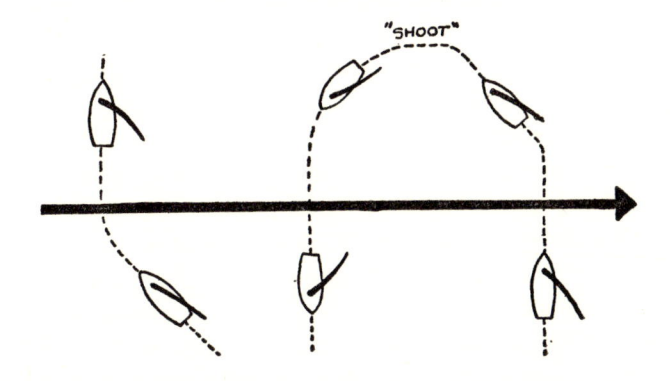

to reach. So sail the boat until it can be sailed no more, come about quickly, and off you go.

By taking it slowly, you have a few seconds to adjust leisurely backstays and centerboard and to shift weight to weather if you wish. Your margin of safety and chances of completing successfully the maneuver are greatly increased. Flying tacks can be made, of course. Indeed, they are justified in racing or to avert collision or stranding. But for plain sailing, especially in the beginning, follow the safe and sane procedure of sailing your boat around from reach to reach.

I hope that I have not given the impression that sailing your boat around is a long or tedious process. It isn't. A little 20-footer in a fair breeze can perform the entire evolution in well under thirty seconds. It is usually not necessary to bother with the jib or the centerboard. The mainsail properly sheeted, plus the momentum of the boat, will provide sufficient drive and headway to give full steerageway.

We have mentioned that sailing on the wind is a safe position because the boat can be quickly luffed into the wind and stood up straight. This does not mean that sailing off the wind is dangerous. However, since it would take quite a swing of the boat to luff, puffs and overblows can be quite as effectively combated by slacking off the mainsheet thus presenting the forward edge of the sail to the wind and causing it to luff harmlessly. As the puff passes, haul in the sheet and you continue on your way. I believe that this practice of adjusting the sail, rather than the boat, to the wind will see you making good a reaching course much better than luffing by steering. Incidentally, while it seems that to let the sheet run while on a reach would put the sail into the sea to leeward, this does not occur. As soon as the pressure is taken off the sail by slacking sheets the boat will stand up and, of course, lift the boom quite clear of the water.

And so, since any sail is more than likely to include all points of sailing, we proceed to the next and final position.

CHAPTER EIGHT

Before the Wind

THE THIRD position of sailing is "before the wind." It is the sailing position of your hat when it blows off or of a scrap of paper whipped downwind on a gusty day, with one important exception. The boat, unlike the hat, is controlled. It does not thunder on before the wind willy-nilly. It is so controlled by the rudder as to maintain the sails presented always flatways to the wind. Without restraining rudder action, a boat before the wind will tend to swing, complete part of a half circle and eventually stand luffing, bow and sail luffs *into the wind*—if she makes it! There are reasons aplenty why she may not, as we shall see.

You sail before the wind whenever the wind comes from over the stern. The correct position for the sails is as follows: The mainsail should be slacked forward until the sail (not necessarily the boom) is at approximately right angle to the wind. This position will usually find the sail itself very slightly, if at all, forward of an imaginary right-angle line from the keel at the mast. The boom, since the head of the sail will tend to sweep far forward of the foot, will be at about a 60-degree angle from the fore-and-aft center or keel. The jib will probably collapse, due to its becoming blanketed by the mainsail. This is its correct natural position. We shall later learn how to rig it so as to draw.

The sloop rig, in reality, becomes a cat rig, before the wind. The jib serves no purpose. It is usual to keep the jib standing, however. Immediately you put the boat on a different point of sailing, the jib will be required for drive and balance. And, as we shall see below, there are still other reasons to leave it standing.

The centerboard is normally not required. Since that part of the wind's force, which is expended in making leeway when sailing on or off the wind, is now expended in making forward motion—which we want—we need no mechanical device to combat leeway. At last we have Mike working *for* us, pushing, helping Tom! So sheath the centerboard. Its skin friction is a retarding force.

The backstays are required in anything but very light winds. On this point of sailing the mast will show its greatest tendency to bow forward, especially in its upper length above the hounds of the lower shrouds. The shrouds offer very slight control against bowing forward; the backstays do most of the job of controlling and correcting when before the wind.

Ballast, especially in the light boat, should be moved aft. This is to counteract the tendency of the bow to bury. Our boat now, you see, is really "heeling forward," and we follow the same ballasting practice that we do when it heels sideways. Place ballast to windward. There is little danger of capsizing forward. (An accident called pitch-poling which,

Before the Wind

when wind and a steep breaking sea join forces, *can* happen.) We ballast aft merely to maintain trim. We maintain trim to keep the boat on her best sailing marks and to keep the rudder submerged and operating. At all costs, we must have rudder, i.e., the ability to steer, when before the wind.

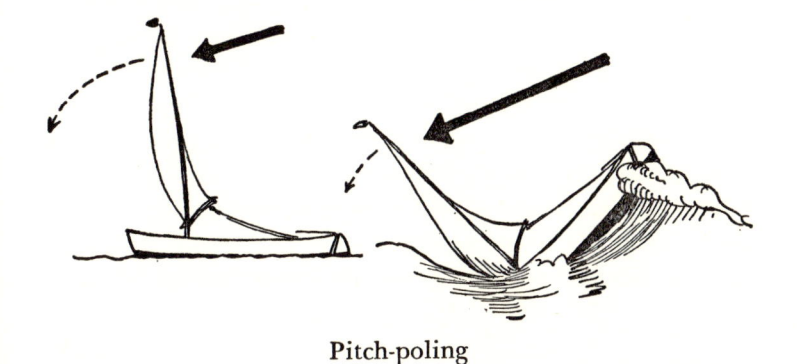

Pitch-poling

The reason that we must be able to steer at all times is that our two forces, that of the wind urging the boat forward and that of the water resisting this force, can never be brought into natural useful balance. Always the wind's force on the sail will be like the force applied to the end of a lever. It will so overpower the force of resistance that it takes charge. The mainsail will simply move rapidly forward and in so doing turn the slower moving hull as a wheel spoke turns the hub. To resist this turning tendency of the hull and keep our boat sailing straight downwind, we must apply another force, that of slipstream pressure against the rudder, in short, steering. To lose the power to steer is to surrender immediately control to these forces which have no point of useful balance and so surrender forward motion of the boat. On no other point of sailing is helmsmanship quite so important as when before the wind. The progress of the boat and our own safety depends upon efficient and positive steering.

If the wind is from *directly aft,* its path parallel with the keel, the mainsail may be carried on either side. In light air it won't always stay on the side you want it, but you can combat this by shifting live weight to the same side as the sail. The sail will then act exactly as a door hung on an out-of-plumb jamb acts, since, what you really have done by shifting ballast, is to carry your mast (the door jamb) from which hangs the sail (the door) out-of-plumb.

The wind very seldom comes from the convenient point of dead astern. Usually it is a few points port or starboard of dead astern. You must then *very carefully* determine the true wind direction and set your mainsail on the side opposite to that from which the wind blows. Be meticulous in this; *carelessness can mean disaster.* From then on you must

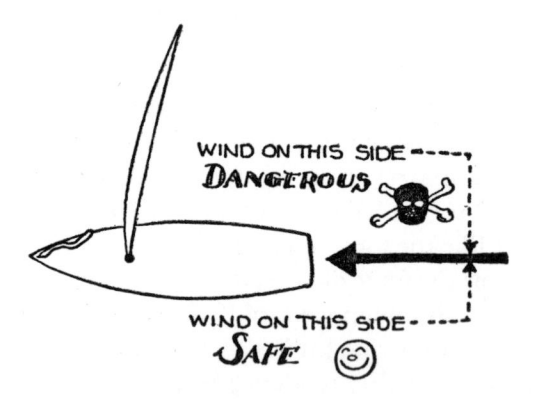

exercise concerned helmsmanship. Your fixed steering order is "nothing to lu'ard"—which means in plain language that you must so steer that the wind never passes around the stern to blow from the *same* side on which the sail is set. For if you steer so that the wind does blow from the same side on which the sail is set, you will invite the first of the three dangers which give sailing before the wind the just reputation of being the most dangerous and difficult of all courses to sail.

Before the Wind

This danger is the accidental jibe. To jibe is to permit the wind to pass from side to side of a sail *by the stern*. There is nothing wrong with jibing, provided it is intentional and

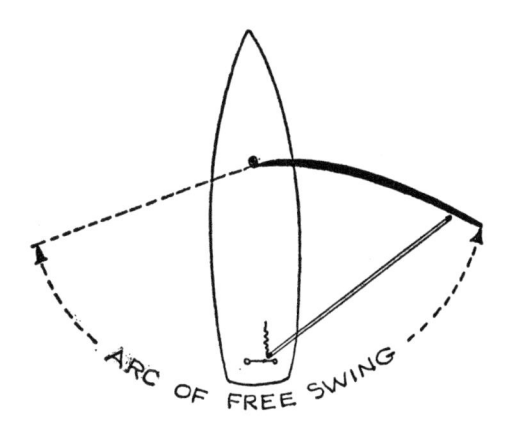

ARC OF FREE SWING

controlled and not accidental. We have seen how, in permitting the wind to pass from side to side of a sail *by the bow* (as in tacking), the sail has acted as a waving flag, its forward edge or luff firmly secured to the mast by hoops or track and slides—a lot of noise and rattling but at no time dangerous. As the wind fills the sail the noise and fluttering subside and the sail quietly goes to sleep, airfoiled and hard as long as you keep it so. In the accidental jibe we have no such control of the sail. The edge over which the wind now passes is the leech, secured to *nothing* from clew to head. When the wind passes over this edge it flutters nothing, it violently fills the opposite side and violently smashes the entire sail forward. The only possible rein is the main sheet but, alas, this is payed out. Nothing can stop this free-swinging, powerful area of wind-driven canvas except the sheet against which it is violently jerked, and the sheet seldom can take this strain, nor can the backstays and shrouds or the mast itself. An unplanned jibe in a strong wind is almost certain to wreck your rigging, likely to break your mast, and possibly capsize the boat.

It is entirely a matter of steering and possibly shifts of wind in gusty weather against which, fortunately, there are some defenses. *The only way to avoid jibing is never to allow the wind to blow from the same quarter as that on which the sail is set.* The moment the wind passes over dead center of the stern toward the side of the sail you are "sailing by the lee." It is always dangerous to sail by the lee. It is far better to practice deliberately tacking downwind, which is setting a downwind course that is slightly toward the side opposite that on which the sail is carried even though this course is not the exact one you wish. At all costs, keep that wind away from the dangerous dead astern quarter and over where it belongs. Only then will the sail surely stay where *it* belongs. You can never accidentally jibe if you follow this rule always.

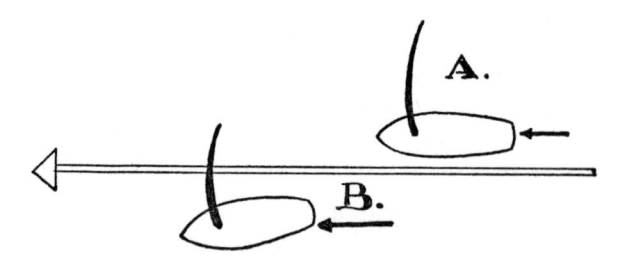

Boat B is "Tacking Downwind"

A hawk on the masthead becomes a necessity. As long as its head points toward the sail, you are in no danger of jibing. And here, we might look into the reason why it is well to let the jib stand when sailing before the wind even though it has collapsed and apparently is doing no work.

The jib serves as a most reliable telltale in informing you of the danger of jibing. As long as it remains collapsed be-

Before the Wind

hind the mainsail, you cannot jibe. However, if it stirs, if it makes *motions* of filling, if it lifts and passes to the side opposite the mainsail, BEWARE! The wind is getting at it, from *in back* of the mainsail, and is likely to jibe the mainsail without warning.

Look out for jibes whenever approaching land, or docks, or when passing other boats. These things often denote an unpredictable change of wind direction. Be careful in puffy weather; wind shifts when sailing before it can be best combated by increasing your margin of safety by tacking downwind. In heavy and confused seas which buffet your boat and force her off course, jibing is an ever-present danger unless you take a broad tack downwind.

Lesser dangers of sailing before the wind are broaching to and rolling. Broaching to is the opposite of jibing. Because of careless steering or improper rudder design or sail

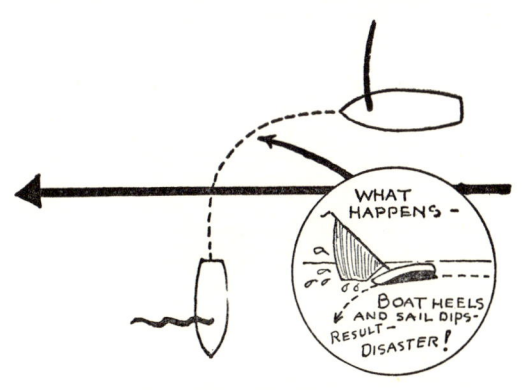

Broaching to

balance, a boat might have a tendency to veer into the wind. She wants to complete a yaw and go swinging off in a wide circle, boom broad off and hull broad to the wind. In this position, she heels sharply as she rounds to, the outboard end of the boom and the clew of the sail may dip into the water, take charge of the steering, and what might happen is any sailor's guess. You fight broaching to by firm and instant helmsmanship upon the first indication of the boat to disregard the rudder and go into a spin. *Allow it nothing.* The forces which cause broaching to marshall with increasing power as the boat swings and quickly become too great to correct by ordinary rudder action.

Here we might take up the matter of rigging the jib artificially so as to draw before the wind, since a jib so rigged tends to discourage broaching to. The stunt is simply to "wing out" the jib by means of a light boom, often made of

"Wung Out" before the Wind

bamboo, on the side opposite the mainsail. This boom is called a "whisker pole." It has a wooden jaw which fits over the mast and, on the other end, a snap hook or lanyard which secures to the clew of the jib or the jib club. By setting the whisker pole and sheeting the jib sheet against it, the jib remains spread before the wind and serves as a powerful additional driving area. A boat sailing like this is sailing

Before the Wind

"wing-and-wing" or, à la Long Island Sound, "wung out." The pressure of a wung-out jib somewhat counteracts the off-center pressure of the mainsail and lessens broaching to tendencies a great deal.

Another warning on this point of sailing is in order here; that is the minor one of the danger inherent in some boats. When sailing with a strong wind on the quarter, which is somewhere between abeam and not quite dead astern, these boats have a strong tendency to veer into the wind and broach to. Usually it is a matter of faulty sail balance or too small a rudder—the effort of the wind on the sails fighting the effort of the lateral resistance of the hull. If the tendency becomes so powerful that it can be controlled only by superhuman strain on gear and tiller arm, there is no recourse but to reduce sail area. On the gaff-rigged boat, merely drop the peak of the gaff until the gaff is about horizontal. Then get sailing. If the pressure needs further reduction, tuck a reef into the mainsail. A jib-headed sail must be reefed.

Since the object is to lessen the sail area aft, the addition of sail area forward will give the same result. Therefore, you can sometimes relieve pressure by setting a larger jib, or a reaching jib or, as I have seen done, adding a jib topsail. Sometimes, too, it will pay to experiment with various settings of the centerboard. For a quartering wind, most boards should be about 30 per cent exposed.

The boat going downwind, especially the beamy boat, is prone to roll since the wind is exerting no stabilizing force on the sails. The seas, traveling in the same direction as the wind and the boat, have free rein to impart a slow, somewhat regular roll, not particularly unpleasant but potentially dangerous. The danger is that the extended boom and sail might dip into the water or the top of a long crest and, acting as a rudder, slew the boat around into a position of jibing.

Such a jibe would be full, a vicious power swing of unsheeted sail through 180 degrees of arc.

There are several ways of combating the dangers of rolling. First, top up the boom with the topping lift to keep it out of water. This will result in more draft or "belly" to the sail but will not reduce the drive in the least. Second (or instead of topping the boom), trim in the boom a few feet, thus reducing its extension outboard. Sail efficiency will be slightly reduced but, on the other hand, there will be a strong funneling tendency off the luff which is easy to gather and utilize by rigging the jib and sailing wing-and-wing.

Roll itself may be reduced by checking it with rudder action. There is a moment to the roll, soon evident, which you can reduce by appropriately timed steering. Roll is accompanied by a regular and predictable swinging of the bow from the course. By checking this swing with careful steering, roll itself is somewhat reduced. The course will not be straight, but a series of long slants downwind, making very little difference in the distance traveled. By averaging these slants, a true course can easily be made good.

Keelboats do not roll as much as keel-less boats. If you have followed usual centerboard practices in sailing before the wind, your centerboard will be all, or mostly all, sheathed and your boat will be keel-less. Drop the centerboard; you will become a keelboat and roll will be enormously decreased. What happens is simply that since a flat underwater plane, like a fixed keel or a centerboard, offers great resistance to being shoved "flatways" through the water by the rolling of the boat, such planes effectively reduce the extent of the roll. The keel has the same steadying effect before the wind as the sails have off the wind.

In the course of an afternoon's sail, you will normally go through many maneuvers calculated to carry you from point

Before the Wind

to point of sailing. In all cases it is wise for the beginner to go through the complete evolution and skip no step. Thus, in coming from on the wind to before the wind, or vice versa, go through and distinctly sail *off the wind* as you make the change-over. I think this is repetition, but it's quite important and will bear repeating.

We have learned how to get from on the wind to off the wind and reverse. This is the way to get from off the wind to before the wind and reverse.

You are sailing off the wind, on a reach. Broaden this reach by slacking off the mainsheet and heading the boat slightly away from the wind. Never mind the jib—it will soon be idle and useless. Then, slowly, slack the mainsheet and head the boat directly downwind. Throughout the maneuver keep the boat under complete control and never steer—not even a little bit!—beyond that point where the wind comes from *dead astern*. To do so is to invite an accidental jibe. You are now sailing before the wind. This maneuver is diagrammed below.

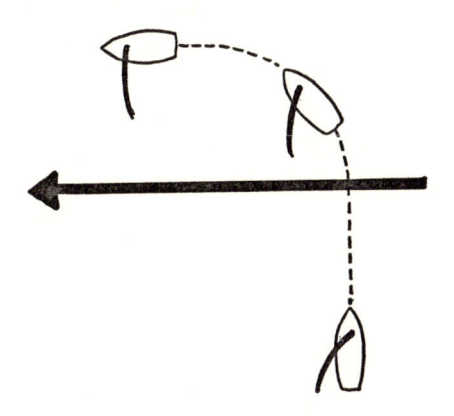

If you are sailing before the wind and wish to get off the wind, do exactly the reverse (Diagram, page 126). This means steer *away* from the side on which the sail is carried and at the same time trim in the mainsheet. The jib will "wake up" and draw; you will be sailing on a broad reach again and in the same direction (or on the same tack) as orig-

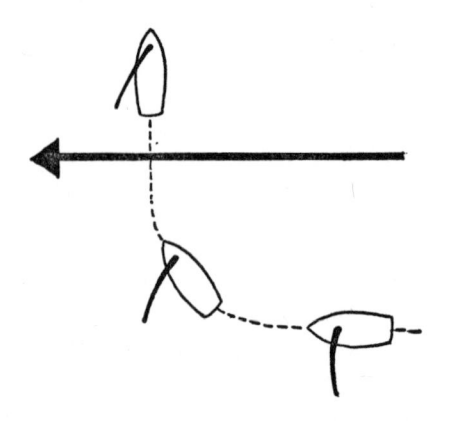

inally. Obviously, from this point of sailing you can trim and steer for a close reach and for pointing, etc.

But you can easily see that this isn't going to give you much freedom. Always the mainsail will be on the same side as it was when you started the maneuver, and you may want to sail a course which will necessitate carrying the sail on the opposite side. There are two ways to swing before the wind from a reach so that *you* and not the wind decides on which side your mainsail shall be carried. The first method is to simply tack onto the opposite board; the second is to jibe, which is neither contradiction nor heresy as you shall see.

To tack to the opposite board before the wind, let us say from a broad starboard reach, you simply close haul her, tack her and ease her off to a port reach—and then to before the wind. The sail will thus be on the starboard side and you must thereafter always keep the wind on the port side of dead astern. This is diagrammed in the sketch on page 127.

Before the Wind

While a slow and somewhat cumbersome method, it is absolutely safe. You can get into no trouble.

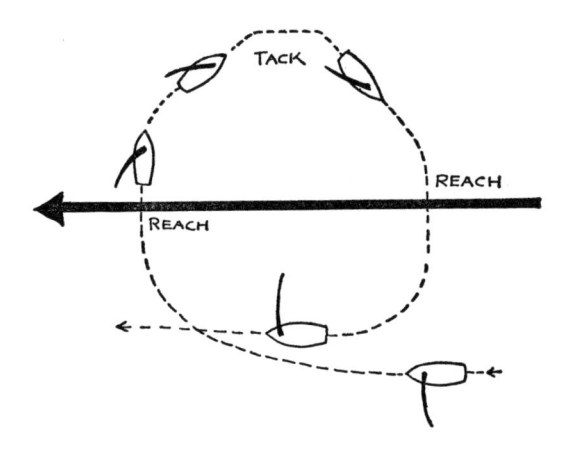

The other method, that of jibing, is fast and handy and must be used in races where time is important or in close quarters where maneuvering space is limited. The jibe, in this case, is *intentional;* there is no danger whatsoever in the intentional jibe. Here is the way to perform it. With the boat sailing before the wind, trim in the mainsheet until the sail is amidships. It is of the utmost importance that during this sail trimming the course of the boat is not changed in the least. Until the sail is amidships, tightly snugged down by its sheet, there is always danger of an accidental jibe. Now, sail amidships, put the helm over slightly so that the wind passes the point of dead astern and blows from the opposite quarter. Then, still carefully steering, pay out the mainsheet until the sail is again broad before the wind and, of course, on the opposite side to what it was.

In this, the controlled or intentional jibe, the wind has passed from side to side by the stern but, since the boom was securely sheeted down, there was no sail slack to bag the power of the wind. The leech of the sail merely flopped from side to side with a gentle sigh and the wind silently filled the opposite side of the sail. So off you are, before the wind, on the other tack.

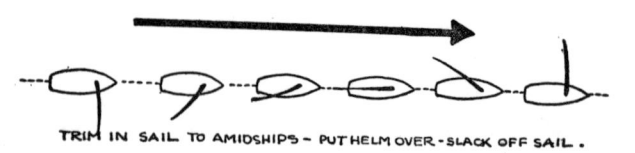

TRIM IN SAIL TO AMIDSHIPS – PUT HELM OVER – SLACK OFF SAIL.

The Intentional Jibe

It is important to sheet in the sail completely. To be careless about this, trimming in the sail to only the quarter and then, helm over, let the wind *blow* the sail across the stern, is called a "flying jibe" or "Bangor River Pop-over." Not only does this place a sudden and very great strain on rigging and sheets but it may result in an embarrassing situation called "goosewinged."

If the sail is not snugged down for the intentional jibe, the boom is apt to lift as the wind passes across the stern. This gives the sail a large bunt (or belly) and only the foot of the sail goes over to the opposite side as it should. The head of the sail remains on the same side, pressed hard against the spreader on its side and crossed by the leech. The result is a hurrah's nest which some people think looks like a pair of spread goose wings. Personally, I never could see the connection between the mess and the beautiful sleek goose wings. Gaff rigs are much more prone to goosewing than jib-headed rigs, due, of course, to the extension of the gaff.

You cannot pull the head of the sail over. The only way to get out of a goosewing is to jibe the entire sail back to the side on which the head is; then, try it again—your

Before the Wind

lesson learned, I hope. If you keep the sail always trimmed in to amidships, you cannot goosewing.

Goosewinged as a Result of a Flying Jibe

Thus, with this final point of sailing, we have become acquainted with all the maneuvers required for complete freedom of movement and direction under sail. The real trick of maneuverability is to understand thoroughly the evolutions from one point of sailing to another. There are short cuts, but for the time being, it is sound sense to concentrate on the safe and sane methods of handling your boat on all points of sailing.

It has always helped me a great deal to carry a mental image of the wind in my mind as I sail. This image is simply a large arrow across the sky, its tail at that point on the horizon where the wind "comes from" and its head at that point where the wind "goes to." This is fixed, steady and absolute; it is the stream of power which I use. The direction of the waves, of currents, of backwinds and eddies near headlands or in inshore bays or of anything else which *seems* to prove the wind false is automatically rejected by my mind. These are merely local disturbances, to be used or combated—my arrow in the sky alone remains always true. To this arrow, this stream of power, I present my sails in the most efficient way I know. As I change from point to point of sailing, it is *always* in relation to this invisible arrow.

Contributing to this mental picture are obvious physical factors. The "feel" of wind is one factor. Always, you feel the wind on your cheek or body and from it deduce its direction and strength. Yet this is not always reliable. There are backwinds from the sails, from fellow passengers and from deck fixtures. Also, the masthead hawk is prone to wander because it is affected by air currents from off the head of the sail and because, especially in light airs, it behaves somewhat like our door hung from an out-of-plumb jamb. The hardness or softness of the sails, especially their luffs, also indicate wind conditions. I think that the safest course to pursue is not to trust any of these things singly but, rather, to take the teachings of each and average them, representing that average by visualizing this vast arrow across the sky.

Naturally, I anchor my arrow to some visible shore or sea mark—a headland, a distant sand bank, an island, a shore mark like a lighthouse or building. (Never to another boat —which may sound a silly caution indeed but, I assure you, I have many times cussed myself out for discovering that I was unconsciously doing just this!) Coasting at night, it is easy and very pleasant to pin your arrow to a distant shore or navigation light or to the stars themselves. Another method is to convert the direction of the wind into a compass bearing and thereafter sail by compass. Indeed, for a long hitch this is by far the best method, since, obviously, you cannot sail too far before you catch up with your marks.

The Sea Scouts have in their Seamanship Manual a simple game which their leaders often use to teach "paper" sailing. It is called "Sail-O" and I include a description of it here because it might assist you in visualizing the various sailing positions and manuevers.

SAIL-O

On a Coast and Geodetic Survey chart, line off, with india ink, all the water areas into squares, say about ½-inch square. Provide several whittled water-line sailboat models, something like shown in the sketches above. These should have a pivoting cardboard sail or a bent nail to represent the main boom. Cut out an arrow of cardboard to show wind direction and go to junior's bureau and borrow his dice; or perhaps you have one of those spinning pointers which come with parlor games.

Now, decide upon starting and finishing points, say at opposite edges of the chart, determine wind direction and indicate it by laying the cardboard arrow on the chart, place a boat or two at the start, and cast the dice. "Sail" your boats toward the objective as many squares as the dice or the spinner indicate. Of course, you must actually sail, setting your sail correctly, avoiding shoals and dangers to navigation, other boats, etc. Go through the evolutions of jibing, tacking, mooring, docking, etc. You will be surprised how much you can learn from doing this seriously and how well the lessons will "stick." Naturally, you can, by playing against an opponent, engage in races and so make it a competitive game.

Incidentally, from this layout, you can easily learn Rules of the Road, the Buoyage System, Racing Tactics and Coastwise Navigation. Perhaps I'll remember, in the proper chapters, to describe such games.

And that's all there is to sailing—on the wind, off the wind and before the wind. You've got the foundation, the fundamentals, the red meat of the art. From now on, we go into the refinements.

CHAPTER NINE

Making Sail

WHEN I was a youngster, a marvelous boat named the *Blue Bird* was presented to me by a boatyard owner who was cleaning up his storage area. He said that the gol-darned thing was no gol-darned good, she was nail sick and ready to spring planks like a lobster pot in Pollack Rip and what's more, she was so tarnation smeared full of pitch and roofing tar that she was a fire hazard to the whole county and if I'd promise to take her gol-darned far away, I could have her—which discouraging words I had no trouble forgetting in my enthusiasm to become owner and skipper of a 13-foot catboat. It was impossible to delay that wonderful first sail more than the few hours necessary to stick a mast into her and hang a dirty sail to her spars. I sailed the *Blue Bird* a long time before the novelty had worn off enough to take the time to bend sail properly, to adjust my rigging and ballast her correctly.

Our boat, too, may be suffering from lack of attention to careful commissioning, and quite understandably so. This book has actually put you under sail and to sea rather quickly. Now, we will take time out to check back and be certain that boat, sails, spars and rigging are in the best possible condition to assure safety, efficiency and long life.

The hull should cause no great concern. A new boat will be ready to sail; her hull smooth and seamless. The old boat should be fitted out to bring her as nearly as possible to the underbody sleekness of a brand new craft. Seams should be filled flush and level with an elastic seam compound, nail holes puttied over, barnacles scraped off completely and the area vigorously sanded, and centerboard bottom, keel and skeg shorn of wood slivers and whiskers. A retarding force to fast sailing is the skin friction of the underwater hull. The smoother it is the less the friction. Even ripples of paint or the careless overlapping of two coats of paint add to skin friction.

By all means, even if you are on fresh water, paint the underwater hull with a paint designed to discourage marine plant and animal growth. On salt water, barnacles, mussels and various breeds of flora and fauna of the deep can foul the unpainted bottom to such an extent that you *can't* sail the boat, all within thirty summer days.

There are many good books available and the yachting journals have been printing the same list of "fitting-out hints" annually since the last century to help the amateur with hull-conditioning work. The subject is beyond the scope of this book.

With this reminder about hull condition, we shall go on to the power plant of the wind boat, which is most decidedly within the scope of this book. The power plant is the mechanism—mast, spars, rigging and sails—which drives the sailboat. Each must be in top-notch condition and balance to perform its part of the task of carrying sail.

Ordinarily, the mast is set at the correct rake, when the heel is in the mast step and the mast itself is centered in the mast hole in the partner. To change it, raking it forward or aft of a centered position, might upset the balance of the sails. Since there is and always will be a difference of opinion between sail designers as to whether or not the mast of a jib-headed rig should rake forward, aft or stand plumb, it is best to assume that centering the mast in the

Making Sail

partner hole will give the correct stand. Once stepped and the mast wedges firmly tapped home, the mast should stand straight, without curve or twist. To check this, lie on your back on the deck and, on a smooth sea or in a cradle, sight upward along the length of the mast on *all* sides.

The standing rigging, which is that rigging made of wire, serves as support and guy for the mast when under the load of full canvas. Setting up standing rigging is a delicate job—never should the standing rigging curve, bend or warp the mast. Rigging is set up at its lower end, by means of a turnbuckle. Remember always that tension

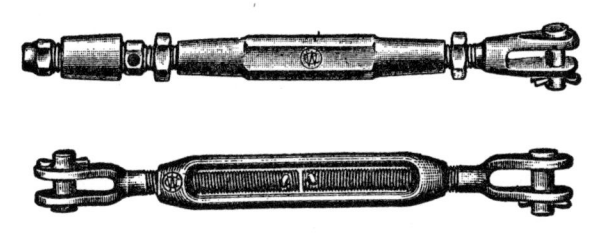

Rigging Turnbuckles

on wire rigging will tend to back open the turnbuckle and that, after adjustment, you must arrange a stopper to secure the barrel firmly. Various devices are in use—a hex nut which sets against the barrel of the turnbuckle, cotter pins which slip into a hole in the top and bottom stud ends and engage the barrel (an unpleasant gadget indeed as various rips and tears in my spinnaker can testify), or a sheer pole or rod which passes through the clevis of the studs on both upper and lower shrouds.

The upper shrouds pass over the spreader and to the deck; the lower shrouds directly to the deck and to the turnbuckle fitted to the chain plate *aft* of the chain plate of the upper shroud. In the way of the spreader, the wire is "adrift," it is *not* secured to the outboard tip of the spreader. However, it should be served to prevent undue wear and loosely secured to the spreader so that it cannot jump out of the fork which forms the tip of the usual spreader. For this use marlin or light copper or brass wire.

Set up the lower shrouds first. Set them up hand-tight only. They should not sing when you snap them but be merely taut. Be very careful to adjust them to equal tensions. Your best indicator for this is to sight the mast. With both sides adjusted, the mast should still be straight and show no indication of curving off to port, starboard or aft. Next set up the lower forward stay, or jib stay. It should be just hand-tight and should not curve the mast forward in the least. If the headstay is not equipped with a turnbuckle you can gain or lose a little length by twisting the wire, with the lay to make it shorter, and against the lay to lengthen it. In this event, the tension on the lower shrouds as well as the weight of the hoisted and filled sail is intended to keep the stay taut.

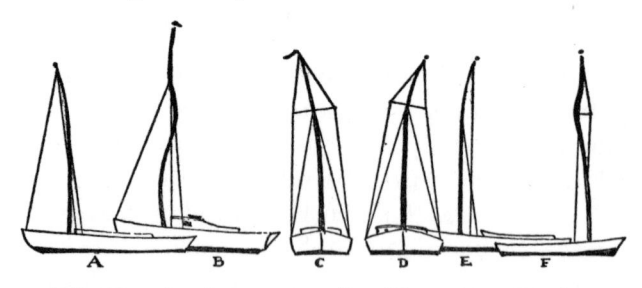

The Results (exaggerated) of Improper Staying

With the lower shrouds, lower headstay and backstays set up the part of the mast below the upper ends of them (usually from the spreaders down) should be rigid and straight. It is often difficult to set correctly the forward stays since they do not pull against an opposing stay as do the shrouds. Try setting the lower forward stay with the

Making Sail

sail hoisted or with *both* backstays set taut but yet not bending the mast aft. The upper forward stay is best set while the boat is sailing (on the wind is better than off the wind and never while before the wind) and with weather backstay set. It is imperative that the forward stays should be so adjusted that they do not bend the mast forward nor that hoisted sails bend the mast aft. Be careful with this. A curve or bow in the mast soon becomes permanent and no amount of staying will remove it completely.

The upper lengths of the mast of a jib-headed sail plan (sometimes called Marconi rig because the staying system looks somewhat like the old-fashioned Marconi wireless antenna towers) should be somewhat supple. Suppleness here imparts a beneficial bow or bend to leeward under canvas which gives an increased and desirable draft to the luff of the mainsail. For this reason the upper shrouds may be somewhat slack—not sloppy, but, on the other hand, far from high G. Under sail, the weather shrouds become immensely taut as they resist the side-thrust of the sail and mast and the lee shrouds hang loose, sometimes quite dismally so. Provided the mast stands straight *without sail* this is perfectly correct and nothing to worry about in the least.

Watch the spreaders. They occasionally sag or press forward. If they do, check the sockets or hinges where they join the mast. See that they are securely screwed home at this point. Iron spreaders are frequently bent. They may be straightened by unshipping them and hammering them straight with a wooden mallet—an iron hammer will chip off the galvanizing.

In setting up shrouds of the gaff-headed rig, make all stays taut. In this rig no suppleness is desirable at the masthead. Unlike the Marconi masthead which must support only a small narrow area of sail, the gaff-headed masthead must take half or more of the full weight of the sail which hangs from the gaff. The peak of this gaff is supported by halyards leading directly to the masthead. There is a powerful tension here both sideways and aft which the masthead stays alone must combat. Undue slack will result in bending and weaving of the masthead, and eventual rupture in the area of the gaff jaws.

Any mast which shows a tendency to bend and weave in spite of proper staying requires a jackstay or a pair of jackstays. These stays reach from the masthead forward to a short strut (like a half spreader) between masthead and main spreader; then to the mast or the deck. Jackstays combat forward thrust. If your boat is equipped with a jackstay, set it up *before* setting up other rigging.

In racing, or at least in certain kinds of racing, a flexible rig is used. Mechanisms are provided to impart certain curves, rakes and bows to both mast and boom which cause the sail to set with maximum efficiency on various points of sailing. Rigging becomes complex. Yet these boats do simply marvelous things in their battles with the wind and each other. It is sailing raised to the nth degree. Star class and other strictly racing craft have many of these devices. Vanderbilt's *Ranger,* probably the last of the America's Cup racers had the famous rubber boom; some modern small classes even have adjustable mast steps. But the most desirable of these features of flexibility in rig is that which permits controlled curves in the upper mast. This feature is possible without special mechanical equipment; it is simply a matter of ideal tensions on the upper stays. Experiment on your own boat. Sometimes a turn one way or the other on a turnbuckle will allow the mast to curve in exactly the right way to give you a very powerful draft in the luff, a draft that will seem suddenly to wake up the whole boat. Uffa Fox and others have written at length about this matter of nth degree sailing.

Making Sail

To this properly stayed mast and its boom we bend our sails, and this, too, approaches being a fine art. In Chapter II we have learned how to bend and hoist sails in somewhat the same spirit as we might hang wash on a line. Let us now make sail in a more professional manner.

The foot of the sail should be hauled out hand-tight and the luff set up smartly as we have seen. In the event that the clew or tack are not fitted with special receivers for the cringles, you must lash these points down with line. Use a laid cotton line, the kind called awning cord on shore. The tack is simply made fast by several round turns between the cringle and the eye in the jaws or on the gooseneck and held down by a square knot. Be sure to lash this so that the sail is as far forward as possible and so avoid a baggy bunt in the neighborhood of the tack.

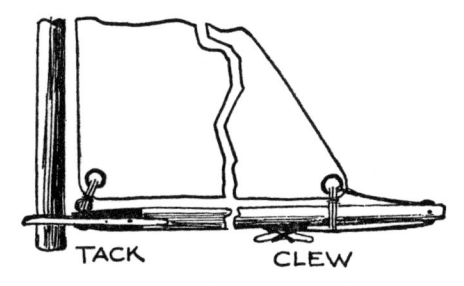

Tack and Clew Holddowns and Clew Outhaul

For the clew of the sail, take a much longer line, say a fathom or more in length. This line is used *only* for hauling the clew aft along the boom. It usually passes over a sheave or through a hole in the very after end of the boom, then forward to a cleat within reach of the helmsman. On large boats, this clew outhaul line might be in the form of a tackle. The clew outhaul is in reality running rigging since it is often necessary or desirable to change the draft of the sail by adjusting the tension of the foot while under way. It is essential that you do not haul the clew aft with too much strength. To do so will stretch the sail, especially a new sail, and forever destroy its "cut." Hand-tight only is the rule always! If the sail becomes wet from rain, or dew or flying spray, immediately slack off the outhaul to allow for the shrinkage of the wet sail. If you set the sail wet, or it dries after becoming wet, be prepared to tighten on the outhaul as it stretches.

It is not good practice to use the clew outhaul also to bowse down the clew to the boom. Use a separate and shorter line for this. If the foot of the sail laces to the boom, or if the sail track in the way of the clew is not of extra heavy gauge, you will *have* to do this. On one of my boats, I used a metal ring, served with marlin, for this "hold down." A snap at the clew secured to the ring. It was a successful piece of forecastle-made gear and saved the annoyance of lashing the clew before every sail.

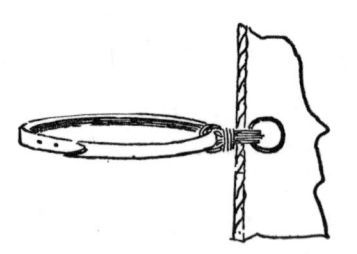

Lashing of a Mast Hoop to a Sail

The gaff-rigged sail must be secured to the gaff in the same manner—head of the sail hand-taut only; throat and peak lashed to the spar securely. In addition, the gaff-rigger requires the luff of the sail to be lashed to the mast hoops. This is done with cotton line or white fish line. Marlin, which is wonderfully strong and durable, has the fault of being tarred and thus soiling sails. Pass several turns of line

Making Sail

between the hoop and the luff-grommets, snug up, then take several turns around the original turns and secure the lashing by laying a square knot on it (See sketch page 140). Be sure to lash the hoops to the grommets, which are distinguished from reef cringles by being smaller than cringles and being located between (not at) reef bands.

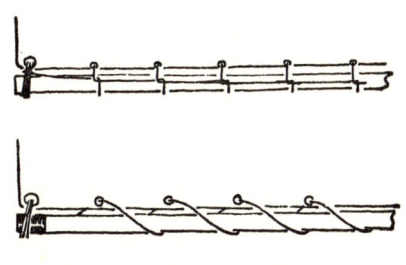

Jib Lashings to Club

The jib foot is also stretched hand-tight only and lashed to the club (if your boat is equipped with one) in the same manner as the mainsail. In lacing the jib foot to the club use either of the two hitches shown above, whichever seems to make the jib set with the least wrinkles. Many jibs will set best "loose-footed"—which means that they are lashed only at the tack and clew, without lacing. This trick often results in elimination of the undesirable bunt in the jib caused by a slack headstay which cannot be set up.

The most important part of making sail is hoisting the mainsail so that it sets properly. Proper setting is a matter of tension on outhaul and halyard, halyard lead, flatness of leech and correct pocketing of the battens. Understand that your sail is not a flat sheet of canvas. It is cut full; it has been designed to have a certain amount of bagginess or bunt. You can never stretch all of it flat at the same time —not and have a usable efficient sail thereafter.

Hoist the sail up to that point where there are distinct

wrinkles running from aloft, parallel to the mast. The luff will not be flat; it will have softness and "fluffiness"; the whole sail will appear to be "bigger" than the triangle in which it is confined by the spars.

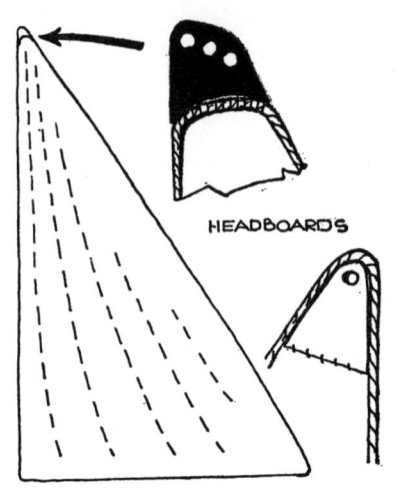

Desirable Wrinkles in a Mainsail

Failing to achieve this looseness in the hoisted sail, look to the lead from the headboard. The headboard has three or more holes to which you can fasten the snap hook of the halyard. Try several holes and thereafter use the one which gives the best "hang" to the sail. If there is a sharp wrinkle passing along the inboard ends of the batten pockets, look first to the length of the battens. These should be *shorter* than the pockets. If the sharp wrinkle persists, try a different lead from the headboard or haul the foot out more. If a series of small sharp wrinkles radiates upward from the boom, haul in on the clew outhaul; the foot is probably too loose. However, distinguish these wrinkles from those caused by the boom lacing or sail slides.

The leech should stand flat, neither sagging off from the

main plane of the sail nor curling inward. To control this, your sail has a light cotton line built into the leech from head to clew. You seldom need it, since most leeches are amply supported by the sail battens. If you do set up on the leech line, watch it carefully. It is a long light line and stretches enormously, and by the same sign shrinks enormously when wet. Improperly set, the leech line can completely destroy the efficiency of the sail. Under sail, the leech should carry aft the airfoiled curvature of the sail. If it does not, use the leech line, and you might check battens. They should be springy and flexible, bending to the curve of the sail and not stand straight and unyielding. Their purpose is to keep the leech from flapping and sagging off and should not cause bunts in the sail between battens.

These remarks are also applicable to setting the jib. Hoist it so that the desirable wrinkles appear immediately aft of the luff and carefully check the leech. A tight or pinched leech on the jib will backwind the mainsail, pouring air against the luff at the very point where the vacuum is exerting its forward pull. Jibs are often cantankerous critters indeed and require a good deal of experimentation with the lead of the sheet or sheets before they set properly.

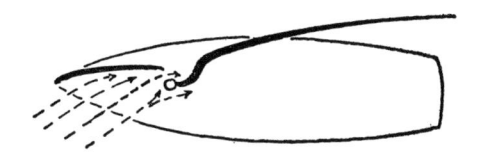

A Poorly Set Jib Backwinding the Mainsail

Clubbed jibs usually set best when the lead comes from well forward of the clew. The trouble is that, while you can easily make a jib set correctly at one point, immediately you trim or slack the sheet, it takes on a new and inefficient set. There is no complete cure that I know of. Sometimes, shortening or lengthening the traveller helps. While it is a great convenience to have a jib which is controlled by one sheet on either tack, the jib will usually set better if rigged with double sheets. I have, on a small knockabout which hangs to one of my moorings, a triple sheet rig. One sheet is rigged from the traveller to the jib in the usual knockabout manner and permits sailing on either tack with one sheet setting. But in addition, I have rigged port and starboard sheets, which when used permit the quite perfect trimming of the jib. This arrangement is ideal for long tacks and for racing, yet for maneuvering in close quarters or loafer sailing, the single middle sheet serves well enough. This rig, which is not my own invention by any means, is shown in the sketch below. The lead of the outboard sheets can be determined only by experimentation on your own boat.

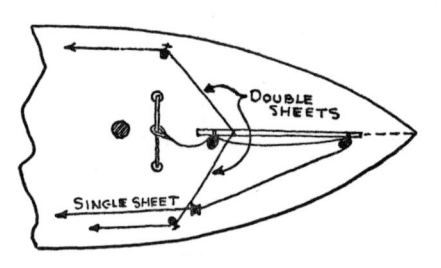

Jibsheets

The overlapping jib must have double sheets of necessity. The lead of these must be very carefully worked out. When sheeted home, there should be no sharp wrinkles from the clew toward the luff. Usually modern headsails are mitre-cut, which means that the cloths of which the sail is made meet at a nearly horizontal seam which runs from the clew to somewhere along the luff. This seam bisects the angle made by the foot and the leech at the clew. On nar-

Making Sail

row headsails, like working jibs, the sheet lead will generally work out best if the sheet does not exactly bisect the angle but has a more acute angle between the mitre and the leech than between the mitre and the foot. For squarer sails, like Genoas and reaching jibs, the reverse will work out better. Too great an angle of lead results in bagginess or slackness along the foot or the leech.

Sheet Lead for an Overlapping Jib

The result of experimenting with the leads of overlapping headsails is often discouraging. Perfection on one point of sailing is far from perfection on a different point. Yet the matter is important—so important that marine hardware manufacturers offer various devices which provide a series of different adjustable leads from a standard fair-lead fitting which may be moved on a track screwed to the deck. Some racing classes are regularly fitted with these devices. Ordinarily about three different locations for the sheet lead will give the required flexibility and, for the average smart sailboat, these leads can consist of three of the several types of deck snatch blocks or open fair-leads.

Yachtsmen follow a standard procedure in making and dousing sail which it would be well to adopt since it avoids much confusion, when, after the sail bag is opened, the search for proper corners of the sail commences.

First, always be sure that your sails are dry before stowing them away in the bag. Remove the battens as the sail is loosely bundled for carrying ashore. On land, sails are best dried by spreading them out over a network of lines either outdoors or in a warm loft or other space. Do not hang them from a wash line with the corners pinned. There is no surer way to stretch them out of shape than this. Drying on a lawn is not satisfactory; only one side dries and when you turn the sail over to dry the bottom side, darned if the top doesn't absorb moisture from the earth again. A wooden platform, like a club veranda or a wide wharf, on the other hand, makes a perfectly satisfactory drying rack.

When the sails are thoroughly dry, use the following procedure in folding them, for reasons which I will present later. Spread the sail out on a clean area. Two can do the job—one at the tack and one at the clew. Each man takes

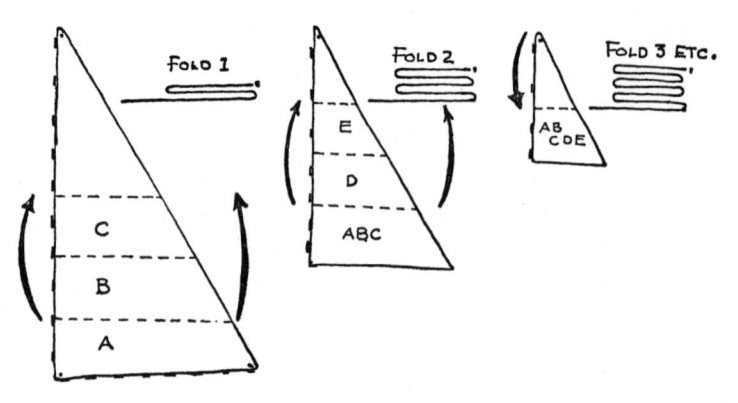

To Fold a Marconi Mainsail

Making Sail

hold of the edge of the sail (one the luff and one the leech) at a point from the foot a trifle less than the depth of the sail bag. Pick up the sail here and carry it upward toward the head the same distance, making three layers of sail the length of the foot and the width of the depth of the sail bag. Smooth out the wrinkles, then, taking the folded bundle at the upper corners, carry it toward the head. You will now have five layers of sail. Smooth these out and continue until the entire sail is a long packet of folded sail.

Now, starting at the luff, roll this packet toward the leech. You will end up with a tight bundle, showing the foot sail slides on the bottom, the leech along the side and folded sail on the top—and it will fit perfectly into the sail bag.

The jib is folded in exactly the same manner if you have taken the batten out of the pockets. If not, and many skippers do not bother removing jib battens, proceed in the same way but fold as if the foot were the luff, i.e., carry the luff toward the leech. Then, when you roll the folded bundle, the battens will lie lengthwise of the packet and the whole stow in the bag alongside the bundled mainsail.

Here is the advantage of folding your sails in this way. Upon bending them, you will find that your sails can be handled as a *bundle* right up to the point of hoisting them, and what that will do in keeping them out of dirty bilges and from under feet is a minor blessing.

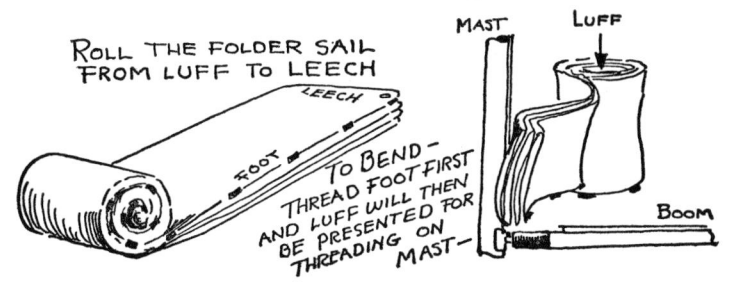

To bend the mainsail, lay the bundle on deck, near the mast, and as you haul the folded leech aft thread the foot slides to the boom track. The bundle will now be a long packet lying along the boom and, on the forward end, the luff slides will be presented exactly where you need them at the foot of the mast, ready to thread. Thus until the moment you are ready to get under way, your sail will remain a bundle, out of your way and safe from soiling or accident. Just before hoisting, break the leech out, insert the battens and you are ready to make sail. The jib is set the same way —lace the foot to the boom, thread the luff snaps and you are ready to make sail.

It is very simple and easy to unbend Marconi sails, quite as simple and easy as furling sail and putting them to sleep under sail covers. However, on a cruising boat, or between sails during the day or week end on the small boat, you might wish to furl sails.

This is the way to do it. As you drop the mainsail pull, or have your mate pull, the leech aft. Then cast off the main halyard from the head and slack the outhaul well. *Take out the battens.* Now, one man aft and the other about amidships to tuck, fold the sail back and forth over the boom (which is now in its crotch) in successive layers. Make the first fold good and wide; this will form a hammock into which you tuck the rest of the folded sail. Now bring this wide lower fold around and over the furled sail to form a smooth cover and secure the bundle with a temporary gasket. Then starting at the mast, work aft, tying a gasket about every three feet. These should go once around the sail only with a second turn around sail and boom, and stop with a slippery square knot laid on top. The after end of the sail is merely rolled on itself and stopped down with short gaskets or a cotton lacing line. Over this spread the sail cover. First fit and lace the mast coat and be sure that

Making Sail 149

halyards are *outside*. Then roll the cover aft, stretching it aft and lace the two lower edges together.

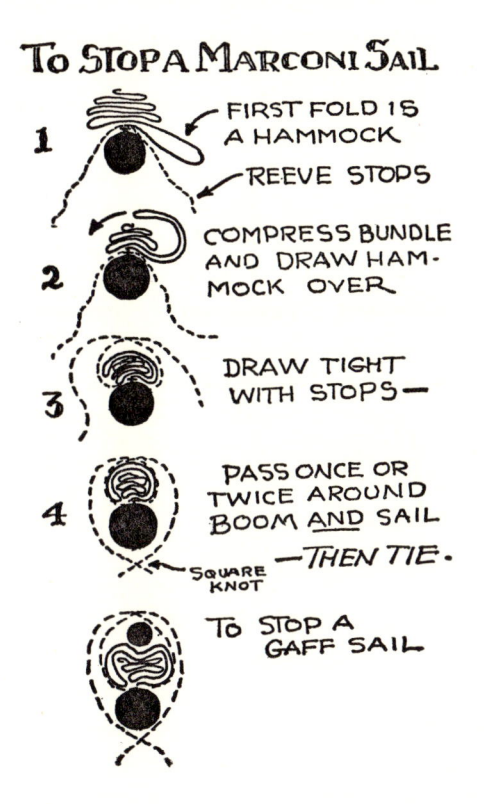

To Stop a Marconi Sail

1 — First fold is a hammock / Reeve stops

2 — Compress bundle and draw hammock over

3 — Draw tight with stops —

4 — Pass once or twice around boom AND sail — Then tie. (Square knot)

To stop a gaff sail

Do not think of leaving your sails furled overnight without a sail cover. Summer night dew will surely shrink the sail against its gaskets and cause trouble, sail trouble of this kind being mildew and stretching out of shape, possibly ripping and tearing. Never cover sails unless they are dry. You can dry them while bent by hoisting them about two-thirds of the way and letting them flap gently in a warm drying wind.

The best place for sails when not in use is ashore; bagged and stored in a dry place. I have never seen a locker or sail bin on a small class boat fit to store sails; always they are damp, warm and too near the bilge. If you must keep your sails on board, keep them bent and between sails furl and cover them. They are far better off in the sun and wind, than under a deck or seat.

MAKE SAIL IN THIS ORDER ⟶
⟵ DOUSE SAIL IN THIS ORDER

The Order of Making and Dousing Sail

In making sail on all fore-and-aft rigged craft, the aftermost sail is made first, doused last. The idea behind this, obviously, is to have our boat behave as a weather vane by streaming herself into the wind until we are ready to sail and, reversing the process, to lay docilely at anchor or dock when we have finished sailing.

I must admit that my little *Blue Bird* never received the care and attention I advise for your boat. I was only thirteen then, learning the hard way. But I recall that, when the time came for my next boat, I got rid of her as I had received her—for nothing. She was worth exactly that for I had not yet learned the lesson that a boat with good power—carefully used sails, carefully maintained spars and rigging and thoughtful working out of sail handling problems—always had value. A perfectly sound reason for heeding the lessons of this chapter, though you may think them merely making a fetish of a simple pleasure, is the crass one of maintaining the value of your boat.

CHAPTER TEN

Carrying Sail

THE ART of carrying sail is a complex one; it extends far beyond the simple making of sail by hoisting canvas aloft and sheeting it so that, somehow, the boat moves in the direction we wish it to move. Carrying sail, as I shall attempt to demonstrate in this chapter, is *using* sail in the most efficient manner possible; it is carrying the right sail at the right time in the right manner; it is achieving and maintaining balance between sails and boat; it is adjustment of trim, of helm, of windage—a happy control and reduction of all the forces which interfere with efficient sailing and the encouragement of all the forces which forward efficient sailing.

With sail made, after bending in the correct manner, the sails might be termed "fixed." Under way, they are capable of no further major adjustment except the adjustment possible by sheeting in or out. Their relationship to the boat itself is alone capable of adjustment. As we have seen, by means of the sheets, we control these "fixed" areas of sail so that they provide power to drive the boat into the wind, across the wind and before the wind. Sheets, however, have one more function and that is to allow adjustment of the sails so that the *mainsail takes from the wind its maximum power.*

Note that it is the mainsail which is so adjusted. All other sails are adjusted so that they too draw the maximum

Carrying Sail

power from the wind, but not beyond that point of adjustment at which they interfere in any way with the maximum drive of the mainsail. In plain words to the sloop sailor, this means set your mainsail to draw its best; then the jib to draw *its* best provided it does not backwind or otherwise interfere with the performance of the mainsail.

The entire surface of a sail is not equally efficient. The most efficient area is one that roughly parallels the mast

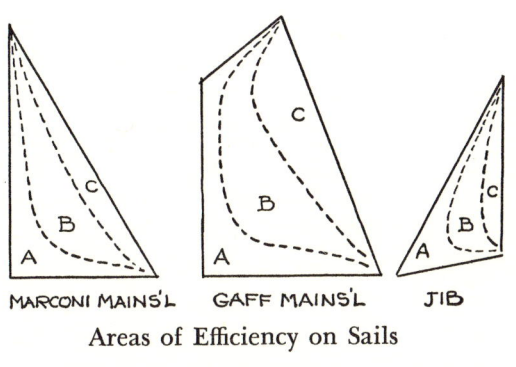

Areas of Efficiency on Sails

(A) Most Drive   (B) Moderate Drive   (C) Least Drive

and the foot. The least efficient area is adjacent to the leech. Between these two areas lies a region of moderate drive or efficiency (See sketch above). The great enemy of complete efficiency are eddies. To discourage eddies, the sail is so cut and so sheeted that it becomes air-foiled, taking its shape, unlike the airplane wing of our earlier chapter, from the component forces of the wind itself. Nevertheless, some eddies always remain and we try to present our sail to the wind so that there remains the least amount of eddies.

Eddies in the wake of the mast and boom attack the leeward side of the luff and foot. These are especially ruinous since it is here that the wind, its direction changed, exerts the all-important forward pull or vacuum. (Vacuum is strictly a layman's term. It's not technically correct but, since it is quite understandable, let's continue to use it.) So, since we cannot completely eliminate eddies at the mast, not even by designing streamlined masts and fittings, we must sheet the sail so that, in spite of eddies, the luff is presented at that angle and that degree of fullness which will give the most drive. Naturally, this position is a compromise between what we'd like and what we can get. Other parts of the book have discussed this in detail—hard luff, but neither too hard nor fluttering, etc.—but remember always that the first step in carrying sail correctly is to get the correct "luff" by correct sheeting.

Obviously, wrinkles at the mast or at the boom cause eddies, which is why the last chapter cautioned about wrinkles of the wrong kind. The right kind of wrinkles (those parallel to the mast) are ironed out by the wind; in the idle sail they represent merely the fullness required to gain a proper, hard, rounded luff when under sail.

In the area of moderate drive, the vacuum begins to taper off in pulling power and, on the windward side, there commences a forward pushing power. Obviously, eddies here would interfere with the free passage of wind aft on the windward side and vacuum on the leeward side and so, too, we try to avoid the wrinkles here which cause eddies. Racing skippers go much further. Many like their sails sewn in certain ways, cloths seamed horizontally, reef points omitted and the like, all so that the sail becomes the smoothest possible non-eddying surface. Interesting experiments with unseamed sails of cellophane some years ago proved the increased efficiency of a really "slick" sail surface. The second step, then, in carrying sail correctly is, in so far as possible but never at the expense of the luff, to sheet the sail so that the central moderate drive area is comfortably full and drawing and not soft or fluttering.

The area immediately forward of the leech is the least efficient. It sags off to leeward because of the long stretch between masthead and the movable boom. This sag is especially noticeable in gaff-rigged boats and accounts for that type being less efficient on the wind than a jib-headed rig. It is here, too, that eddies off the windward edge of the leech curl backward and tend to destroy the remaining vacuum on the leeward side. It is to keep the leech flat and reasonably well airfoiled that we introduce battens here and have a leech line with which to control somewhat the leech. The third step in carrying sail correctly is, in so far as possible but never at the expense of destroying the efficiency of the moderate drive area, to sheet the sail so that the leech area is flat, airfoiled and drawing.

It is seldom possible to do this unless the sail is correctly bent, the battens of sufficient number and length, the leech line correctly adjusted and clew and head correctly secured. Therefore it is of the utmost importance that sail is first made correctly. Efficiency, we might say, stems from the luff and spreads aft, but it does not usually reach the leech area. We require "artificial" means to stimulate efficiency here.

The perfectly setting sail appears to be modelled of a precious substance, alabaster or jade or obsidian. It is a beautiful thing, a full drawing sail, and very seldom seen —no humps, no flats, no bunts and not a wrinkle from clew to head. Try, by carefully making sail and carefully carrying sail, to achieve this smooth, modelled beauty. If you do, you have an efficient sail, exerting its maximum drive.

And remember—first maximum efficiency for the mainsail and after that the jib.

The jib can rarely be sheeted for its maximum power. To do so would, as we have seen, backwind the mainsail which we must have 100 per cent efficient. So we carry the jib sheeted at a "compromise point." It, like all other sails, has the three rough divisions of degree of drive. While, in view of the above remark, the jib might seem quite a useless sail, the opposite is true. The jib is amply justified because it performs in several ways which contribute to the general drive.

First, it contributes the rather mighty drive of its own long luff, especially when sailing close-hauled. The efficiency of this luff does not vanish too quickly as the sail is slacked to leeward to avoid interference with the mainsail. It always pulls *some*. Off the wind, or wung out before the wind, the jib needs no apologies.

Further, the air spilling off the leech of the jib destroys some of the eddies from the mast which normally invade the luff area of the mainsail. Thus it helps the mainsail drive. And, still further, the jib creates a "funnel" through which the wind rushes with increased velocity reaching the mainsail at exactly the point at which velocity is needed most—the leeward side of the mainsail luff. It is these two features which have led to the development of the modern overlapping jib. The overlapping jib contributes to mainsail drive very much. Its own large area, as such, contributes very little to the drive of the boat. It is essentially a device to increase wind velocity on the luff of the mainsail.

The fourth step in carrying sail correctly is to sheet the jib so that it draws in its own right as much as possible but also assists the mainsail in drawing. Under no circumstances must it interfere with the proper drawing of the mainsail. As I have pointed out in Chapter IX, this ideal setting can seldom be achieved by ordinary jib sheets. You will probably have to experiment with various jib-sheet

Carrying Sail

types and directions of lead to reach perfection. But the efficient jib, too, seems to be modelled of a solid. By no means, does sheeting at the "compromise point" mean that the jib is sloppy, or partly luffing. The adjustment is delicate, but perfectly possible if sail is carefully made and carried.

Sail carrying is also a matter of sail balance. If sails are out of balance it is reflected in helm. The helm which must correct a major unbalance of the sails interferes with the free passage of the hull through the water—inefficiency.

Balanced sails will be reflected in a light helm. At no time will you need continuous acute rudder angles to keep the boat on course. She will seemingly steer herself with an occasional and *very slight* effort on your part if, that is, she is a correctly designed boat, correctly sparred, canvased and ballasted.

However, no boat but for the rare exception, is designed to balance perfectly. Boats are quite deliberately designed

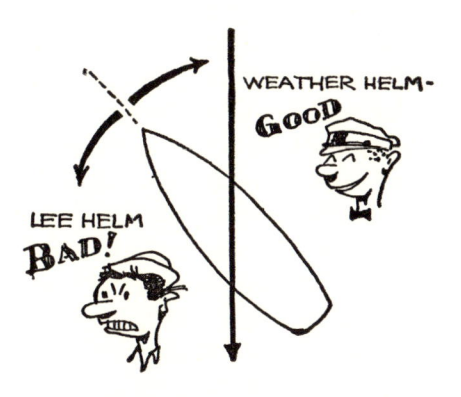

to have a tendency, without rudder action, to head slowly into the wind. Obviously, this is a safety measure. If for any reason the helm is left unattended, the boat will head into the wind, stand up straight, luff and cease sailing. Her *inclination* is always to head for safety, the position of luffing. The boat which will do this is said to have a *weather helm*. Within reason, a weather helm is desirable. It becomes out of reason if the boat has so much weather helm that it requires excessive rudder action to keep her sailing and from heading into the wind. We want our sails a *little* out of balance but not too much.

A boat which, without rudder, tends to head away from the wind is said to carry a *lee helm*. A lee helm is undesirable. If the helm is left unattended, the boat will fall away from the wind, heel sharply, perhaps knockdown and fill, eventually wear, jib and careen about in dizzy gyrations. She will never stop sailing while the wind blows. Lee helm is not only undesirable, it is dangerous.

Mild cases of excessive lee or weather helm may be cured by fairly simple means—ballasting, trimming, adjusting mast rake, etc. Severe cases lead to inquiring into hull design and sail balance. Few hulls worthy of the name are so poorly designed that proper sail balance cannot correct the faults. But let's have a look at sail balancing, briefly, before we discuss adjusting these balances to cure helm trouble.

Let us visualize your boat, sails hoisted and close-hauled centerboard down, lying broadside to the wind. If the sails were mounted on a pivot running horizontally to the exact center of their area, the wind would blow with equal pressure on all sides of the pivot and the sails remain broadside to the wind. They would not, since they are balanced on the pivot, go flying off like a weather vane or a hawk. This pivoting point is called, by naval architects, the center of effort of the sails—the theoretical center of the wind's effort on them. It is abbreviated CE.

Now forget the sails for a moment. Think of the hull. A force is trying to push it sideways through the water. The

Carrying Sail

force is applied at such a point that the resistance of the hull to being pushed is exerted with equal strength on each side of this point somewhat like our pivot, you see. The boat moves sideways; it does not go flying off bow first or stern first like our weather vane would in wind, since the force is equalized. This balancing point at which the force is applied is called, by naval architects, the center of lateral resistance of the hull. It is abbreviated CLR.

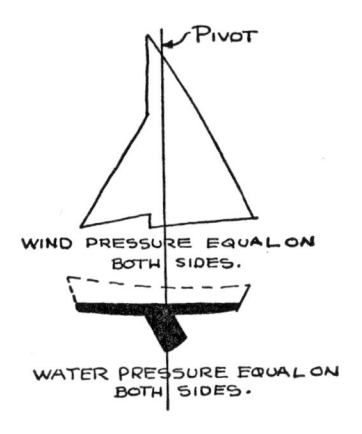

WIND PRESSURE EQUAL ON BOTH SIDES.

WATER PRESSURE EQUAL ON BOTH SIDES.

Now let's combine the sail and the hull, joining them together with masts, stays and sheets. Neither hull nor sails, when the force of the wind or the force of resistance is applied, may now move independently. They must move, or resist movement, together. It is obvious that unless the CE and the CLR are occupying a position along an identical vertical line, there will be unequal pressure, resistance or both and the whole out of balance. The assembly will not remain balanced on the pivoting line; it will fly off, like a vane in the wind. If it is greatly out of balance it will fly off quickly. If it is only slightly out of balance it will fly off slowly.

However, if there is balance, CE and CLR matching, we

need no corrective force (like the rudder) to achieve balance and, theoretically, the boat should sail without steering, the position of the sails alone "setting the course." A boat which has these centers of effort coinciding should sail herself, and she would if all other factors affecting balance were stable and fixed.

The reason that we want balance is so that we require a minimum of corrective rudder action as we sail. When the rudder is in any position but straight amidships, it is using power, power that should be used only for going ahead. If the unbalance is severe, we will *always* require the use of the rudder and the boat *never* will or can go its fastest.

We do not want the boat in absolute balance. We want it to tend very slightly toward a favorable unbalance so that the bow of the boat will veer gently into the wind; into safety. To achieve this we design the boat so that the CE is slightly forward of the CLR. Then, with very slight rudder, we can keep the boat in balance as we sail.

To know the centers (or balance) of your boat with complete accuracy, it is necessary to consult with a naval architect. This gentleman applies an exact and complex science with a good deal of practical experience and has no difficulty in arriving at a cure. I might mention that there are many factors entering into the calculation which make a universally correct answer impossible. Always, because the sea changes and your spars change and your sails change, the answer must be approximate only. And for all practical purposes, since we can apply several local correctives, the approximate answer is quite satisfactory.

This is the way (if you are not a naval architect) to check the balance of your sails. Work it out graphically, to a convenient scale, on paper. Graph paper, a scale ruler, compass and pencil will do nicely. First, draw the outline of your sails to scale in correct relation to each other and indi-

Carrying Sail 161

cate the mast. Then work out the CE of each sail; then the total (or combined) CE. The sketch below suggests how to do this.

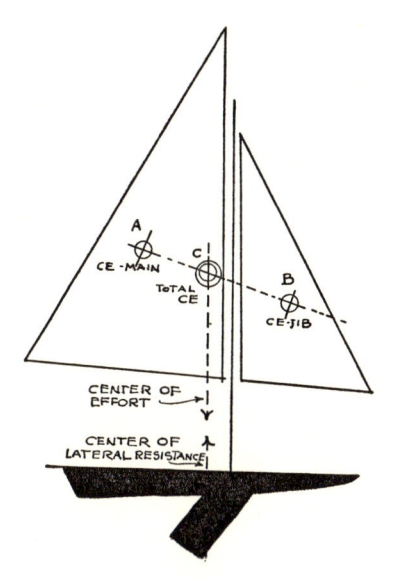

Drop a vertical line, square to a water line to which the sails have been correctly related, down from this total CE.

Note that in arriving at the total CE, the areas of the individual sails must be known. In figuring sail areas do not consider the area of roaches or of the overlapping parts of overlapping sails. Areas are figured as shown in the sketch, page 162. Next, draw to scale the exact *underwater* profile of your boat. Show the centerboard all the way down, and the skeg but not the rudder unless it is very large (like a catboat rudder) and then draw only the forward half of it. Be sure to indicate the water line and the location of the mast step. (Here is where we leave theoretical naval architecture completely and use a dory shop method for finding the CLR.) Transfer this drawing—which, by the

TO LOCATE CENTER OF EFFORT

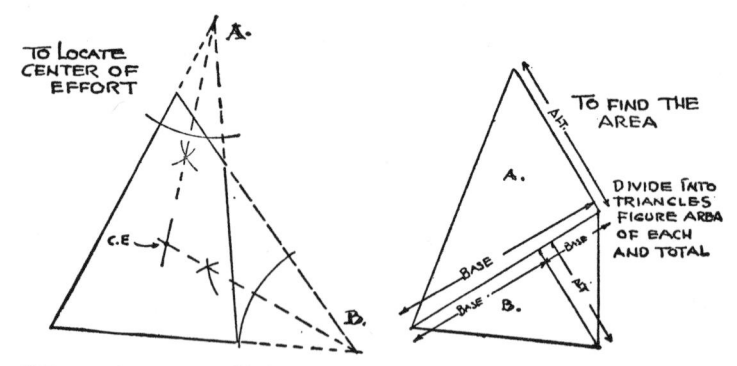

EXTEND THE FOUR SIDES TO FORM 2 TRIANGLES. BISECT EACH ANGLE AS SHOWN (A & B) THE INTERSECTION OF THE BISECTING LINES IS THE C. of E.

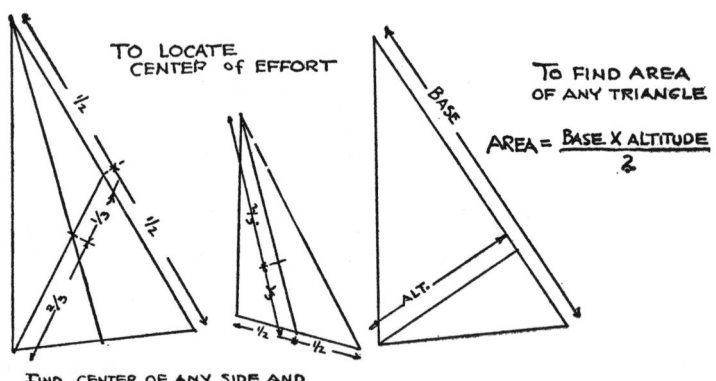

TO FIND THE AREA

DIVIDE INTO TRIANGLES FIGURE AREA OF EACH AND TOTAL

TO LOCATE CENTER of EFFORT

FIND CENTER OF ANY SIDE AND PROJECT LINE FROM IT TO OPPOSITE APEX. ONE THIRD THE LENGTH OF THIS LINE FROM THE SIDE DIVIDED IS THE C. of E.

TO FIND AREA OF ANY TRIANGLE

$$AREA = \frac{BASE \times ALTITUDE}{2}$$

way, is drawn to the same scale as the sails—to a piece of stiff cardboard, sheet metal or plywood. Then with scissor or band saw, cut out this shape.

Now balance this shape on a knife edge held exactly at right angles to the water line. Where the knife edge touches

Carrying Sail

the water line, make a pencil tick. This is the CLR (See sketch below).

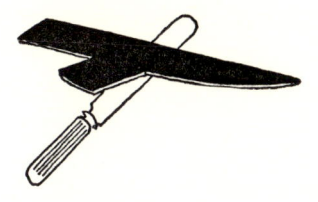

Place this shape under your drawing of the sails, with the water lines matching and the mast heel coinciding with the mast step on the profile of the hull. Then extend the CLR upward by a vertical line parallel to the one representing the CE. You now have the relationship of the CE to the CLR as it is in your boat.

Unless the CE is *forward* of the CLR, your sails are definitely out of balance, probably dangerously so since you must carry a lee helm. The CE must always lead the CLR, but by what amount varies with every design. Ideally, the amount of separation is about 6 per cent of the *water-line length* of the boat. The important point of this check is to be certain that the CE is forward of the CLR.

If it is, your boat is essentially in balance and minor corrections are possible with little effort as we shall see.

If the boat is seriously out of balance, you must re-design the sail plan or underwater features which affect lateral resistance. This, obviously, is a job for experts. Usually balance can be obtained by changes in sail plan. Such changes include larger or smaller sails, together with new or altered spars, or relocated existing sails, alterations to sails by adding or subtracting area. Sometimes an additional headsail, or substituting an overlapping jib for a plain jib, will cure a faulty helm. Great care must be exercised in making the commonplace change-over from gaff to jib-headed rig. These two types of sails seldom are found interchangeable without upsetting the balance of the sail plan. I have seen some change-overs which resulted in a new rig entirely; one was from sloop to yawl rig.

Sailmakers of reputation are usually capable of re-designing sail plans and are often called upon to do so. Boatyards are generally not, although some of the larger yards have engineering talent available which can do such work. Naval architects, of course, are thoroughly able to assist, specify and supervise such alterations.

It is highly unlikely that you will acquire a boat which needs much more than minor adjustments to be put quite in balance. But most boats will sail better after some concerned attempt to reach perfect balance. Here are some hints, and remember that a combination of several is more likely to produce results than reliance on only one method.

To Cure a Mild Lee Helm—
1. Loosen all stays, knock out mast wedges and reset mast so that it rakes aft. Be sure to *rake* the mast aft, not *bend* it aft! If the headstays become too short, insert a link or two of chain; if the shrouds become too long, twist them with the lay to shorten them.
2. Reduce the headsail area by cutting down on the jib area, or by substituting a plain jib for an overlapping jib or starting the jib.
3. Increase the mainsail area by sewing another cloth to the foot or leech, or to the head of a gaff-rigged sail, assuming that you have the room on the existing spars. If not, it is hardly worth building new spars except as a last resort.
4. Relocate the centerboard or adjust the centerboard pennant so that the centerboard sets *forward* of its present position or drops deeper and further forward.

Carrying Sail

To Cure Lee Helm — To Cure Weather Helm

5. Reduce, if possible, the area of the skeg or (be careful here) the rudder.
6. Shift ballast forward.

To Cure a Mild Weather Helm—
1. Reverse number 1 above; rake the mast forward.
2. Increase the headsail area by adding cloths to the jib, or substituting an overlapping jib for a plain jib, or adding another headsail on a bowsprit or trimming in the jib.
3. Reduce the area of the mainsail.
4. Adjust the centerboard pennant to prevent the centerboard from swinging too deep and too far forward.
5. Increase, if possible the area of the skeg or the rudder.
6. Shift ballast aft.

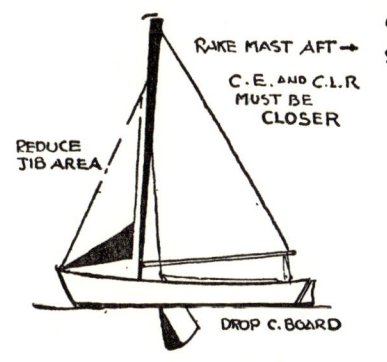

The keelboat lends itself peculiarly well to increasing or decreasing the lateral area, since area may be added to or cut from the deadwood or leading edge without serious structural changes. Quite often a faulty helm, particularly a heavy weather helm, can be cured by the simple expedient of getting new sails. Old, baggy sails shift their centers of effort as they stretch. Sometimes, too, what seems like faulty balance is merely the inability of the rudder to correct designed weather helm without excessive steering angles. If the rudder seems small in area, try adding to it a shallow shoe or a feathered scantling on the after edge.

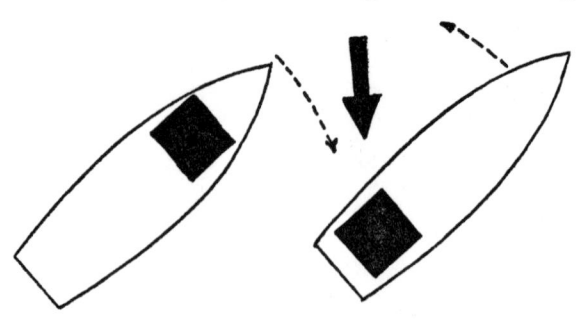

The Effect of Ballast on Helm

In boats up to 24 feet or so, especially light boats, the correct use of ballast, which includes live ballast, will often cure a bad helm. Ballast aft will bring normally related centers together. Ballast forward will separate centers. As you see by the sketch below. It does not take much ballast either way to make a great difference in the relative positions of the CE and CLR.

In this matter of balance, I do not suggest that it is

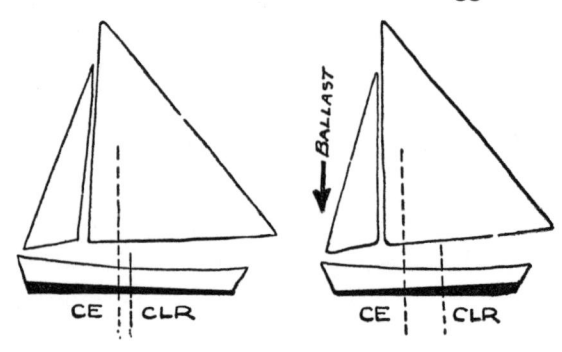

necessary to go deeply into naval engineering to balance sails and so carry sail efficiently. Most of us are not even aware of a lack of balance, but, if you will experiment a bit in a moderate breeze and deliberately search for unbalance, you will probably find it. If it is so trifling that you must look for it, the cure will also be trifling. Indeed, I think that most boats are quite in balance but that we upset the balance by carelessness in small matters such as the disposal of our live weight, anchors, ground tackle and other heavy gear and, of course, the matter of pumping bilges dry to get rid of water weight. If you balance a fixed weight in the bow with an equal weight aft, you won't get into trouble.

An excellent check on balance is trim. The boat should trim—which means the painted water line and the actual water line should be parallel—with its full sailing load on board, including passengers in the seats they will occupy during the sail. Without the passengers, the boat which is in

balance will probably trim slightly down by the head. Keelboats, of course, are less affected by weights on board than centerboard boats.

And now one more item in this matter of carrying sail,

windage. On every point of sailing, except before the wind, the windage of passengers, topside hull, cabin houses, spars, rigging, etc., adversely affects the speed of the boat. Keep windage to a minimum. I do not think that streamlining is necessary for an ordinary afternoon sailor or small cruiser, but neither do I think that much deck gear and rigging does anything but hinder her. Certainly, carry what is necessary but always in such a manner that a minimum windage is created. Thus, on the small boat, anchors and coiled lines forward, navigation lights and light boards, open hatches or skylights, objects on the deck and passengers draped all over the boat, like British tars manning the yards in Lord Nelson's time, create drafts which affect the drawing of the sails and use up power best conserved to drive the boat. In a race, these small matters often decide the winner.

You will go faster if you expose as little of your body as possible above the rail. When you climb to windward, for ballasting, lie out on the waterways, do not sit on them, back to the wind. I shall always remember a little Snipe in which four husky adults sat perched on the windward waterway. They completely blanketed the foot of the sail and presented a solid phalanx of broad backs to a fresh breeze, and never moved a fathom. Discouraged, they asked me for a tow, which I told 'em wasn't necessary at all, and they became very angry when I suggested the cure. Eventually, crowded into the tiny cockpit, they were sailing along with the rest of the fleet.

Excessive heeling, with the topsides and part of the bottom exposed to the wind and the rail creating ruinous eddies all along the foot of the sail, is another form of windage to be discouraged. There is a point where heeling will assist the boat. It is just beyond that point where the windage of deck fittings, combings and open cockpit equals the

Carrying Sail

windage of the heeled hull but never to that point where eddies reach the sail itself.

I recall a lovely, salty little ketch which used to moor near me. A great deal of her charm was in her old-time deck and rigging appointments—smoke heads, a dory in chocks, several rugged deck chests, a square yard for a raffee, husky North Sea light boards, gallows frame and a very salty set of hammocks slung under her bowsprit. One day I found her stripped. There wasn't a thing movable or protruding left on her except a few essentials. The yard was gone; the spinnaker pole which used to hoist alongside a shroud was chocked on deck; flush hatches were battened over her forecastle companionway and cabin skylight. "Windage," grinned Cap Seavy when I told him I thought he was getting ready to haul for the winter, "I'm going up to west'ard to race."

The point is that you can't carry sail efficiently if you must fight windage.

CHAPTER ELEVEN

Too Much Wind

So far we have been sailing on beautiful blue seas in a gentle summer breeze, say about a Force 3 wind, which the scale devised by Admiral Beaufort calls a "gentle breeze capable of keeping leaves and small twigs in constant motion and extending a light flag." Force 5, which blows 19 to 24 miles an hour instead of a mere 8 to 12 is a good deal more fun but, on the other hand, begins to approach the forces designated as strong breeze, moderate gale, fresh gale, etc., in other words, too much air moving too fast—Heavy Weather.

Heavy weather poses some problems for the sailorman. There is wind.

There are often large and powerful seas kicked up by the wind.

Most of us don't mind heavy weather very much—not really. We can do something about it; reef or heave to or scud before it, put out oil to quiet the surrounding waters or anchor in some lee. What bothers is that undecided weather characterized by puffy winds and overblows, by varying and fluky breezes which leave us as undecided as it is itself. There isn't much danger in steady strong wind which definitely makes us take steps to sail safely in spite of itself; there is a good deal of danger in the spotty wind which howls a three-reef gale one moment and falls to a zephyr the next.

Too Much Wind

The only method of combating steady heavy wind, since we cannot reduce the force of the wind, is to reduce the area of the sails upon which it blows. This is done by shortening sail, a process called reefing. In strong wind which presses the boat beyond the limits of efficiency and safety, you *must* reef.

But in the fluky breeze, which is usually a land breeze that reaches the sea as a mass of eddies of varying directions and velocities because of passing around mountains and through areas of different thermal characteristics, reefing would see us safely through the blows but becalmed in dangerous positions when it doesn't blow.

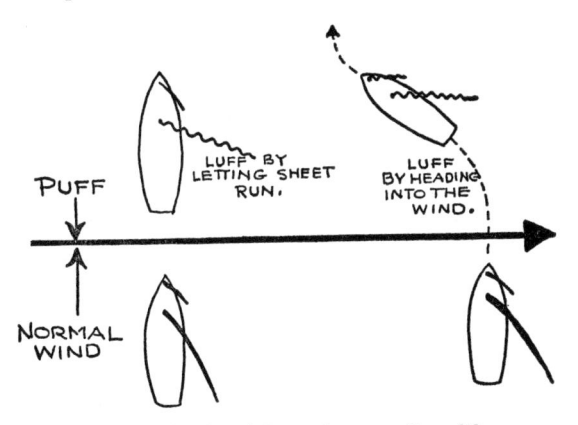

Two Methods of Parrying an Overblow

There are several ways to parry the puffs and overblows of a varying breeze. One, which we have discussed, is to luff the boat as the wind bears down upon it. Provided the puff is not of too long duration, the momentum of the boat will carry it ahead to windward and you can soon put the helm up and sail again. This method is generally used as a foil when sailing on the wind since there is but a short arc of swing from close-hauled to luffing. When sailing off the wind, it is probably better and quicker to let the mainsheet run out a few feet as the wind burdens the boat. This is called spilling the wind. Do not spill *all* the wind. By reason of the boat being well heeled to leeward the sails are spilling *some* of the wind over the leeches; just a little more spilling on your part will vastly relieve the pressure and see you quickly, sheet trimmed in, sailing again.

It is of paramount importance that you do not lose headway during this parrying process. Keep the boat sailing a little, always. To lose headway completely, and therefore steerageway is to invite disaster, for no one knows from what quarter a varying puffy wind will next attack. If you can steer, even a little bit, you can keep the sails presented to the most likely quarter from which the wind might blow. And if it does attack from another angle, you may, since you can steer, quickly adjust yourself to it. To be pressed by the wind without steerageway is to risk a knockdown.

A knockdown is almost always dangerous. None of the wind's force is expended in giving the boat forward movement. Every pound of its power is devoted to pressing the sail to leeward and down. A knockdown places enormous strains on rigging, spars and canvas and often breaks them. It is likely to fill the hard-heeled boat, shift inside ballast to the very worst possible position, to leeward, and throw passengers about or into the water. Your best defense against a knockdown is to keep some steerageway no matter how hard the puff.

If the puffs are of long duration or you don't relish the prospect of reefing because you are in crowded waters or quite near the safety of your home mooring, try this well-known trick of the wind sailor called "sailing by the luff." Sheet the jib in amidships. Slack the mainsail off until it luffs over most of its area. The flat jib will kill the power of the luff of the mainsail and that part of the main still drawing will just about balance the power of the jib. Keep the boat footing, not pinched too close to the wind, and you will sail right through even very hard puffs.

Be very careful when running before the wind in puffy weather. Wind force won't bother you much, but its varying direction lays you wide open to an accidental jib. By all means, tack downwind, with the wind and its possible future direction always on the quarter opposite the mainsail. At the slightest indication that the wind is going to veer to the same side as the mainsail, put the helm down, but not so far down as to risk broaching to. Prepare for this eventuality by topping the boom even though it does not seem necessary while sailing before the wind. Far less dangerous than running with mainsail set, is to take off all sail aft of the mast and hoist your spinnaker, or wing out one or two jibs. A lone jib or small spinnaker before a heavy wind will produce a speed almost equal to that possible with the full mainsail. This phenomenon is due, oddly, to the fact that before the wind, a given hull is capable of a certain speed—and no more, no matter how much sail is carried. Strong winds impart sufficient power to the jib or spinnaker to move the boat at its maximum possible speed; more power is simply superfluous.

When wind becomes heavy and even its minimum velocities press the boat too hard, it is time to reef. You reef for the heaviest wind, not the lightest. Fortunately, strong winds are apt to be steadier than puffy winds containing strong overblows and, while reefing reduces speed, it obviates the necessity to luff or let sheets run at frequent time-consuming intervals and results in constant headway and more than likely better time.

Reefing is accomplished by actually reducing sail areas by mechanical means. The most common method of reefing is to lower sail, tie a portion of the foot into a tight bundle along the boom, then hoist sail again. For this purpose, sails are provided with reef bands to which have been sewn short cotton lines, called reef points, or into which brass grommets have been inserted.

This is the way to reef a sail. Head the boat into the wind, drop the jib, then the mainsail. Now overhaul the sail so that it all falls on one side of the boom and lay the reef band to which you plan to reef along the boom. Toss all the sail between this band and the boom on the opposite side from the rest of the sail. (The depth of the reef—one, two or three bands—will depend upon your judgment as to the proper sail area to be carried under the conditions.)

At the forward and after ends of the reef band is a large grommet, sometimes punched into the sail, sometimes spliced to the boltropes. These are the reef cringles. Make them fast to the tack and clew just as you did when bending the mainsail, using short cotton-line lashings. Do not forget the special attention needed at the clew, a clew outhaul and also a hold down lashing. Haul the foot of the sail aft hand-taut.

Now, assisted by the crew if possible, roll the sail between the boom and the reef band into a long tight sausage, parallel with the boom and lying snugly against it. The reef band should be close against the boom.

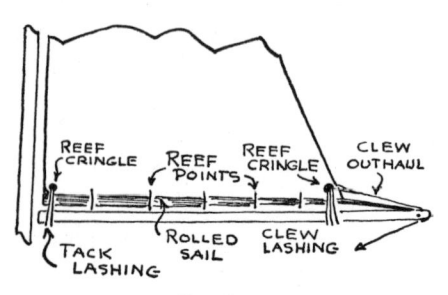

Reefing

Too Much Wind

If your sail is provided with reef points proceed as follows. Starting at the tack, work aft tying the two ends of each reef point together after passing one under the sail. Points pass under the sail! Never, if you wish to be classed a real sailor, tie these under the boom. Be certain that you are tying together the ends of the same reef point and not some stray point that has fallen nearby. Tie points with a slippery square knot with the closed bight on the top. As you tie the points, smooth out the rolled sail, pinching it into a small tight roll and pulling it gently toward the clew.

If your sail is provided with reef grommets only (no cotton points) proceed as follows. Take a long cotton lacing line, half again as long as the length of the reef band and secure one end to the tack. Now, lace it aft, spiralwise, through a grommet, under the sail (not the boom!). Repeat, repeat and so on to the clew. Draw the loops tight so as to hold the furled excess sail securely.

Now, either method of tying in the reefs having been completed, set up the outhaul, re-lash the clew to the boom, bundle the excess sail between the clew and the end of the boom into a roll and lash it down with a short length of line and you are ready to hoist reefed sail—after you do one more important thing.

But before we get away from the mainsail, here are a few additional thoughts. If your boat is provided with a receiver at the gooseneck and on the clew outhaul slide, omit the hold down lashings at these points. Slip the pins from the receivers and insert the reef cringle in place of the regular tack and clew cringles.

If several reefs are required, tie one on top of the other, each on the side opposite the one below it. Thus, since when the wind begins to slack it will do so gradually, you are then prepared to shake out a reef at a time to meet its waning force. In each reef use separate tack and clew lashings and outhaul lines. It is a simple matter then, since each reef is complete, to shake a reef out without lowering sail and so lose no great amount of time or make undue leeway.

Roller reefing gear is becoming more common each year. This gear is simply a mechanical device which permits you to roll the excess sail around the boom, just as a shade is furled on its roller. The boom is carried by the gooseneck and secured by the mainsheet so that it can be freely rotated by means of a gearing device. The sail is wound around it to any depth desired. A good roller reefer is a good shipmate indeed. Not only does it conserve a lot of effort and hand work (which is anything but pleasant in rain or icy weather) but it permits you to reef without lowering sail and while under way.

This is that important thing I mentioned.

Remember always that when a sail is reefed, its center of effort is dislocated and the entire sail plan is thrown out of balance. To set a reefed mainsail, then hoist full jib and be off will probably result in a heavy and dangerous lee helm. The boat will show a strong inclination to fall away from the wind and get into all that horrid mess we recited in the last chapter. The jib is the culprit. It's too powerful. Its wings must be clipped.

Not many small-boat jibs are built to be reefed. It is much more common to find the sail bag stocked with a smaller storm jib to be used in place of the regular jib. Surely, it's easier to hank on a new jib than reef the regular one. Always use a smaller jib when you reef the mainsail. The order of use is this: Number 1 storm jib goes with the first reef in the mains'l; number 2 storm jib with the second reef, and no jib at all with the top reef. No matter how many reef bands your mainsail has, the top one is used without a jib.

All plain sail

Reefed main and storm jib

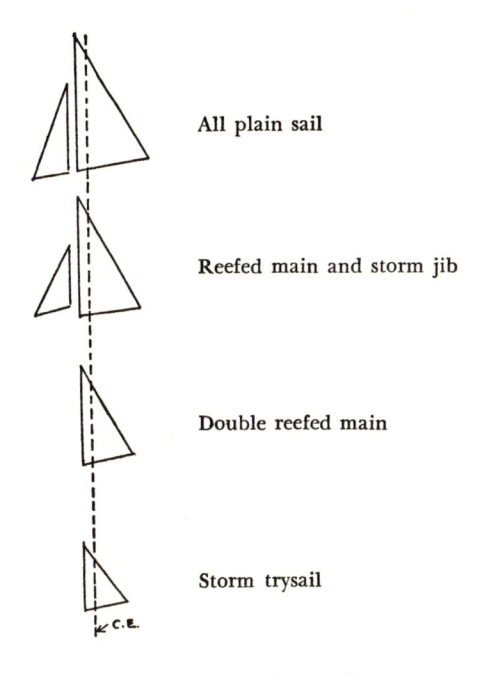

Double reefed main

Storm trysail

The Order of Reefing a Sloop

The loose-footed jib, of course, cannot be reefed and must be replaced by another. However, the jib equipped with a club but not reef points may sometimes be reefed by rolling it around itself on the club, lashing down the tack and clew reef cringles (with which it should be equipped) or by "scandalizing" it, which is lashing at tack and clew as above but not rolling it on the club.

Under reefed sail you handle the boat just as under full sail. It will probably not point as closely as before and may feel somewhat sluggish on the wind. But you will make better time in the long run, sail with a far greater margin of safety and with little or none of the nervous energy and tension required to battle and parry constantly heavy weather under too much sail.

There are no rules as to when to reef. It depends upon your boat and its characteristics. Certainly, when you find that you are regularly parrying puffs and luffing instead of making steady forward progress, it is time to tuck in a reef. In steady hard blows, the angle of heel becomes the indicator. If the boat sails continuously with her rail submerged, if solid water sweeps the lee deck or if the boat *feels* dangerous, reef. You reef for the hardest blows. Caught offshore in a rising wind, it is wise seamanship to recognize that the wind will increase and to prepare for its maximum estimated strength. Thus, while at the moment a single reef might adequately ease the boat, the double or triple reef, soon required, is better seamanship since, first, you do not know exactly when or how hard the gale will blow and, second, the wind may kick up such violent seas as it increases that reefing then will be almost impossible. A perfectly sound habit to develop is to observe what other boats are doing. If they are reefed, it behooves you to reef also. This is an especially good indicator when an offshore breeze is blowing. Wind from the land is very deceptive. It is a blue sky wind. The day doesn't necessarily feel stormy, there are no heavy seas building up, the barometer may not be down, but offshore, in open water, the little cat's-paws which ruffle the harbor from time to time, may have real force. What the boats offshore are doing about shortening sail, is what you should do also.

The land breeze is generally a squally one. On lakes the breeze which blows the *length* of the lake is apt to be a good deal steadier than one which blows *across* the lake. Lake breeze from a mountainous area nearby is usually puffy and varying. The onshore sea breeze, in spite of the large seas which it sometimes builds up, is by far the most predictable

Too Much Wind

and friendly. You can feel it and see it (or its force) and therefore judge and estimate it with fair accuracy. As you get further into the game of sailing, study up on the laws of storm and weather prediction in any good book on navigation or seamanship.

When the wind decreases while you are under sail, you will want to get under full sail again speedily. The following is the way to shake out a reef. You need not lower all sail unless you are single-handed and cannot man the tiller. Sailing on the wind (so that the boom is inboard where you can reach it) untie the middle reef point. Pull the fall of the reef knot *down*—which is why the slippery square knot is tied with the bight on the top. It won't mean much to you in pleasant clearing weather. But at sea, at night, in fog or when rigging is covered with frozen spray, it is a vast comfort and convenience to know exactly how the knot has been tied and how to cast it off. So, starting with about the middle reef point, untie them all, first working forward to the tack, then aft to the clew. Next cast off the tack lashing, then the clew outhaul and finally the clew lashing. Re-insert any battens which you have removed. Check to be sure that all reef points are free or, sure as Davy Jones will someday get you, you'll have a torn sail. Then luff her and hoist full sail again.

At any time *after* you have made full mainsail, the jib may be replaced with the regular working jib or the jib reef shaken out. If you have tied down several reefs, cast them off one at a time and hoist sail as far as it will go; then start on the next lowest reef. A carelessly reefed sail, in heavy wind, is subject to stretching that will completely ruin it for plain sailing in a few hours. Be very careful to make a snug job, with strain equally distributed over the length of the foot. The greatest danger of stretching the sail is while the tack and clew lashings are supporting the entire load. If you want to be absolutely sure of not harming the set of the sail, drop the sail while untying a reef, but be sure to get bow to the wind before trying to again hoist it. You simply can't hoist sail with the wind on the beam or aft. An ancient seaman's precept becomes appropriate here—"rope is expendable." So, in order to reduce the length of time in which a sail is supported by only the tack and clew when untying a reef, *cut the lashing*—six seconds of stretch instead of several minutes.

In very heavy weather it may be impossible to carry even a completely reefed mainsail. For this, though the small afternoon sailor is unlikely ever to use such a sail, a storm trysail is carried. This sail is smaller in area than the fully reefed mainsail and is set flying between mast and the strapped down boom after the other sail has been completely furled and gasketed. With this sail (or with a fully reefed mainsail) it is possible to "put the boat to sleep" in heavy weather by a maneuver called laying to. I include it because of its interest to sailors; not for its practical value to the small-boat skipper. After all, laying to is a deepwater practice; you need plenty of ocean and few small boats get outside where there is plenty of ocean.

With a minimum of mainsail set, just enough to sail *some,* head the boat into the wind (luff her) until she begins to make sternway. Lash the helm down so that, as she makes sternway, the head falls off on the wind, she starts to move forward, luffs, makes sternway, falls off, sails, etc., ad infinitum. The trick is to adjust the helm and the sheets so that a minimum of sternway and a minimum of sailing ahead takes place during each cycle. This point can be found only by experimentation but once the point is found, other factors such as ballast and windage on parts other than the sail remaining fixed, the boat will rather quietly lie still. In practice, the sail will be fluttering, sheets slightly started and the boom in about the same position as when sailing a close reach. On small boats, once hove to and "in the groove," live weight cannot be shifted or the balance will be upset. Quite small keelboats can lay to fairly well; centerboard boats hardly at all because of wave action. While hove to the boat will make a good deal of leeway and possibly drift because of current and tide. The small world-girdlers which must frequently lay to during their lonely passages often make several hundred miles leeway and drift while a great storm blows itself out. Obviously, there's not much sense in laying to in Long Island Sound or Monterey Bay.

A part of heavy weather, a big part, is the state of the sea—waves. It is the waves rather than the wind which often drive the small boat into protected waters. Inshore, where waves are steep and surly, they buffet the small boat about so that wind is shaken from the sails. Offshore, where waves are long and steep, the small boat usually completely loses the wind while in the troughs and, upon rising to the windy crest, finds herself without steerageway and subject to a knockdown.

For ordinary sailing in heaving seas, the best defense is careful handling of the boat. Sail in such a manner that the boat makes steady progress yet is as easy as possible on her gear and her passengers. Avoid sailing into steep headseas; they will stop most boats dead in their course and if very powerful will throw the boat backwards. Alter course to take the seas on either bow. The boat will ride easier and throw less spray than stubbornly bucking into them.

In a beam sea, take the same precautions as when sailing on a reach, i.e., sheet in the boom or top it to prevent dipping the sail as the boat rolls to leeward. Before the wind, the danger from waves is in becoming pooped. Pooping is being boarded by the stern by a breaking or crested sea while coasting down the windward side of a wave which has passed under her. The danger is from the following seas which might attack while the stern is buried in the preceding wave. There is not much that can be done except to alter course so that the windward quarter is presented to the waves. Waves striking the quarter are somewhat divided upon striking and part of their force destroyed. Do not take seas on the leeward quarter; that will place you in danger of jibing. Sometimes you can outrun waves by pressing on all canvas; or enough to keep you sailing up the backs of seas instead of wallowing helplessly on them, vulnerable to the full attack of the next following sea.

Comfort in heavy seas is closely related to dryness. Dryness is the ability of the boat to throw spray off along the beam rather than on deck. The quality of dryness is designed into the good hull and further somewhat controlled by correct ballasting.

Ballast (other than the fixed ballast on a keelboat) location makes an enormous difference in the handling abilities of many boats. Generally, if ballast is concentrated amidships, the boat will steer well and be quick in stays. But on the other hand, in a heavy sea, the boat with ballast amidships will probably hobby-horse and pound quite badly and throw sheets of spray from under the bows. Such spray is flat and not solid and, were it not for the wind, would likely not even wet the deck. If ballast is concentrated in the ends, the boat will pound less and throw less sheet spray. On the other hand, should she plunge because of ballast weight in the bow, she will throw solid water in generous quantities, which the wind will deposit in bucketfuls in the cockpit. Again there are no rules. Ballast by experiment. Unfortunately, the very ballasting method best

Too Much Wind

for heavy weather is the worst for ordinary sailing and ballasting, on your boat, must be a compromise. However, since most of us sail only in reasonably fair weather and are not likely to be caught offshore for extended storm periods in a small boat, it seems sanest to ballast for ordinary sailing and let the spray fall where it may for the few times we must ride a storm.

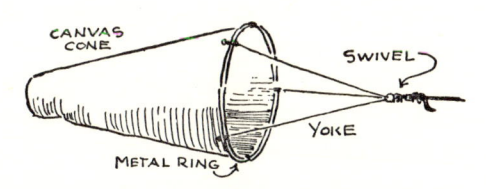

A Sea Anchor or Drogue

Waves may be combated by the use of a sea anchor or drogue, provided you have sea room. Take all sail off and set a sea anchor. A sea anchor is a canvas or wooden device which offers resistance to being pulled through water. It is rigged from the bow of the boat by a very long warp and, like a conventional anchor, keeps the bow headed into the waves. Of course, the anchor makes leeway and the boat moves over the bottom, necessitating open waters. Emergency sea anchors may be made by lashing together bundles of spars, timber or boat furniture, by swamping the dinghy or laying to a long fouled line. But, again, the sea anchor is not a practical device for the small boat and few small boats carry one.

"Oil on the waves" does really somewhat calm the sea, not by flattening the heave but rather by preventing the waves from breaking and engulfing a hard-pressed boat. Any heavy oil will do—engine oil, olive oil, or commercial storm oil. It is applied by immersing an oil soaked sponge or rag or a canvas bag or tin can pierced with small "weep holes" to windward. Its greatest usefulness is when hove to or when riding to a sea anchor. The sailing boat overruns the oil slick before it is of much use. However, when before the wind, oil dropped from the bows will effectively lessen the dangers of being pooped by breaking following seas. If lying to a sea anchor, or a regular anchor, in dangerous white water, put an oil bag ahead of the bow, attached to the warp, to quiet the sea in the vicinity of the boat itself. If sailing off the wind, rig a bag to a boomed-out spinnaker or whisker pole, on the windward bow. The cruising boat can introduce oil into the seas by pumping it overboard via the galley sink or water closet. The only time I ever used oil, I dropped it, a dollop at a time, through the centerboard slot and it proved quite effective in the following sea which was running. But, in a real coastal storm, I wouldn't put too much faith in the calming properties of the small quantities of oil possible for the small boat to spread. An ocean-going vessel, forced to use oil, pumps many gallons per minute into the sea, about as much per second as the average small boat has stowage room for.

Thunderstorms might be termed "temporary heavy weather." Generally thunderstorms are wind and noise. Seldom do they last long enough to build up large seas. And always they come from the land. The time to prepare for the thunderstorm is when the thunderheads begin to pile up to leeward. Wind, a lot of it, is shortly going to come from that quarter. The wisest course, since after the storm there will be confused and shifty winds, *if any*, is to get back to your home mooring and watch the storm from the club house veranda. If you can't do that, get off a shore

Too Much Wind

which will be a lee shore when the thundersquall breaks and anchor. Douse sail and make everything snug.

The wind will come first with a chilly and wild swoop, short steep seas will build up, then the rain suddenly falls in torrents, completely kills the wind and the seas, and the danger is over. Except, of course, that from lightning. To avoid that danger, keep away from the mast, shrouds and wet halyards and get yourself stretched out under the forward deck near or under the water line. But surprisingly few boats are ever hit by lightning; it's something to respect but not unduly fear on the water.

Since the force of the wind which foreruns the thundersquall is often very great, put out the heaviest anchor and stream behind it on your longest warp. The rule for warp length is five times the depth of the water anchored in—which double for the thunderstorm. A light anchor and a long warp is better than a heavy anchor and a short warp. If, as is likely, the storm finds you in deep water where you can find no bottom for the anchor, take comfort in the knowledge that there are very few truly deep spots in 'longshore tidal areas. Your normal anchor cable, plus mainsheet, spare lines and, *in extremis,* the halyards, should find bottom and safe anchorage, or at least a slow drag. I'd use 'em all rather than try to ride out a thundersquall anchorless in limited quarters.

A good way to ride out a thunderstorm, if there is sea room to what will be leeward when the wind comes, is to take in all canvas and scud before it. Here an emergency sea anchor will stand you in good stead and somewhat reduce the rate of drift to leeward. But in general since, to repeat, there will likely be no sailing wind after the storm, it is best to ride out the storm by that method which finds you nearest your home mooring when the storm is over.

Incidentally, beware of the split storm; the one with two centers, or a "double storm" which occurs at the turn of the tide. In all probability you will have to fight them both, and each will attack from a different direction.

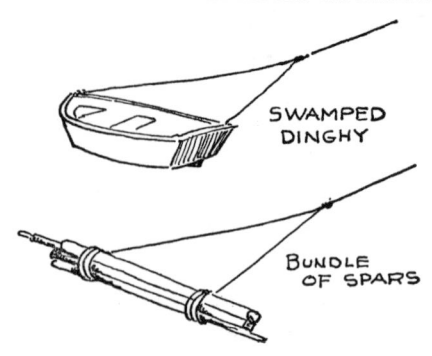

Emergency Sea Anchors

Your sails need special attention—the thunderstorm being also a rainstorm. Be sure to slack off the clew outhaul and unshackle main halyards as you furl the sails in preparation for the blow. Your sails are going to get wet and are going to shrink. And when you hoist them again, take it easy; haul them out to original positions only as they dry and stretch.

But cheer up! It's not heavy weather all the time nor most of the time. In the log of *Altair,* which I sailed almost every day from June to mid-September last summer, I find the following weather posted:

Heavy long-duration line storms	9 days
Thundersqualls	(on) 2 days
No wind, clear	1 day
No wind, fog	6 days
Good all day sailing	47 days
Fair all day sailing (rain on some days)	25 days
Fair half day, calm half day	12 days

On one of those last twelve days, I did not reach my mooring until 4:30 A.M., having started home from an offshore island when the wind showed signs of foo-ing about 2:30 P.M. Light winds, calms and head tides did the business to me. So I feel peculiarly qualified to write the next chapter which is concerned with "Too Little Wind."

CHAPTER TWELVE

Too Little Wind

WHEN the breeze becomes a breezelet, and when working sails, which are the jib and mainsail, no longer drive the boat fast, it is time to spread more sail. The sails which are used in light winds are called "light airs" or "light sails." They are the spinnaker in its various cuts, the balloon jib and the Genoa jib.

Before we identify these sails with light air sailing too much, I should explain that they are by no means used only when the breeze fails. All, and especially the spinnaker, are regularly used as working sails by yachts. They fill in that power gap present when the wind does not press the boat to the capacity of her plain sails, the jib and mainsail. I urge you to get into the habit of thinking of the so-called light airs as regular sails, to be used whenever possible.

The typical spinnaker is deliberately cut to be a baggy sail; a wind holder. Its designed use is for before the wind, and it can be used on a broad reach to advantage when it's not too windy to carry it. In fact, some modern spinnakers are cut less full than their originals and so serve as a combination sail before and off the wind. Light air fashions dash in and out of the yachting scene in colorful array—the ventilated spinnaker, the parachute, the twin parachute, the Genoa, the Annie Oakley and that delightful Greta Garbo, which is characterized by an exceptionally long foot—but they all amount to attempts to gather what power there is in the breezelet or less, so that our boats may continue to sail.

For the small boatowner, the spinnaker and the Genoa, and sometimes a ballooner, comprise his bag of light airs. Whenever it becomes apparent that the boat is not moving fast because of lessened sail drive, additional sail area in the appropriate form is indicated. Most of us do not set our light airs soon enough; we are prone to delay using them until a flat calm descends and, then, the best additional drive can be obtained only from a friendly tow-rope or an auxiliary engine. If you want to sail fast and far, get the light airs working just as soon as it becomes apparent that the wind is dropping and that the addition of sail area won't overtax spars and rigging. The western Long Island Sound skippers are the bravest of all light air carriers as far as I've observed. In no other area do skippers fly light airs in what most of us consider a reefing breeze.

First let's attack the problems of light breeze sailing from the standpoint of the working sails. The mainsail will draw best in light wind if set just the opposite for drawing in steady wind, that is, quite full and almost baggy in the luff area. To give it this desirable fullness slack off on the clew outhaul and pull the foot forward so that it *almost* puckers along the boom, then drop the main halyard several feet, pull the slack sail down toward the tack and rehoist the sail—but not as high as before. The flat leech area, so necessary to ordinary sailing efficiency, can be deliberately destroyed by adjusting the leech line and by removing one or all of the battens. Thus the fullness will extend over the entire sail.

The jib foot is probably all right as is but the halyard may be dropped a few inches to give its luff more draft. Keep weight to leeward so that the boat heels slightly away from the wind. Be very careful about moving. Quick motions and sudden shifting of live weight all tend to shake the air out of the sails so that you lose steerageway, and without steerageway you are licked. In a confused sea such as runs during the typical calm after a thundersquall or is kicked up in active boating areas by passing powerboats, it is almost impossible to keep the boat headed on a course. Drop the centerboard; that will be a little help against rolling and improve steering and, by ballasting, keep the sails out to leeward. The mere weight of the sheets in a ghosting calm will tend to swing the sails inboard. Cast them off and rig a piece of light fish line for a jibsheet and a cotton lacing line for the mainsheet. There is quite likely to be moving air above the surface of the water and you might try hanking the jib to the headstay and hoisting it to the masthead with a long single sheet secured to the clew. More than ever dispose yourself and passengers to offer the least wind resistance and eddy making; sit still on the cockpit floor with only your head above the coamings. Make an effort to use the current and tide. Tide against you is least powerful close to shore; tide with you is strongest and most helpful in mid-channel or offshore. Study the patches of wind-ruffled water about; go hunt a breeze and do not be ashamed to scull yourself to a ruffle with the rudder, or paddle with a floor board or an oar. In shallow water, the spinnaker pole used as a "settin' pole" will help. If nothing moves you closer to your objective (which should be home when it falls calm) or if you are losing ground, frankly anchor.

Following is the universal gesture signal to get yourself a tow. Go forward, rig a tow line and, perched on the very bow, wave the end of the line to passing power boats going your way.

But if you have a spinnaker in your sail bag . . . ah! You will find it useful whenever the wind is aft of the beam. Here's the way you set a spinnaker. Lay the spinnaker out on the forward deck, being very careful that its three corners (top is the head, boom corner the tack and inboard corner the clew) are in the clear and will lead straight when secured. Now unship the spinnaker pole and lay it along the deck, jaws aft and tack eye forward. Snap the tack to the eye, also the guys, one forward and one aft, though many skippers do not bother with

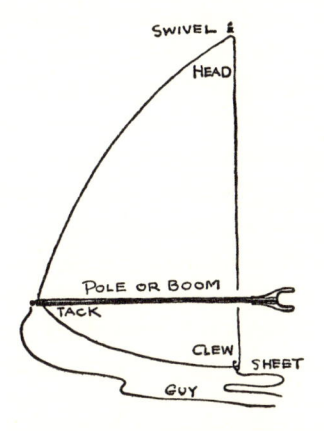

The Gear of a Spinnaker

a forward guy. Pass the after guy to the helmsman *outside* the shrouds and backstays. Now overhaul the foot of the sail until you get to the clew and belay its sheet to a convenient cleat or the bitts *forward* of the mast. Now overhaul the leech of the sail, which is that edge which is not roped, until you come to the head swivel and shackle the spinnaker halyard to it.

Hoist the head of the sail and belay the halyard. The spinnaker will hang from aloft like a curtain in a sea fog;

quite lifeless. Upon signal from the helmsman, slide the spinnaker pole forward, set the jaws against the mast at about the height of the gooseneck and pull it outboard—aft and toward the shrouds until it is athwartships. At the same time the helmsman will haul on the after guy. The spinnaker will then fill. Helmsman will belay his guy and you will adjust the sheet so that the sail has the greatest possible draft. This belaying point for the sheet will vary, depending upon the wind angle.

For a stern wind, the pole will be about 90 degrees off the keel line and the sheet belayed somewhere forward of the mast. The further the wind on the windward quarter, the further forward will be the pole and the further aft will the sheet be belayed. As the spinnaker pole goes forward, it will show an inclination to lift, which you can control by rigging the forward guy from the spinnaker pole end to the foot of the headstay.

If the wind blows from aft of the beam, at an angle permitting a broad reach, let the spinnaker pole lay fore and aft, parallel to the keel, lash it to the headstay and set the spinnaker on the same side as the mainsail. If the pole projects beyond the bow, forming a short bowsprit, so much the better. In this case, you would have to have the sheet passing around the leeward shrouds and perhaps backstay and belay aft of the mast on the leeward side. Set so, the spinnaker makes a powerful and picturesque sail.

When sailing before the wind with a spinnaker, let the jib stand. If you sheet the spinnaker well forward, you will find that wind from the mainsail spills into the spinnaker and the wind from the spinnaker spills into the jib, giving the boat a very efficient combination of sails. On a reach, of course, the jib should be doused.

Before the wind, sheet the spinnaker loosely so that it has great draft (or belly). On the wind, sheet it flatter but

Too Little Wind

not so flat that the foot or the leech curls inward. In passing the spinnaker from the windward side to the leeward side, it will have to pass forward and outside of the headstays, which is a good trick if you can do it. A great aid here is a double spinnaker sheet, a short one for sheeting when sail-

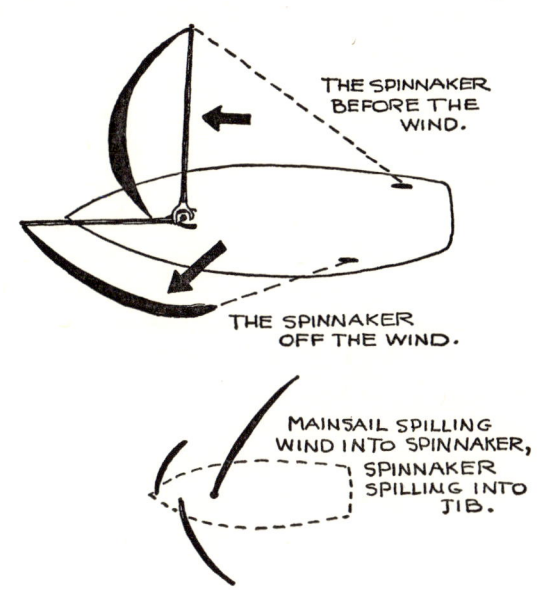

THE SPINNAKER BEFORE THE WIND.

THE SPINNAKER OFF THE WIND.

MAINSAIL SPILLING WIND INTO SPINNAKER, SPINNAKER SPILLING INTO JIB.

ing before the wind and a long one to pass around the headstay and leeward shrouds to a belaying point *before* the short sheet is cast off when you want to sail on a broad reach. At all costs the spinnaker must be kept always under control in this maneuver. If you cannot do it by controlling the sheets, there is nothing to do but lower the sail, pass it around the headstay in a *bundle,* hoist it and then sheet it in, just the same as you set a jib.

Underway with a spinnaker, the course must be kept rather faithfully. A collapsed spinnaker is a distinct drag; a backwinded spinnaker actually drives the boat backwards.

Sometimes the lazy spinnaker will stay filled if you sheet in the mainsail or top the boom slightly and spill wind into it.

Spinnakers are set on large yachts and on all classes of racing boats by putting them in stops. This method permits you to rig the spinnaker whenever you wish (before leaving the mooring if you want to save time later turning a racing mark for example) and is a neat and seamanlike trick to institute on the smartly manned boat.

On shore, or on the waterways of the boat while at anchor, lay the spinnaker out with the luff and leech edges matched to each other. Then roll the sail tightly toward these, making the spinnaker into a long roll with the head swivel forward and the tack and clew corners exposed at the foot of the roll aft. Now, at intervals of about 2 feet, tie stops around the roll, using one turn of cotton thread. Use a thread only strong enough to hold the roll together and no stronger; the wind must be able later to break these stops. Do not stop the spinnaker within about four feet of the head and at the foot take a few extra turns. At any time prior to use, hoist the rolled spinnaker aloft and lash its foot to the mast.

Sometime before you are ready to use it, snap the tack to the end of the boom, pass the guy aft to the helmsman and

Setting the Spinnaker in Stops

Too Little Wind

rig the boom just as if you were setting the spinnaker. Be sure that you have belayed the end of the sheet someplace forward of the mast. The spinnaker roll will now hang from the head to the pole end. Whenever you are ready, yank the sheet and, as the thread stops break and the sail fills, haul in on the sheet until the spinnaker is drawing properly. The advantage of this fast method of spreading sail while racing can readily be appreciated.

Another method of setting a spinnaker in stops is to prepare it as described and immediately rig it to the spinnaker pole. Let the pole rest on the forward deck, its guy passed aft. The rolled spinnaker will now hang between the spinnaker halyard block and the end of the pole on deck. Be sure the sheet is belayed. To set it quickly, put the pole against the mast, shove or pull it aft while the helmsman hauls in on the guy. As the stops break the sail will fill and draw.

To douse a spinnaker do this: Slack the guy so that the spinnaker pole swings forward and inboard and the sail collapses. Quickly unship the pole from the mast and lay it on deck. Then unsnap the tack and throw off the sheet. Bundle as much of the sail as possible in your arms and then drop the head by slacking off the halyard. Belay the halyard, haul the spinnaker guy aboard and secure the pole. Do not set the spinnaker in stops again unless you plan further use for it immediately. Always dry the sail before stopping it down; a wet sail, rolled and stopped and put in the sail bag, will mildew in a few hours.

It is a good plan to bag the spinnaker in stops so that it is always ready to use. If you prefer to set the spinnaker flying, as described in the first method, fold it as shown in the sketch on page 196. This fold will always present the clews just where you want them—tack outboard and down, clew inboard and down and head on top—and it will not be necessary to overhaul the foot and leech before setting to be sure that there is no twist in the sail. Before bagging, tie the bundle lightly with small stuff.

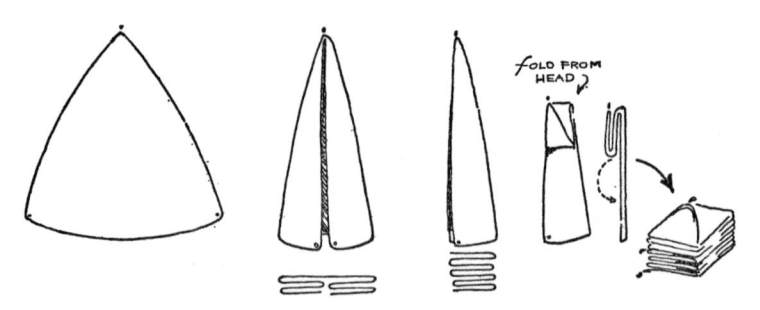

To Fold a Spinnaker for Stowing

On small boats it is best to have the sheet permanently spliced to the clew. Always keep the pole guys with the spinnaker so that they are at hand when you need them and not doing duty as spare rigging about the boat. These should be fitted with snap hooks on one end which slip into an eye or eye-fitting at the outboard end of the pole. If you sometimes use a forward guy, rig it even though you do not plan its use at once, leading it from the pole end to a cleat near the inboard end of the pole. Then, should you require the forward guy, it's ready at hand and you won't need to send the spinnaker pole forward to snap it in place. A most necessary fitting for the spinnaker head is a swivel. Be sure that yours has one.

The other light airs are simply larger jibs. The ballooner, which is used for reaching, is somewhat smaller than the spinnaker and is cut less full. The Genoa is cut flatter and is used for close windward sailing. Both sails hank to the jib or headstay and are sheeted outside the leeward shrouds. They are set, hoisted and sheeted just as an ordinary working jib. However, since they are very power-

Too Little Wind

ful sails and pull like a bag of atoms on the loose, it generally requires a stout tackle or a winch to sheet them in flat. Both are darn nuisances when tacking. A hand must go forward and pass sheet and sail around shrouds, headstays and opposite shrouds as the boat comes about.

For racing, the ballooner and Genoa are necessities and their greatest use is as racing sails. A common and very clever rig for setting them consists of double headstays, the ballooner hanked to one and the Genoa to the other. Thus, both sails may be kept hanked at all times during the race and set at will without the necessity of first removing the one presently in use. Both the ballooner and Genoa, like the spinnaker, are sometimes set in stops. A pull on the sheet and they break out and instantly draw, the seconds thus saved being valuable in a race but hardly worth the effort for afternoon pleasure sailing.

Light airs are fine shipmates, but seldom are they used as they should be, as additional working sails. It is a fallacy to

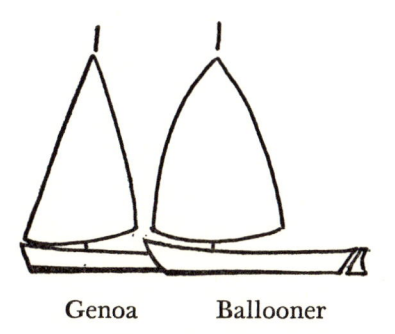

Genoa   Ballooner

regard the light airs, especially the spinnaker, as cure-alls for those late summer afternoon calms. When the wind has vanished, no sail in the bag will revive it. Get into the habit of setting light airs whenever it appears that the boat will sail better and faster with them. But after the ghosting calm has descended, not one of these light sails will make much difference in your progress. You have lost steerageway and probably are in the clutches of the tide—which may be favorable, of course, but seldom is for me. There is no recourse but to anchor, or row. It is at such times that most of us straight wind sailors wish we had an auxiliary engine tucked under the cockpit floor!

In normal summer weather there comes a time of calm, near sunset, which can be predicted. It is good sense and good seamanship to sail, with this predicted time in mind, so that your sail ends before the calm at your mooring or destination.

CHAPTER THIRTEEN

Setting the Course

THOUSANDS of sailors do not understand navigation in its finer points. Thousands of little boats sail innocent of charts, compasses, taffrail logs, parallel rules and dividers, the intricate tables required to forecast tide and current and the other physical equipment necessary to professional navigation. They set courses and successfully sail them in clear weather, nor does occasional darkness or fog worry them greatly. After all, the day sailor is limited to an area within a radius of perhaps twenty miles from the home mooring, which figure I arrived at by multiplying half an average sailing day of eight hours (four hours for the voyage out and four for return) by an average top speed of five miles an hour, twenty miles of range. It is not at all difficult to develop your own local knowledge of the waters within such a small area and never have to refer to a chart when sailing in them. In other words, you can sail happily and safely without being an expert navigator.

I have no desire to be left wing or plain screwball about the matter of navigation for the beginner. The subject is not only necessary for the cruiser but desirable for even the day sailor. You will sail better and safer under certain circumstances if you understand navigation. But you *can* sail without it, and it seems that at this time, with a strange new boat on your mind and your hands, you will be better off solving but one problem at a time. By all means and as soon as possible investigate the subject with the aid of a good book on navigation or by taking one of the courses offered by the United States Power Squadron or the local yacht club. Meanwhile you require only enough information to sail in ordinary weather in the ordinary sailing season in ordinary waters.

"Navigationless sailing" (which isn't a very good name at all since there are plenty of good navigators who don't know *north* from a rudder gudgeon) has its foundation in intimate local knowledge of the waters you sail in. You become acquainted with local waters by sailing in them, aided by the local chart and a knowledge of the buoyage system. You set your course always in the light of the physical limitations of the area and choose the course which will see your boat sailing fastest and safest to your objective.

For many years I was confounded by the uncanny ability of eastern Connecticut lobstermen to find their way home from the offshore grounds in thick o' fog without benefit of compass. They never missed their landfall. Of course they intimately knew the tides and currents but that did not account for their unerring sense of direction. Eventually their secret was revealed. They simply took a *general* direction toward their home ports and listened for the whistles of the heavy railroad traffic which skirted the shore. Locomotives whistled almost constantly as they negotiated drawbridges, the stations and yard limits of the many coastal towns and industrial sidings. It was a simple matter, by timing the whistles, to identify the particular stretch of unseen shore off in the fog and then take sound ranges from the successive whistles of a passing train. Homer Wincenpaw, who had lobstered for nearly sixty years, told me the only time he had ever used a "chart" was once when he went to the White Mountains in his daugh-

Setting the Course

ter's automobile! "Charts," he snorted, "warn't very good when I was a minnow."

But charts today are "good" and there is no better way to become acquainted with your local waters than detailed study of the large scale chart of the area in which you sail. Charts are published by the United States Government and are sold by ship chandlers, marine supply houses and bookstores. The local Customs House will supply the name of the nearest dealers upon request. Charts cost from 50 to 75 cents and give all the information necessary to navigate the waters they cover. They are regularly corrected and have the date of the last correction stamped on the lower left margin. Catalogues listing all charts are free from one of the following agencies, which also publish and distribute them.

U.S. Department of Commerce, Coast and Geodetic Survey, Washington, D.C. or any U.S. Custom House—coastal and tide-water charts and publications; all U.S. coasts, but not foreign.

U.S. War Department, Engineers Office, 540 Federal Building, Buffalo, N.Y. or U.S. Lake Survey Office, 649 Federal Building, Detroit, Mich.—Great Lakes, Lake Champlain, New York Canals, and Lake of the Woods charts.

Mississippi River Commission, P.O. Box 80, Vicksburg, Miss.—The Mississippi River and its tributaries.

Charts show in accurate detail *everything* which might be of interest or possible aid to the mariner, including the depth of the water, character of the bottom, the near-by shore line, land contours and objects which may be used to take bearings and ranges, aids and dangers to navigation, tidal and other currents, anchorages, Coast Guard stations,

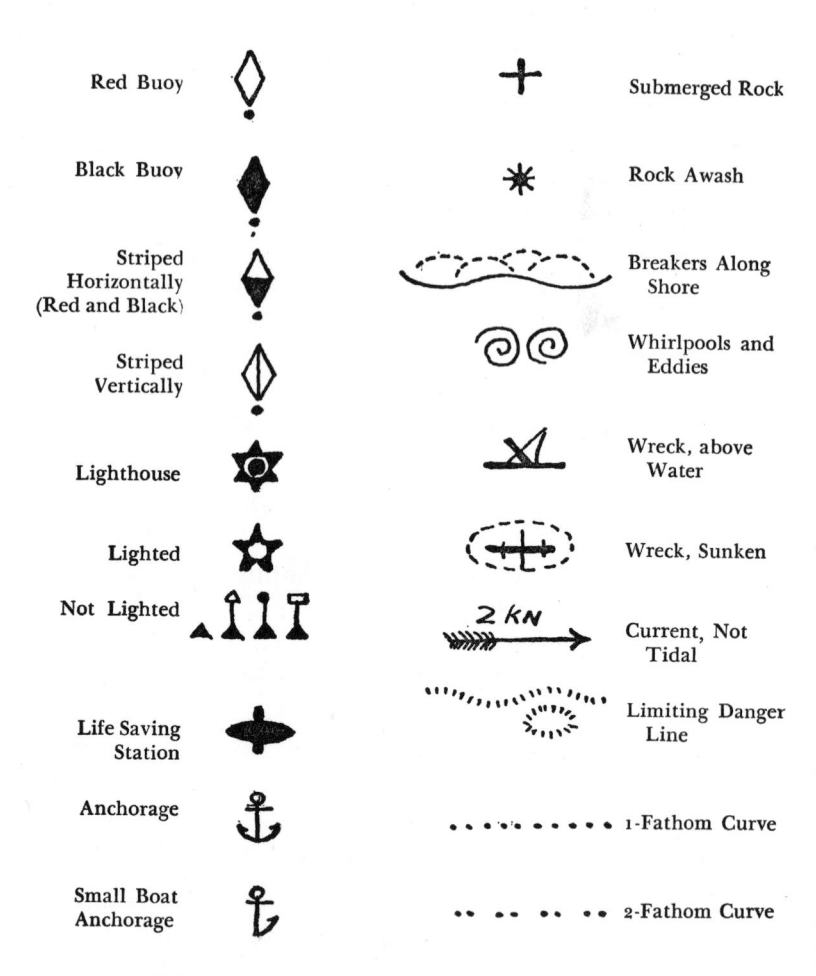

Symbol	Name	Symbol	Name
	Red Buoy		Submerged Rock
	Black Buoy		Rock Awash
	Striped Horizontally (Red and Black)		Breakers Along Shore
	Striped Vertically		Whirlpools and Eddies
	Lighthouse		Wreck, above Water
	Lighted		Wreck, Sunken
	Not Lighted	2 KN	Current, Not Tidal
	Life Saving Station		Limiting Danger Line
	Anchorage		1-Fathom Curve
	Small Boat Anchorage		2-Fathom Curve

Some Symbols Used on Navigational Charts

Setting the Course

tidal height and interval and many other things. Standard symbols and abbreviations are used on all charts. The following pamphlets interpret and explain chart symbols and may be obtained free of charge by applying to the agencies which publish them.

Aids to Marine Navigation. 23 pp., illus. U.S. Coast Guard, Washington, D.C.

Buoyage of the United States. 1 p., illus. U.S. Coast Guard, Washington, D.C.

The Use and Interpretation of Charts and Sailing Direction. U.S. Navy Department, Hydrographic Office, Washington, D.C.

Study the chart as you do a road map before an auto trip into strange territory. The practice of outlining in red, as suggested in Chapter I, areas which are closed to your boat because of depths of waters is an excellent dodge for the embryo navigator. Depths are shown by figures representing soundings in feet at normal low tide. If your boat draws three feet, mark off all areas showing less than five feet depth. You will be in safe sailing waters during normal tides if you stay outside the red areas. Search for isolated dangers outside of the red areas. These might include rocks and ledges, wrecks, fish weirs, fishing net stakes, breakers and the like. Mark them plainly with red crayon or waterproof red ink. Fix firmly in your mind the picture of the shore and the bottom under the water of your sailing limits.

The United States government has established a buoyage system second to none in the world. It is comparable to the State and Federal system of road signs which warn of hills, S-curves and the dangers and hazards to autoists. It is entirely possible to navigate in clear weather by these aids to navigation without the use of charts. At night an inter-

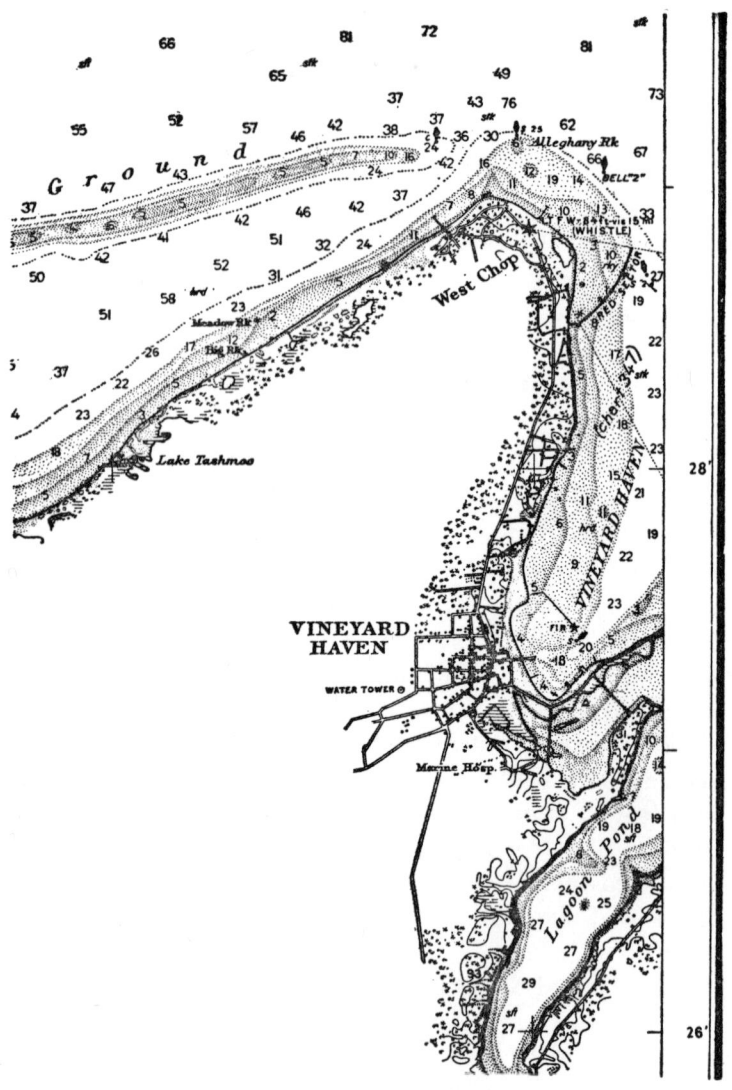

Section of a Typical Chart

Setting the Course

locked system of lighted aids and lighthouses serve the mariner; in thick weather sound and radio signals mark the safe highways of the sea.

Even the casual day sailor should understand the message of the buoyage system. In all cases buoys denote either submerged shoals, ledges and unseen dangers to navigation or best and deepest channels. Buoys may be floating, or fixed (in which case they are called beacons). From their color, shape and number their message is read.

The principle colors used are red, black and white. A black buoy, called a "can buoy," is always shaped like a tin can and is numbered with odd numbers. A red buoy, called a "nun buoy," is always shaped like the business end of a lead pencil, conical in shape, and is numbered with even numbers. Multi-colored buoys may be either can or nun buoys and are not numbered.

Buoys are numbered in sequence, starting from seaward. Red nun buoys will always mark the limits of safe navigation on the starboard side. Black can buoys will always mark the safe limits of navigation on the port side. The first seaward buoy of either color will start with number 1 (if a can) or number 2 (if a nun). Numbers on the buoys progress upward, marking the channel and safe waters from seaward toward land or from large bodies of water into smaller bodies. The rule is: When entering a harbor keep can buoys to port and nun buoys to starboard, when leaving a harbor keep can buoys to starboard and nun buoys to port. The lanes defined by can and nun buoys are the best channels to or from the sea.

Red and black buoys have special significances. If horizontally striped red and black, it means junction, middle ground or obstruction. Pass on either side but *not close aboard*. Such buoys mark underwater dangers like rocks and ledges of small area. They may be either nun or can.

How to Sail

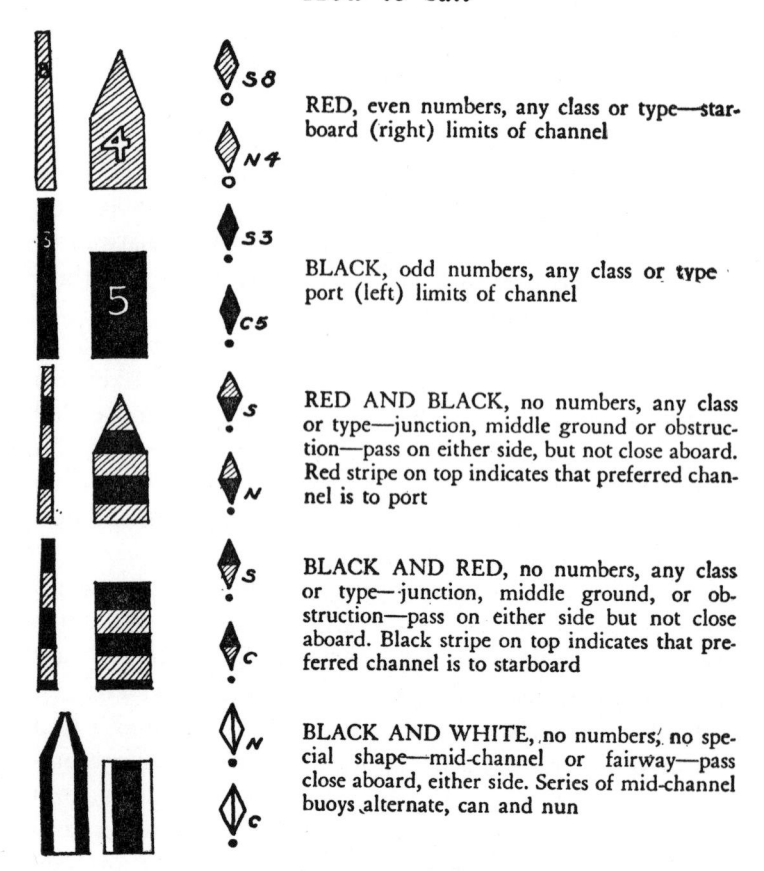

RED, even numbers, any class or type—starboard (right) limits of channel

BLACK, odd numbers, any class or type—port (left) limits of channel

RED AND BLACK, no numbers, any class or type—junction, middle ground or obstruction—pass on either side, but not close aboard. Red stripe on top indicates that preferred channel is to port

BLACK AND RED, no numbers, any class or type—junction, middle ground, or obstruction—pass on either side but not close aboard. Black stripe on top indicates that preferred channel is to starboard

BLACK AND WHITE, no numbers, no special shape—mid-channel or fairway—pass close aboard, either side. Series of mid-channel buoys alternate, can and nun

U.S. and Canadian Buoyage System

If the black stripe appears on top, the preferred channel is to starboard when entering the harbor.

Black and white vertically striped buoys mark the center of the best channel. Pass either side *close aboard*. A series of mid-channel buoys will alternate, can and nun. They do not have numbers.

Special buoys are in occasional or temporary use. White buoys bound an anchorage area, or a torpedo or naval ex-

Setting the Course

perimental range or may be experimental buoys. A white buoy with a green band around the top indicates a dredging area. A yellow buoy marks a quarantine area. They may be of any shape or size.

Buoys are further divided into classes of various sizes and types so that a navigator may recognize them as coastal, harbor, river and local buoys. The size or type does not in any way change the meaning. Color and number are the final indicators of the meaning of the buoy, be it a can, nun, spar, lighted, sound, beacon or spindle. Many aids to navigation are fitted with reflectors so that they may be picked up with a flashlight or searchlight. Reflector coloring follows the order of the coloring of night lighting of navigational aids. Deep inland, beyond the limits of commercially navigable waters, private marks are often in use. These may be in the form of bush stakes, stakes on which are mounted painted oil cans, barrels, fish baskets or floating cans and barrels. Their colors follow the practice of the standard buoyage system. If colorless (like a bush stake) they generally mark the starboard limits of the channel when entering, serving the same purpose as a red nun buoy.

The Intracoastal Waterways have a system of buoyage better suited to the generally shallow water and winding channels of inland waters. These are shown in the sketch on page 208.

Buoys may be lighted or may be equipped with a gong, bell or whistle but for day use their color and number alone will denote their meaning. The use of the buoyage system at night or in foggy weather is explained in any good book on navigation or in the free government publications listed before. An especially appropriate publication is *Light Lists,* published by the U.S. Coast Guard, Washington, D.C. Six *Light Lists* are available, without cost, covering the North Atlantic Coast of the U.S., South Atlantic

Aids to Navigation on the Intracoastal Waterway

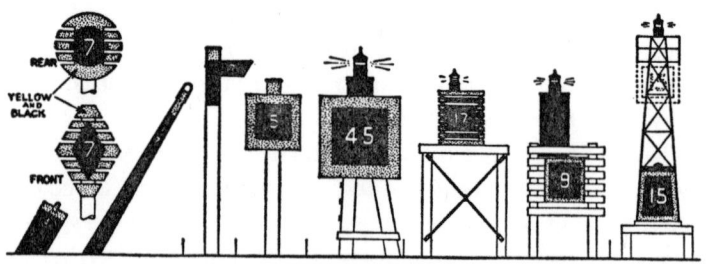

Marking port side of channel when entering from north and east and traversing from south and west respectively.

Color is yellow and black and shape of ranges, markers, etc., is square. Reflectors are square and green. Navigational lights are white or green, either fixed or flashing. Numbers are *always* odd.

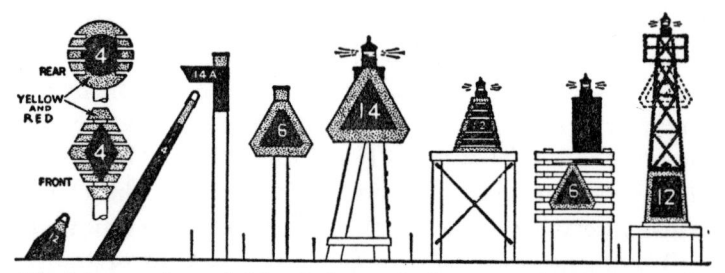

Marking starboard side of channel when entering from north and east and traversing from south and west respectively.

Color is yellow and red and shape of ranges, markers, etc., is triangular. Reflectors are triangular and red. Navigational lights are white or red, either fixed or flashing. Numbers are *always* even.

Ranges for either hand are diamond shaped on front and circular in rear, appropriately numbered and colored in conformity with the above. Structures are painted white or aluminum and their color has no significance. When markers are used in combination (as on structures to right) the top, or day-mark, is used by navigators.

Setting the Course

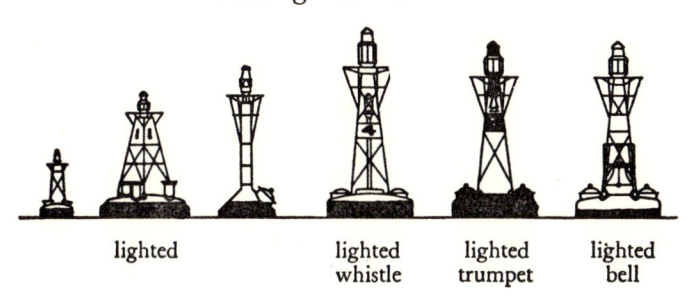

| lighted | | lighted whistle | lighted trumpet | lighted bell |

Lighted Buoys

and Gulf Coasts of the U.S., Pacific Coast (United States, Canada, Hawaii, Midway, Guam and Samoa), the Great Lakes, and the Mississippi and Ohio rivers and their tributaries.

The water in which we sail is not "standing still," not even on the inland lake where current in some amount is generally present. In tidal areas it rises and falls and in so doing creates currents which must be taken into consideration when setting a course. Local knowledge of tides and their currents is essential. While there are various tables to predict tide and current, they are only generally accurate for inshore areas. Wind strength and direction and the stage of feeder creeks and rivers all affect the current and its velocity, strength and direction. The Coast and Geodetic Survey of the U.S. Department of Commerce distributes (25¢) the following printed aids: *Tide Tables, Current Tables* and *Tidal Current Charts*. These show and predict for one year in advance the tidal and current conditions for various sections of the coast. Local knowledge, which may be gained by observation and experience during a few sails, stand the average "harbor" sailor in greater stead than reliance upon published tables and diagrams. However, the racing skipper can often use tide and current to his advantage by careful study before the race.

We have not gone into the matter of navigation at all professionally. I think the important thing now is to be able to read a chart accurately, to understand that current is present with or against us, and to be able to set and make good a course by sight, sound and the lessons learned by actually sailing the boat.

It is not at all difficult to "find our way" around on a chart. Innumerable features of the shore, the shore line and the buoyage system help to orient you as you make good the local course. The only method of establishing a "fix" without a compass or pelorus is to establish a line of position. A line of position is obtained by taking a range on any two objects which "line up" as you view them from the boat. Find these objects on the chart (bold headlands, light-

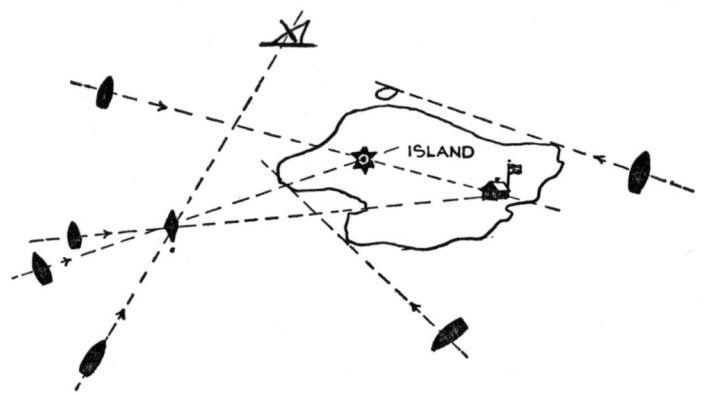

Lines of Position to Obtain a Fix

houses, buildings, buoys, etc.), draw a line through them with a pencil and extend it seaward. You are somewhere along this line. You may be fortunate enough to be able to find two other objects lined up on either side of this line of position. If so, that line extended and crossed with the first line gives you your exact position along the first line of position—a fix.

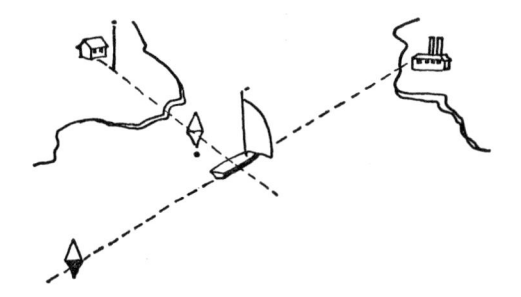

Example of Obtaining a Fix by a Range and a Bearing

However, a cross range is seldom possible. Objects do not conveniently line themselves up for you very often. Accurate bearings are impossible unless you have and understand the use of a compass or pelorus. Yet by estimating ranges and bearings *by eye* you can soon learn to define your location at the moment down to a small area. A large part of estimating such a position is determining where you are *not*. From the practical viewpoint, you are not as much concerned in sailing the shortest course possible to your objective as in avoiding hidden dangers. You want to know broadly where you are and where you're going so that you don't strand or wreck the little ship. Therefore, an exact fix is seldom necessary for ordinary sailing.

Depend always upon the buoyage system to warn of the major hidden dangers. A straight line drawn between two successive buoys on the same hand will give you your shoreward sailing limits. Do not go inside such a line. Check your course between the buoys by sighting ahead and astern, and do not sag from a straight course. Once you have established a fix, it is simple to establish a danger bearing from your location to an area you wish to avoid because of submerged hazards. Draw a line from your position which clears the danger. Extend this line to the shores ahead or astern. Note any possible ranges suggested by this line. You are bound to find one, and thereafter

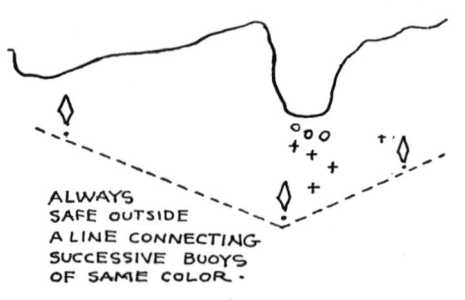

ALWAYS SAFE OUTSIDE A LINE CONNECTING SUCCESSIVE BUOYS OF SAME COLOR.

"Running" Buoys

everything right (or left) of that line spells danger so you do not go right (or left) of that line.

The sketch below demonstrates a danger bearing. The range line A-B extended from lighthouse to the prominent cliff definitely "clears" the wreck which lies on the submerged reef. Our boat, C, would not alter her course to starboard until the lighthouse can be seen beyond the cliff, nor would she ever sail inshore of this line.

Innumerable ranges present themselves in the course of an afternoon sail. One overlaps the other frequently. Each contributes to the final answer to: Where am I? A com-

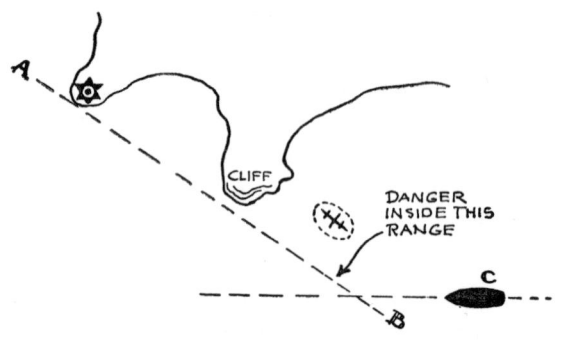

A Danger Bearing

Setting the Course

bination of sight ranges and sensed bearings, each understood and heeded, will give you remarkably accurate fixes in inshore waters. Indeed, as you sail and become versed in "local knowledge," you will hardly be conscious of taking observations to establish position . . . automatically you carry in your mind an ever-changing picture of the waters and what's beneath them. You always know where you are.

Contributing to the picture will be the "signs" known to every navigator—the same kind of signs, insignificant in themselves, used by woodsmen and native islanders on their amazingly long ocean voyages. The color of the water, the character of the waves, the set of the current, the presence or absence of lobster pot buoys or fish weirs, anchored boats, where other boats are sailing, breaking fish, back eddies, floating seaweed and debris—all these "signs" carry a message to the local skipper. In Maine, lobster pot buoys indicate deep water because we who sail there know that traps are set in at least 15 feet of water. In Gardiner's Bay, large boats sail right through a maze of oyster stakes driven into the bottom, knowing that oyster beds are on sandy soft bottom and always at least 16 feet deep. You can crawl into any boat anchorage without fear by following the line made by the largest of the anchored boats. In Muscongus Bay the islands run Sou'west-Nor'east, so you can sail close aboard the sou'west sides where the sea has eroded the land but better stay off the nor'east sides where broken ground will stretch far underwater. Blue water usually means deep water, dark green water might mean deep or it might mean patches of kelp or rockweed (and rocks) below, yellow or "thin" water probably does mean sand bottom and that not too far down. Porpoises play generally in deep water, but kingfishers and heron fish in shallow water. Become acquainted with your own local signs. In confined areas, especially in thick weather or at night, local knowledge is far more important than a knowledge of formal navigation. On short hitches, in varying currents and eddies, the compass course is anything but reliable. Local knowledge is so important, in fact, that the insurers of commercial vessels specify that upon entering strange ports, the vessel must take on a local pilot. These men rely not on the compass but on secret ranges, signs and intimate knowledge of their waters.

With the course selected and visualized, the sailor must decide how best to reach his objective—beat, reach or run. Very seldom can the sailboat set out for her objective like a power boat does. She must make the best course allowed by the wind and tide of the moment, so the general course is broken down into many smaller courses or tacks. She must confine the length and direction of each to the limitations of the sailing waters.

The first step is to settle the boat down to sailing her best on any given course. We have, I hope, learned how to do this from previous chapters. Once "in the groove," select any two points on the boat which are approximately the same distance port or starboard of the keel and sight over them to some object ahead. Thereafter keep the boat sailing on this course but be prepared always to alter course as dictated by shifts in wind or current so the boat sails her swiftest. The target may be a conspicuous landmark or a mere distant patch of ocean. The "sights" must be doubled. A single sight is accurate only if you do not move or move your head. The sights will vary on each boat, of course. When I sit to starboard of the helm on my boat, I line up the starboard edge of the companion slide with the target. When I'm steering from the port side, I line up the top of the Charlie Noble (which is the smoke head from the galley stove) with the port fluke of the chocked anchor on the foward

Setting the Course

deck. For variety, I often watch the wake—straight wake, straight course.

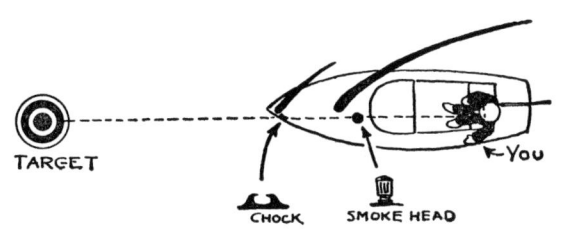

Sighting a Course

A perfectly reliable method of holding course is to steer by compass. The trouble is that you're looking at a compass all day instead of contemporary marine life, your best girl and the luff of your mainsail. After each tack, select another target and keep your boat headed that way. Targets broad on the bows or on the beam are unreliable since their bearings change rapidly as the boat moves. Naturally, there will be some veering from the course as the boat rolls and plunges. But a good helmsman soon gets the hang of "averaging." If the bow veers to starboard he will bring her to port for an equal length of time. This soon becomes quite automatic; you don't have to think about it or do it consciously. It is a matter more of the feeling of the helm than actual sighting or counting time.

In tidal waters, in some lakes and on most rivers current will be an ever-present force which you will have to consider. You sail through moving water, which is current, just as you sail through any other water. It makes no difference whatsoever (unless it is enormously strong like in the Bay of Fundy or the Niagara River) in the handling of the boat or setting of the sails. However, since the water is moving *en masse* over the bottom to which your objective is "fixed," it will greatly affect the matter of course.

If the tide is foul and *directly* against you, it will slow the boat but not affect course. If the tide is fair and *directly* astern of you, it will assist the boat but not affect course. If it is neither fair nor foul, even by a little bit, it *will* affect course and you must make allowances for it. Tide on the beam will sweep you to either side of a direct line from starting point to objective. You must "aim" an appropriate distance left or right of the target to reach the target. The course, we might consider, has been laid out on the bottom but we are going to sail it through moving water passing over the bottom. Obviously, we are going to "miss" the target by the distance the tide has moved us in the time required to sail to the target.

To compensate for this error the professional navigator takes from various tide and current tables the data necessary to predict direction, velocity and periods of current flow in the area to be traversed. He then calculates an appropriate course which will see him reaching his landfall by a course which is the shortest line between starting point and objective. But he does not bother attempting to correct a course for current unless it is a very long one. River mouths, back eddies, depth of water, submerged topography and wind all contort tidal currents into fluid masses of unpredictable habits, masses which vary by the minute and yard in drift, set and behavior and by no means decently reverse themselves upon the turn of the tide. Inshore and in harbor areas, he must, like you, rely chiefly upon local knowledge of the habits of tide and current.

What the professional navigator does by calculation on a long course, you and he must do by estimate on a short course. Make a mental estimate, taking into account the current habits as you know them, of the distance the current will move right or left of the objective during the time you estimate it will require you to reach the objective.

Setting the Course

For example, let us assume (as we have in the sketch below) that the distance A-B is 4 miles. It is going to take you, sailing on a broad reach, 1 hour to reach B. However there

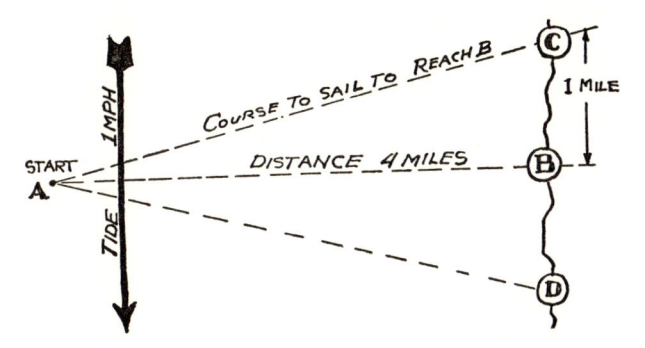

Allowing for Current in Setting a Course

is a tide on your port beam which you know flows at 1 mile an hour. Hence during the hour required to sail from A to B, the tide will be moving you 1 mile away from B. To compensate for this "loss" you must alter the course so that it is "aimed" 1 mile *toward the tide* above the objective, B. By sailing this course you will, obviously, reach the original objective, B, by the shortest possible course. If you did not make this allowance and sailed without regard to the tide you would land at D, 1 mile below your objective and have to beat up against the full flow of the current to B.

But the tidal current does not decently confine itself to fixed direction and velocity. Over a 4-mile course, it may reverse itself, back eddy, run very strong or very weak or not at all, and you must forecast the total effect upon your course for all the time you will remain on that course. Judgment and first-hand knowledge alone can give you an estimate of the plus and minus factors you must consider.

Current vagaries are most pronounced near shore and in the vicinity of shoals and bars. Often rotary currents are present in the neighborhood of submerged obstructions and headlands, the favorable side of which can be used to your advantage. Tide usually runs stronger in mid-channel than 'longshore. For a time between the stand and the slack of a tide, you may find opposed currents, one of which might help you along the way. There is an island in Penobscot Bay which has a "thoroughfare" through which the tide always runs in the same direction whether flooding or ebbing. There are ways to sail through Plum Gut at the eastern entrance to Long Island Sound even against the savage 6-knot current, which sometimes runs there, by using certain backwaters and eddies. Local knowledge alone can give you an understanding of your own tides. Fishermen, coast guardsmen, ferrymen and boatmen are experts. It will always pay to talk with them about the matter.

The only situation in which you can utilize a foul tide occurs sometimes when sailing to windward. If possible, take the tack which brings the tide against your lee bow. It will carry you to windward much more than leeway will carry you leeward and result in a course much closer into the wind than otherwise possible. It is called lee bowing the tide.

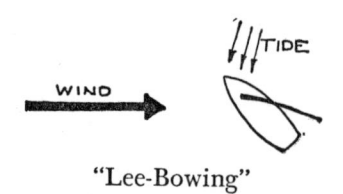

"Lee-Bowing"

In setting a course you will also have to make some allowances for leeway. Our boat, as we have seen, sails not only forward but sideways as well. Leeway is seldom very

Setting the Course

great but it usually is strong enough to require, in still water, that you set the course somewhat to windward of the objective. Experience alone will suggest the amount of alteration in course necessary. Wind forward retards, wind aft helps, wind on the beam causes the greatest leeway, wind on the bow or quarter, the least. Deep boats make less leeway than shallow ones. In rough seas, leeway is greatly increased. A rough estimate of leeway may be made by observing the angle between the wake and a length of line towed astern. Leeway can be somewhat reduced (as I have suggested elsewhere) by being careful about the matter of windage.

Dangers to navigation, tides, currents, leeway, the sea, the wind—all these, plus one more thing, determine your course. That thing, too, is a variable—other boats.

Federal law regulates procedure when two boats approach one another so as to involve risk of collision. Specific boats are given both rights and responsibilities as follows—

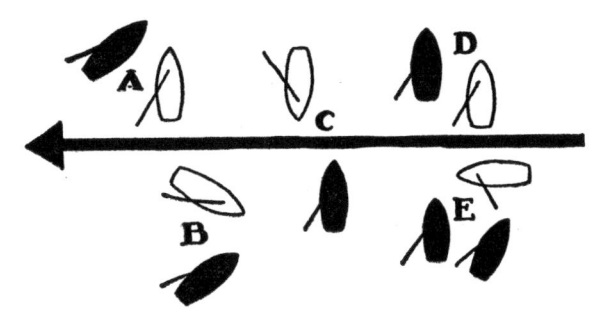

Rules of the Road for Sailboats

A. A boat which is running free shall keep out of the way of a boat which is close-hauled, i.e., a boat off the wind shall keep out of the way of a boat on the wind.

B. A boat which is close-hauled on the port tack shall

keep out of the way of a boat which is close-hauled on the starboard tack.

C. When both are running free (reaching) with the wind on different sides, the boat which has the wind on the port side shall keep out of the way of the other.

D. When both are running free (reaching) with the wind on the same side the boat which is to windward shall keep out of the way of the boat which is to leeward.

E. A boat which has the wind aft (running before it) shall keep out of the way of other boats.

When a boat under power or oars and a boat under sail are proceeding in such directions as to involve risk of collision, the boat under power or oars shall keep out of the way of the boat under sail.

Where, by any of these rules, one of the two boats is to keep out of the way, the other shall keep her course and speed.

Every boat which is directed by these rules to keep out of the way of another boat shall, if the circumstances of the case permit, avoid passing ahead of the other.

Every boat, whether under power, oars or sail, when overtaking any other shall keep out of the way of the overtaken boat.

Plain, specific and exact—that's the law. Only one situation can legally suspend its application. If a boat is in danger of collision or running aground by keeping on the course legally assigned to her, she may demand and must be given the right of way.

Sailboats have the right of way over power and steamboats. A pleasant bit of special privilege for the wind skipper, but one not to be abused. It would be perfectly silly to scrap out the right of way with an ocean liner. Just as silly as that gentleman who some years ago forced

Setting the Course

a great railroad to recognize his legal rights to the use of a bridged creek. After removing the bridge, inconveniencing thousands of train passengers, upsetting freight schedules and causing the railroad to spend several thousand dollars, this gentleman sailed his little bang-bang boat through the bridge, crossed the river for a hot dog and a bottle of pop and returned. He had won a moral victory of dubious value, about the kind you win by making a great liner change course or slow down. (If she does!)

Sailboats never exchange sound signals to signify their intentions in a right of way situation. However, power vessels might signify their intentions to you or to each other in a situation which might involve you, and it is well to understand their whistle signals.

Whistle Signals Used by Power Vessels

One blast means: I am directing my course to starboard.
Two blasts mean: I am directing my course to port.
Three blasts mean: My engines are reversed and I am going full astern.
Four or more rapid blasts mean: Your course not satisfactory to me. Danger.

Three blasts plus one blast means: I am towing. ('Ware the tow—it may be strung out for a mile behind the whistler!)

Racing sailboats navigate under special racing rules. They have no special legal rights, of course, but common decency dictates that you do not argue "legal" rights with other boats while racing. Keep off their race course and always well to leeward of them so that you don't steal their wind. Most right-of-way situations resolve themselves into situations of courtesy and gentlemanliness, the interfering boat giving way *before* a situation involving risk of collision develops. This is as it should be from the decency angle as well as quite a practical one. After all, amateur skippers are not licensed nor have they been examined for an understanding of right-of-way rules. It is safest to assume that the other boat does not understand the rules and would not recognize either your or its rights or responsibilities in any event.

Setting and sailing a course at night or in fog requires considerable technical knowledge which is beyond the scope of this book. You must, by law, carry certain lights, sound certain warnings and navigate by certain rules; you must have considerable special knowledge at your comand to sail in safety. We shall touch only upon the matter of lights and fog signals.

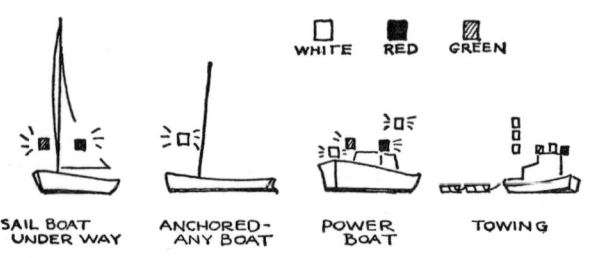

Navigating Lights for Boats

Setting the Course

Under sail, you are required by law to carry special lanterns—a red one to port and a green one to starboard. These are constructed so that they show light only from dead ahead to two points abaft the beam. In addition, you should have handy a flashlight or lantern which can be thrown upon the sail as other boats approach and to show over the stern to an overtaking boat. At anchor in a fairway you must show a single white light. On sailboats this anchor light is usually attached to the headstay about six feet above the deck.

Other sailboats will show lights just like your own. Keep away from them; it is foolish to risk creating a dangerous situation calling for the application of right-of-way rules at night. If you see red and green lights at the same time, you are directly on the course of the other boat. Make a light signal on the sail and scoot!

Colored lights (called running lights) together with one or two white lights means a power boat. Assume that she has seen you and recognized you as a sailboat and will give you proper clearance. However, do not confuse the situation by suddenly changing course and, when within range, flash a light on the sail to *prove* that you are under sail. A power boat which displays a set of two or more lights hung vertically is towing—and it may be a very long tow. Keep clear. If you are towed yourself, show only regular sailing lights, red and green.

In fog sailboats make the following signals on the horn:
Underway—One blast when on the starboard tack.
        Two long blasts when on the port tack.
        Three long blasts when before the wind.
At anchor—Ring the fog bell for five seconds.

The interval between sound signals is not greater than once each minute.

Fog Signals for Sailboats

Power and steam vessels make the following signals:
Underway—One long blast.
Stopped but not anchored—Two long blasts.
Towing or towed vessel—One long blast followed by two short blasts.

This is the chapter in which I should suggest calling into use the game of Sail-O which I earlier presented as a help in learning the sailing positions. The same basic equipment, plus a few models of power boats, barges, and steamers, can be utilized to assist in visualizing the problems of setting a course. Establish a wind direction and try a few courses from here to there. Then add a tide and make the estimates to allow for it. As you sail, throw in a power boat or another sailboat and create a few rules-of-the-road

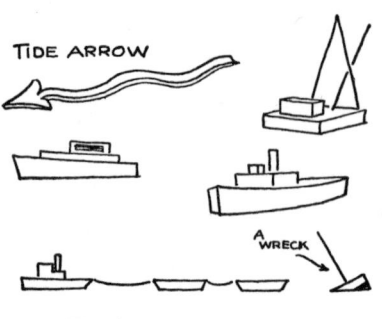

Equipment for Sail-O

Setting the Course

situations to solve. Now assume that it is thick o' fog or night and make the proper light and sound signals. Either worked out by yourself or played as a game against a nautical-minded opponent, Sail-O should assist some readers in picturing and solving the situations arising from setting and sailing a course.

CHAPTER FOURTEEN

Mooring, Docking and Maneuvering

WHEN maneuvering to pick up moorings or docking or anchoring, you will need a thorough understanding of the capabilities of your boat. Inches often count. As I have suggested in an earlier chapter, your boat has a forward, a neutral and a reverse and, in addition, speed control in the forward movements. Just as you automatically use throttle and gearshifts when driving a car, you use the rudder and sails to control the boat. Not always do you want to sail at top speed over the water; many sailing situations will call for slow speed, for stop and for reverse.

Forward speed is obtained by sailing in one of the three sailing positions. Forward speed is controlled by sheeting the sails in various positions of drive or in reducing or adding sail area.

Your "neutral" is always in the position of luffing, boat and sails aimed directly into the wind. In passing from forward speed to neutral (or stop) you must always give consideration to the amount of momentum inherent in the boat and allow for its forward drive even after the sails have ceased to exert their force. In light, shallow boats this momentum, or "shoot," is apt to be very little; in heavy keelboats it may be from four to eight times the length of the boat. You must know the distance of the shoot with fair accuracy and based on experience in various wind

Mooring, Docking and Maneuvering

strengths and sea and tide conditions. The only control you have of shoot are these.

You can quickly send live weight forward, whereupon the boat will become logy and rapidly slow down.

You can put your rudder hard over, first to port, then to starboard, but not for long enough periods to steer the boat actually into a sailing position again. This rudder action serves as a mild brake.

You can, in shallow water, drop the centerboard so that it drags in the mud, holding it down with a mop handle or stick inserted in the centerboard slot if necessary.

You can wing out the jib, making it into quite a bag, holding it first to port and then to starboard, but not for long enough periods to swing the bow on the wind and into a sailing position. This action serves as a windbrake.

The shoot which has been misjudged and is too long is not particularly disastrous when picking up a mooring. With the boat hook, pick up the mooring pennant and quickly snub it to the bitts or deck cleat and the boat is brought sharply to rest. However, when coming up to a dock, the misjudged momentum may prove ruinous to the boat, the dock or both. Your only defense is to fend off

Fending Off

with feet or with the boat hook. The correct manner of doing so is shown in the sketch above.

If the shoot has been misjudged and is too short there is nothing to do but allow the boat to bear off, sail away and try the maneuver again. Fortunate circumstance might discover a willing hand at a dock to whom you might be able to heave a line. If so, you are saved from trying again.

The last position, sailing a boat in reverse, is a very neat trick and requires first-class judgment and seamanship. Sailing in reverse can be done by trimming both jib and mainsail *absolutely flat amidships*. Hold the tiller (or lash it if you are single handed) *very slightly* to port of starboard, an inch or less is sufficient. Then shove the boat off straight to windward. The shove must be *straight!* If you're a centerboarder, raise the centerboard. During the maneuver maintain trim; do not heel the boat either way. She will continue to sail slowly backwards until you put the helm all the way over, whereupon she will fall on the wind—at which point you start the sheets, put the helm over the opposite way and you will soon begin sailing forward. It is seldom possible to sail backward for long. Trim, waves and wind eddies usually quickly destroy the delicate balance required for a boat to sail in reverse.

Another method of sailing backward to leeward, at least for the short distance you would normally wish to sail backwards, is to strap down the mainsail hard. With the tiller amidships, hold the jib first to port then to starboard, continuing this fanning motion by reversing the side on which you hold the jib as the boat shows signs of veering from a course straight to leeward.

Maneuvering requires plenty of practice and I suggest that you reduce the penalties of failure by experimenting, not at the dock or mooring, but in open water, using a dinghy or a floating mark as a target. The secret of successfully handling the boat under all conditions is first to understand that your "throttle" is the position of luffing. Luff-

Mooring, Docking and Maneuvering

ing while sailing slows the boat and luffing when not sailing stops the boat. Therefore, no matter at what place or thing you want to stop, the approach *must be made from leeward and directly to windward*. Otherwise the boat will continue to sail and she will never stop completely. The second secret is to know absolutely the amount of shoot in your boat.

Once secured to the mooring or dock, it is best to drop the jib immediately and, with mainsail luffing, the boat will lie streamed to the wind, quite docile and with no inclination to sail ahead.

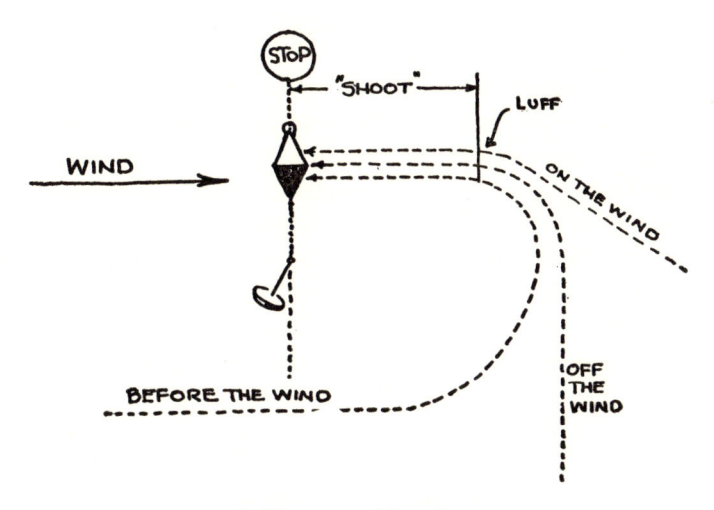

Sailing to a Mooring

The steps in picking up a mooring are shown in the sketch above. Note that, no matter from what sailing position you approach the mooring, you always sail down to leeward of the mark and round up, luff and shoot to the target. Try to approach the mooring buoy so that the bow will make a lee against wave direction, which is generally somewhat different from wind direction. You will have to judge carefully, striving to have the bow of the boat come to rest precisely at the buoy so that you can quickly belay the mooring line and permit the boat, which is about to move backwards, to sag against it.

Making a Mooring under Sail

A little thought about your mooring tackle will assist greatly in making the maneuver smooth and troubleless. To make unnecessary the hasty tying of knots (with wet rope!) during this critical moment, splice a generous eye in the mooring pennant which can be quickly thrown over the bitts. I never saw great need of large metal cans or chunks of logwood as part of the mooring equipment for the small sailboat. Generally the mooring is in fairly shallow water and it is much simpler to attach a light wooden or

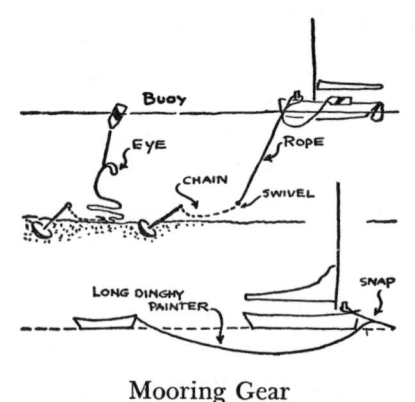

Mooring Gear

Mooring, Docking and Maneuvering 231

cork marker buoy to the main cable by a small line. Thus, upon mooring, you may quickly pick up the buoy, overhaul its line to the eye splice of the main cable and belay it. To become fouled up with heavy mooring casks, knots, a dinghy painter and a few fathoms of kelp is, unfortunately, "snafu" for too many of us. Not the least advantage of the rig I have described is that the buoy may be kept on deck between sails. In calm weather, the small boat which constantly "nurses" the mooring buoy soon has a paint sick and scarred bow.

The dinghy problem, too, must be given careful thought. Seldom do we tow the dinghy astern of the afternoon sailor. We leave it at the mooring where it becomes the very devil of an obstacle to a smooth pickup. The only completely satisfactory stunt that I have found to solve the dilemma is to moor the dinghy to the mooring cable by a painter that is a few fathoms longer than the shoot of the boat. Then you may sail to the dinghy, shoot without interference from it to the buoy, pick up the cable and belay it, and when you're all finished there's the dinghy bobbing gently astern where she should be. Obviously, too, mooring it so greatly simplifies getting under way; no dinghy will be chafing your topsides, fouling her painter in keel or between sternpost and rudder or misbehaving in the many ways that only dinghies can.

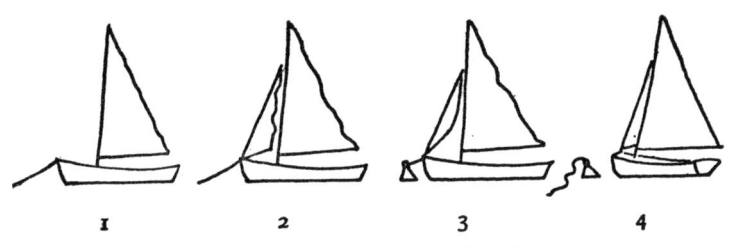

Getting Away from a Mooring

To cast off from a mooring (the boat being manned and ready to sail), you simply drop the buoy overside on the side which is to be the windward side on the first tack. If you don't care what tack you go off on, cast off the mooring cable from its cleat or bitts and carry it toward the stern on whichever side is most convenient (since it is a nuisance to pass the mooring cable forward and outside of jib and headstays). Your boat will fall off on the same tack as the side on which you carry the mooring, i.e., if you carry it aft on the port side, the bow will fall off to starboard and you will start sailing on the port tack. As soon as the boat gathers headway, cast the mooring overside.

Anchoring a sailboat is accomplished by the same maneuvers required to pick up a mooring. Luff, shoot and stop . . . and when she has completely stopped, drop the anchor overside off the forward deck. Do not throw it—more "snafu" will result! Drop it over, crown down and stock rigged and keyed, and pay the anchor line out until the anchor touches bottom. By then the boat should be drifting to leeward. Momentarily snub the anchor line, throwing the anchor toward the boat, and then pay out

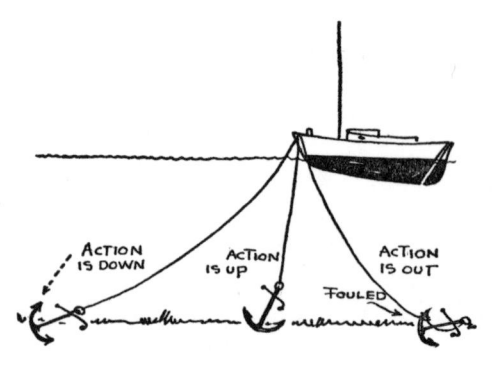

Action of the Anchor

Mooring, Docking and Maneuvering

line as the boat sags against it. Recommended scope for the cable is at least five times the depth of the water you anchor in.

To sail away from an anchor, haul the cable up short—almost straight up and down. Put the boat on the wind and, as she gathers headway, she will throw the anchor forward and break the palms out of the holding ground and you may then haul the anchor aboard. If it is stubborn, sag back on the taut cable and get off on the tack opposite from the first. A few such "yanks" will break out the stubbornest of anchors, unless it is fouled in rock. To rig an anchor to trip, which is what it will have to do in order to break away from rock, follow the instructions in the sketch below.

Anchor Tripping Rig

In attempting to reach a floating mark or buoy, you must always take into account the tide. It may help or hinder you, lessening or increasing the shoot or making it necessary to allow for its affect upon the beam. Steer for a point toward the direction from which the tide sets when you must cross the current to reach the mark. Since the dinghy will probably stream with both the tide and wind, it may hover halfway between their forces and prevent a nice approach on its side. However, by the same sign, it leaves the opposite side clear and you will want to take this into account as you lay your plans for the maneuver.

Sailing up to a dock requires nice judgment—and a good deal of luck. The luck is not necessarily in the handling of the boat; the luck is in the wind. Always inshore in the vicinity of the dock, buildings, land contours, trees, other boats and beach thermals, cause wind eddies and flukes which are humanly unpredictable. A wharf area even directly to leeward is liable to odd winds and wind currents.

Whenever possible approach a dock from leeward, shooting to it with sails luffing. You can make a leeward landing on three sides of a rectangular dock or float, the leeward side and on each end. After docking, the boat will lie on the leeward side to a short painter. To moor to the ends, since one side of the boat will be parallel to the end of the dock, you will require fenders to protect the topsides. Hang these from the *boat* in tidewater, from the *dock* in still water. The boat will lie better and with less chafing if you put out proper mooring lines. These are shown below. The "spring line" is the line which makes the boat behave.

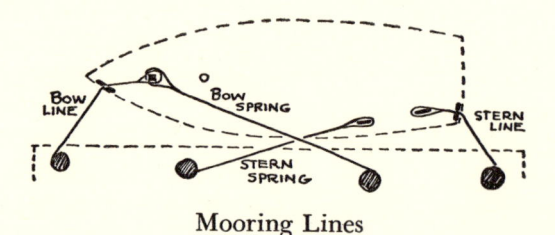

Mooring Lines

Be prepared always when approaching a dock to fend off in the event that momentum is too strong. Wind shifts and flukes are not so easily combated. If you suspect them, give yourself wide berthing room so that if anything goes wrong you will not go berserk amongst your sister ships. At all costs follow the advice of earlier parts of this book—keep steerageway on. Without it you are surely headed for

Mooring, Docking and Maneuvering 235

trouble if those nasty shore winds want to sail you when you want to luff and vice versa. Rather than run chances in a situation of doubt, swallow your pride, lower sail and row or pole the boat into the dock.

The steps required to get away from a leeward berth on

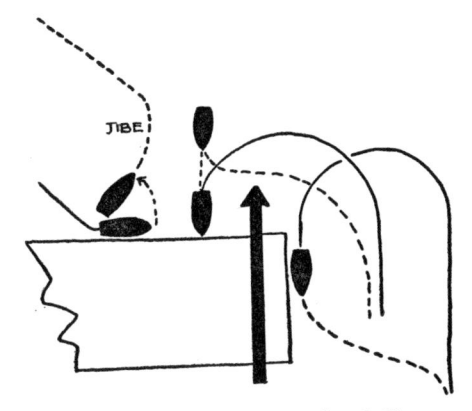

Leeward Landings under Sail

a dock are shown on this sketch by the dotted lines. Note the use of a "swinging warp" when getting off *to* leeward. A swinging warp may be controlled entirely from the boat by using a double line, passing the standing part through a ring or over a pile on the dock and leading the fall back to the boat. When the line is no longer required, simply cast off the fall and haul it aboard. If bound between other boats and there is no room to swing, you can here resort to sailing backwards by fanning the jib.

When boats are thickly tethered to the leeward side of a dock like so many pods on a vine, you must drop to leeward of the sterns of surrounding boats before attempting to sail. If you mistrust your ability to drift or sail backwards and begin sailing correctly in clear water (or, as is more likely, you haven't got maneuvering space), rig a swinging warp from your bow to the stern of a boat on your flank. Drift to leeward on this, make sail, let the warp run and get off on a broad reach until you have cleared.

Windward landings at docks and floats are never desirable, but they are often necessary because of water depths. You always need room for this because you must approach the dock so that you will come to rest parallel with it. In other words, approach the dock on a reach. Such a landing is a matter of neat timing and a thorough understanding of the habits of your boat. Plan the maneuver this way: Some distance before the actual stopping place, get solidly on a reach and then let all sheets run so that the jib and mainsail are both luffing over the leeward side. The shoot should carry you to the exact stopping place and windage then carry you into the dock. There are dangers such as dragging sheets over float cleats and bollards and getting under way again in tight quarters if you miss. Naturally, you can do this only if the dock or float is lower than the distance between main boom and the water.

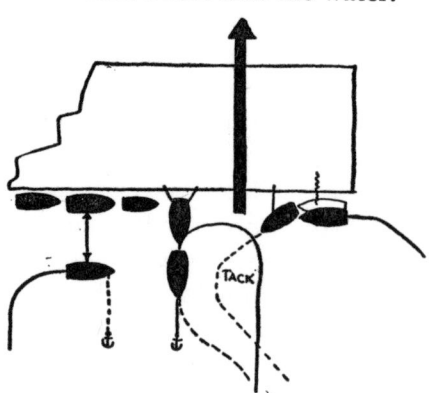

Windward Landings under Sail

The use of the anchor is good sound seamanship in making a windward landing. At some distance off the wharf,

Mooring, Docking and Maneuvering

luff and anchor; then sag back on the cable and make fast to the dock with stern lines. If you wish to lay broadside to the dock, or snuggle into a berth between two other boats, anchor, snub the cable and douse all sail. Then let windage carry you to the dock. In getting away from the windward side of the dock, haul yourself out to the anchor, make sail and sail away just as you do from a normal anchorage.

If the dock is low, you may be able to get away, to windward, in this manner. Make sail. Let sails luff with the main boom extending over the dock. When all ready, shove the boat from the dock to windward by the main boom, give it some headway, jump smartly aboard and quickly trim sheets.

Tide and current must be reckoned with if present. Carefully forecast the affect of tide. It can very often be made to assist a docking maneuver. It is often possible to reverse the heading of a take-off so that the tide will help control the boat. Sailing *against* a strong tide, you can sometimes work a boat out of confined quarters in such a way that tide and leeway neutralize each other and the boat moves directly sideways. I used to sail regularly through a narrow drawbridge using this principle. Some situations to which it might apply are shown on page 238.

There is one more situation (and I hope you will never meet it) which might require quick and expert maneuvering. That is when the cry "Man overboard" goes ringing over the ship. Toss the victim a life preserver and go after him immediately, even if he is a swimmer for he may have been hurt in falling overboard. Be careful not to pinch the boat into a circle smaller than her normal turning radius. Otherwise you may oversail your man and have to get downwind of him again, for you approach him just as you do a mooring, planning for the boat to come to rest precisely alongside of him. Make a lee from the waves if possible. Take him aboard over the bow. If you are alone and must go into the water after him, lash a line around your waist and to the boat. Should you fall overboard while sail-

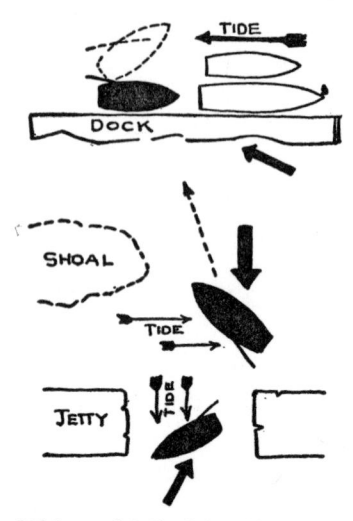

Using Tide and Wind in Tight Situations

ing alone, do not swim frantically after the boat. Unless the helm is lashed, she will soon luff, drift to leeward and commence sailing again. There will be a recognizable pattern to these repeated arcs of sailing—a series of semi-circles—and you should have no difficulty in estimating the time and place of a luffing period and in swimming there with all speed.

Throughout these chapters on handling sail and maneuvering I have been aware of a pedantic quality in my presentations which I would rather see abolished. But I find no other way to convey my meaning or facts. Perforce I must graph it out and lecture like a third mate to the apprentices. Nevertheless, the art of sailing has no quality of the pedantic about it. It is a free, spontaneous and natural art; good sailors sail naturally, just as good swimmers swim naturally and good hikers walk naturally. I urge you not to accept this as a spelling book but rather as an alphabet book—from the letters you can construct the words. What I have said in these chapters is all subject to your own personal experiences, in your particular type of boat, sailed in your particular kind of sailing waters. The art of sailing cannot be neatly defined and catalogued, not in practice anyway, and is always composed of an admixture of experience, study and opinion. Never are there situations under canvas which can be solved as neatly as sailing books solve them. The divisions of the art of sailing overlap and intertwine and complement and cancel each other. You never simply dock a boat; you must at the same moment sail her, reckon tide and wind, plan ahead, observe other boats, be aware of the dangers and limitations of navigation, prepare dock lines, shift ballast, perhaps must be host or captain or guest. Unlike in the book, "everything comes at once."

So digest these facts separately, but understand that you will require them in endless combinations of emphasis when you sail. In time, they will cease to be separate facts and become a subconscious entity ready to be brought forth and utilized as circumstances demand. You will then be a natural sailor, sailing the pleasant watery highways, rules and facts forgotten as such, just as you breathe or walk or talk.

CHAPTER FIFTEEN

For Better or for Worse

> ... for better or for worse,
> for richer or for poorer,
> in sickness and in health. ...

WHEN you become the owner of a boat you take unto yourself practically another wife. "Marriage" in the nautical sense isn't far removed from the one you have made with the girl of your choice—you have an implied contract with the boat to see it through joys and troubles of all kinds. This chapter will deal with some of the troubles which might mar the bliss of life with your other wife, your boat.

When trouble develops in any situation, it is only human nature to call for help. Nautical trouble often means danger, both to the boat and its human cargo. Few of us like to admit shame or defeat by asking assistance when we get into boat trouble. But any trouble which is potentially dangerous, like capsizing or stranding, should see pride swallowed, and a good lusty signal for help go out. Seafaring folks are notoriously generous in offering help to their troubled fellows; if they are in a position to help, they seldom fail. Call upon them freely for serious emergencies, as they might call upon you.

The universal signal for help is three of anything, repeated—three blasts on the foghorn, three gunshots, a light flashed three times, etc. Navigation rules, understood by

For Better or for Worse

professional seamen but not necessarily by amateur boatmen, provide for fixed distress signals as follows:

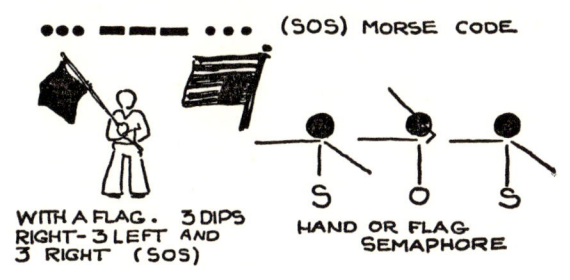

•••   ▬▬▬   •••   (SOS) MORSE CODE

WITH A FLAG. 3 DIPS RIGHT - 3 LEFT AND 3 RIGHT (SOS)

HAND OR FLAG SEMAPHORE

Distress Signals

By Day—

1. A gun or other explosive signal fired at intervals of about one minute.

2. The International Code signal of distress indicated by NC.

3. The distance signal, consisting of a square flag having above or below it a ball or anything resembling a ball (basket, bundle of clothing, water jug, etc., on the small boat)

4. Continuous sounding with any fog signalling apparatus.

5. The signal SOS (three dots, three dashes, three dots, or . . . ▬ ▬ . . .) made by radiotelegraphy, or by any other distress signalling method (such as emergency mirror heliograph, flashlight, on foghorn, semaphore, wigwag, etc.)

By Night (Same as above, plus)—

Flames on the vessel, as from a burning barrel, etc. (For example, on the small boat, oil-soaked burning rags on a stick held overside or contained in a bucket, etc.)

Rockets or shells throwing stars of any color or description, fired one at a time, at short intervals.

I have included these International Distress Signals chiefly for the other fellow's sake. Should you ever see or hear one of them you are bound by honor and tradition to go to the assistance of the maker, if by so doing you do not imperil the lives of those on your own vessel. But we must approach the question as realists. More than likely distress signals used by amateurs will be of the common "land" variety, three of anything or a lusty yell for help. The unofficial signal, the United States ensign flown upside down, is universally understood. It is best to assume that fellow skippers do *not* understand the signals specified by maritime law and to make the commonly accepted ones which *both* the professional and amateur will understand.

Aircraft may summon aid for a ship in distress by flying to another ship, circling it several times and flying off in the direction of the vessel in trouble. It will repeat this until followed. So the circling plane may not be merely a stunt flyer; it may be calling you to the scene of a capsizing, a fire, or persons floating in the water.

Submarines of the United States Navy which may be in need of assistance release a red smoke bomb. If you sight such a bomb, communicate at once (preferably via a power boat which you hail) with the Coast Guard, giving time and exact location. Yellow smoke bombs mean that a submarine is about to surface. Keep clear of such bombs.

But most trouble will have to be solved by no one but yourself. Help is not always conveniently at hand nor, unless there is real or potential danger in your situation, are you justified in bothering other folks. It's fair enough to request a tow if becalmed in dangerous current or a yank off a ledge on a falling tide but quite the opposite if you merely lose a rudder or break a fixable halyard. Here are the common troubles and their cures.

CAPSIZING

Keelboats of proper design are, of course, non-capsizable. Always the weight of the keel will eventually bring them upright again. However they are quite sinkable unless fitted with air tanks or watertight bulkheads or watertight self-bailing cockpits. Unless your keelboat has some flotation features, she's a dangerous "other wife" indeed. Capsizing her means sinking her; once sunk you can do nothing about the matter—death has thee parted! Fortunately there are few keelboats built which do not have one or several of the features required to provide flotation in the event of capsizing and filling. Whenever the weather gets boisterous make a careful check of these flotation chambers. Be sure that air vents are closed and hatches not only shut but battened or hooked down. In the cabin boat, the cabin itself is the flotation chamber. Main hatch, portholes and any deck openings (except possibly small ventilators well above the deck) should be closed and kept closed. Openings in the cockpit floor leading to engine space or lazarettes should be closed and their hatches secured from inside (or by dogs outside) so that they do not float away or fall away in the event of knockdown and filling.

I have never filled by the beam in my boat but I have several times been pooped by the stern. The cockpit fills up, like a big bathtub, and soon begins to scupper off. The boat meanwhile is logy and somewhat down by the stern. Providing hatches are closed, the whole experience is merely amusing, and very wet. Fear it not.

The centerboarder is liable to genuine capsizing, which means, once past the critical angle of heel, going all the way over, filling and staying there, fortunately afloat. About her you can do something. First get wet; jump in the water and get it over with for you'll have to sooner or later. Then cast jib and main halyard off their cleats (never at the heads of the sails or your halyard ends will be aloft when you right the boat) and haul the sails down, or rather toward, the deck. Then get all the live weight possible upon the windward side, even stand on the tip of the extended center-

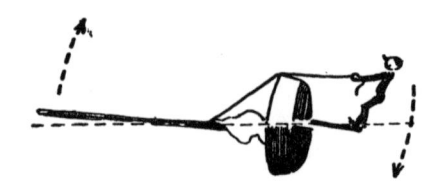

Righting a Capsized Centerboard Boat

board to gain leverage, and she'll stand up. Bail her out and make sail, forgetting not that your sails have been soaked and will need to be slacked off along the foot.

Before righting the boat, since she will begin making leeway as soon as righted, retrieve your spilled and floating gear, particularly the tiller and rudder. If you have spilled in a tideway, do not hesitate to anchor.

If the boat is stubborn about righting there is nothing to do but pull the mast out of her. Knock the pins from the clevises of the standing rigging turnbuckles, slack off all running rigging and quickly pull the mast clear of both the step and the partners. Passing boats can assist in righting by lifting the masthead as you apply your weight or, in the case of power boats, taking a hitch on the masthead and hauling to windward. Once the mast is free of the weight of the sail and slightly clear of the water, the boat will usually right readily.

In bailing the boat, keep weight off her until you have

For Better or for Worse

gained a few inches on the water. As she becomes buoyant, get into her and find your pump or a pail. If you have lost these things, you can bail by a "shirt scoop"—assuming that you have not also lost your shirt. The sketch below shows how to rig this. You can sometimes "rock out" the first few inches of water by rolling the boat (in unison if

the crew helps) from side to side and so dashing some of the water over the beam. This works best, of course, in open boats like dinghies or sharpies.

If while sailing, you fear capsizing, by all means distribute and have your people don life preservers. Place passengers on the windward side of the boat. If the boat does go over, she will throw your passengers on *top* of the sail. The reverse would be the sad truth if thrown from the leeward side. Boats capsize slowly and an alert man can easily crawl to the exposed topside as she goes over.

It is pleasant to remember that few boats capsize and that capsizing, if the crew can swim, is seldom a tragedy. The best defenses against capsizing are:

Keep live weight to windward in strong blows.
Reduce canvas by reefing *before* it becomes necessary.
Always keep steerageway to avoid knockdowns.
Guard against accidental jibes and broaching to.

LOSS OF RUDDER

By reason of capsizing, or storm or breakage, you may find yourself without a rudder. That is not necessarily the calamity it may first seem. A little ingenuity and imagination will soon produce a jury rudder, made of a floor board, oar, spinnaker pole, etc. You can steer quite well with a bundle of rope or "sausage" of furled sail dragged from the quarters. Another dodge is to tow a bucket into which you have punched a few holes. All these forms of drag rudders steer the boat *toward* the side on which you drag them.

The sketch below shows some jury rudders which have been used on small boats.

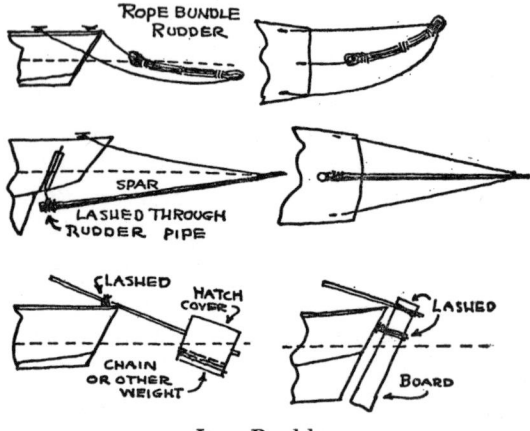

Jury Rudders

It is quite possible to steer by the jib, setting it so that the boat stays on an approximate course. Corrections to this course are then made by shifting live ballast to change the relations of the center of effort and center of lateral resistance and produce a lee or weather helm. Careful adjustment of the centerboard, jib and appropriate ballasting will often result in steady courses, sans rudder, on or off the wind. Before the wind, these measures are not so effective. However, if you can fly all your canvas forward of the mast (like a jib and spinnaker) steering is not difficult if you carefully adjust thwartship and for-and-aft trim. When my son was ten and master of his own 11-foot sailing dinghy he used to sail rudderless through the fleet at Lloyd's Harbor every week end at absolutely no peril to the fleet. He was an expert at shifting his weight and dipping a foot or hand into the water at the appropriate moment to make good his course. He claimed it was easier than finding the rudder in the forepeak of our cruiser and shipping the darn thing! And Bob has big feet too—

STRANDING

In spite of reasonable care in navigating, there are times when you find yourself in thin water and the danger of stranding suddenly looms. Stranding on soft bottom in a lake or on a rising tide is seldom more than annoying. Stranding on a falling tide can be dangerous, especially for the keelboat. Striking a ledge or boulder hard, or stranding on rock under certain sea conditions, can mean disaster.

Let us consider the problem from the viewpoint of the owner of a centerboard boat first. His boat is fairly flat. On mud she will be borne by a considerable area of underbody and do little damage to the hull. It is unlikely that, should she have struck on a falling tide, she will capsize as the water leaves her high and dry.

If the tide is rising, she will soon float off without help. If the tide is falling or there is no tide, she will need your help.

The simplest and quickest thing to do is to get a few passengers overboard, (since the water is shallow) and shove the boat backward along the path by which she slid onto bottom. You *know* that there is deep water in that direction. The mere unburdening of several hundred pounds of live weight will bring the boat up and afloat. Since most boats are deepest at about the heel of the rudder, it will be here that she probably will be "bound." If the boat is balky about coming off bottom, rock it from side to side so that the skeg and keel make a "wallow" in which

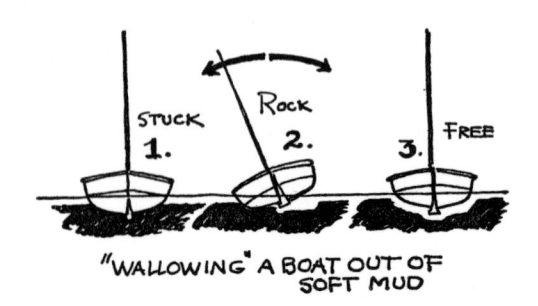

"WALLOWING" A BOAT OUT OF SOFT MUD

these parts can slide. Be sure that the centerboard is all the way up. Unship the rudder if it is deeper than the keel. Unless the wind is favorable, douse all sail. Shift the live weight remaining on board toward the bow or stern as required.

The best and safest way to push is with your back. Get set against the boat with your legs bent, straighten your legs and lift at the same time if necessary. Pushing, with the tension all on your arms or chest, can cause serious strain.

If the boat fails to come off bottom, try walking a halyard off the beam on which the water is shallowest and heaving down the mast. The boat will roll on her bilges and possibly skitter off into slightly deeper water. If the wind is right, the same thing can sometimes be accomplished by sheeting all sails in flat so that the boat heels sharply. Natu-

For Better or for Worse

rally, the deepest water should be to leeward since it is in that direction that the boat will slide—if slide it does.

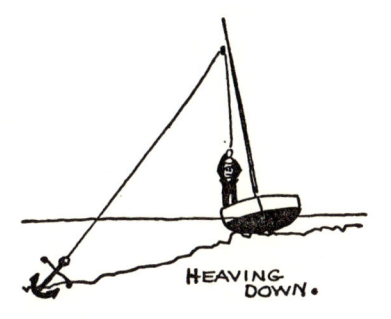

HEAVING DOWN.

If the boat must be taken off the shoal by the beam because of obstacles ahead or astern, a parbuckle will often prove effective. This is simply a line, its end hitched to the base of the mast, led under and around the boat, over the deck and off to some form of power (See sketch below). Such power could be a motorboat, hauling from deep water, or a tackle made fast to an anchor or to a pile, wharf, or anchored boat.

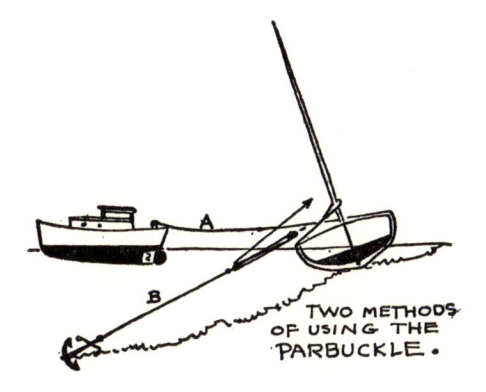

TWO METHODS OF USING THE PARBUCKLE.

The use of a spar or oar as a lever will increase power if a lift is required. A single lever will perform best if you can get its heel well under the forefoot or stern so that, as you lift, the boat will also be moved toward the direction of deepest water. Twin levers applied from opposite sides against the keel or the turn of the bilge will exert a powerful lift which can be converted into a shove deep-waterwards as you lift.

TWO METHODS OF USING A LEVER.

In a stubborn case, carry an anchor as far from the boat as possible, set it and lead a cable from it to the boat. At the boat end attach a tackle (which could be a backstay tackle temporarily requisitioned) or lead the cable to a winch. Rig this tackle so that you pull from *off* the boat and in the direction you want the boat to move. You thus not only use the greatest power of the tackle but relieve the boat by your own weight as well.

If none of these means moves the boat off the shoal, there is nothing left to do but lighten her as much as possible. Send *everybody* overside, or into the dinghy if you have one. Pump the boat dry. Put overside all heavy gear, anchors, ballast, spars, etc.

In thick harbor ooze, it is, of course, impossible to go overside. In this case, you can perhaps wallow the boat by rocking while remaining on board. If favorable, use the wind to drive you backwards over the route by which you came to grief. Consider the use of the spinnaker pole or the main boom as a setting pole. Lash a bucket, pan or flat

For Better or for Worse

board to the outboard end and, using your back muscles, exert all possible power. As you shove, try to rock the boat, or jump so that she hobby-horses, and have the crew assist in this. I once backed myself off an oozy mussel shoal by inserting the spinnaker pole under the forefoot as a lever and applying the power from the boat, which did not work at all until I led a line from the lever aft to where I could apply the power and still have my weight over the stern where it was needed instead of directly over the fulcrum of the lever itself.

Last summer a sloop hung up on a ledge which we call The Keg, off Ragged Island. Quick as a flash, since the tide was falling, the skipper hauled his dinghy close under the stern, lashed it short and piled his crew of three far aft in the dinghy. The dinghy's bow raised just enough to lift the stern of his sloop clear and he sailed serenely on. Ingenuity, which will solve most stranding situations, plus speed, which is necessary on an ebbing tide, saved a lovely little boat from wrecking and her passengers from perhaps real danger.

However, the centerboarder has very little excuse for stranding. The centerboarder itself is a reliable indicator of shoaling water. If it "pops," or suddenly rises in the trunk, it is dragging bottom; danger. Put about at once and head for deep water which, obviously, is where you were before you hit.

The stranded keelboat presents some special problems. She will strand in deeper water than the centerboarder, water perhaps so deep that you cannot wade around her to free her. She is also very heavy and cannot be shoved around with as much ease as the shallow draft boat. Your first defense is, again, to lighten the boat if possible. Get your people into the dinghy or send all the swimmers into the water. Rocking and heeling down with flattened sheets will often quickly free her since, unlike the centerboarder, she has probably hung up at only one point on the deep keel rather than on a broad area of the hull. Usually the keelboat is best backed off because of the common sloping forefoot.

Even a slight heel on a keelboat will greatly reduce her draft and therefore heaving down or the use of a parbuckle is of particular importance to the keelboat skipper unfortunate enough to ground. Because of the fairly deep water surrounding her, a power rescue boat can get quite close—close enough at least to heave a line—and outside aid is therefore open to you. If you have a dinghy, you can carry out a storm anchor and from it rig a tackle to the masthead. The boat can be heeled almost to filling in this way. There is no reason why you could not douse sail, top the boom and swing it broad off and, while a man hangs from the outboard end of the boom, shove the boat off with the spinnaker pole.

If you strand in any kind of a boat on a falling tide and cannot get off, there is no recourse but to make the boat ready for her day aground. Using anything at hand, prop the boat in such a position that she does not fall over, possibly against rocks and so become stove. The shallow boat won't turn over. Get buckets under her bilges, props under her guard rail or a line from mast to a distant anchor rigged at once. If there is a sea running, or likely to run, protect

For Better or for Worse

the hull at danger points by cushions, life preservers, floor boards or pads of sea weed. When the tide goes fully out, you will probably be on dry land. This is the time to stake out the best channel to deep water and, if necessary, to dig a channel in the mud or sand to it. Beyond that you might as well go clamming.

The keelboat which must hang up for a tide is liable to topple over. Get the scupper holes plugged at once so that she does not fill via them. Then see to propping her up so that she will remain reasonably upright. Shifting ballast will help here as will rigging guys from the mast to anchors or surrounding rocks. Keep off the boat unless she is braced in position beyond possibility of shifting. When the hull is exposed, make an inspection for underwater damage.

In general mistrust casual single-stick props and braces. As the boat settles these often are either relieved of strain or given too much strain. If at all possible construct a horse, on the order of the one shown in the sketch below, and shove it under the side toward which the boat will

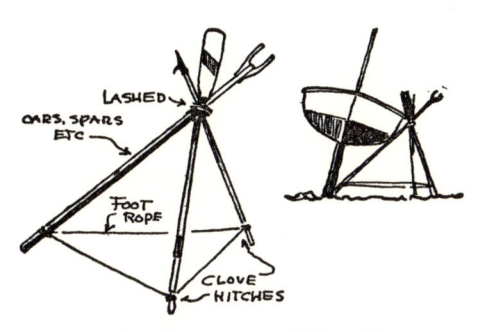

An Emergency "Horse"

lean. Such a rig is a solid unit and does not depend upon a compression strain to keep it in place. The keelboat will usually settle by the head as the tide leaves her, so arrange props to allow for this. Needless to say, if it becomes apparent that the boat will assume a sharp heel or pitch as she settles, put out all fires and carefully plug vents to tanks so that gas does not spill into the bilges.

If, in spite of all that you can do, the boat takes an acute angle of heel, prepare her for becoming waterborne by stopping scupper holes and battening down all hatches. It is possible that the rising tide may flood her before she lifts unless you exercise extreme care in this matter.

In any stranding you are morally bound by the unwritten law of the sea that human life is more valuable than a vessel or its cargo. Your first duty, if your people are in danger, is to them. A stranding in a heavy sea can be dangerous. Do not hesitate to make distress signals and do all in your power to save your passengers. It takes calm and measured judgment in a moment of disaster and confusion to recognize correctly real danger from mere inconvenience. But if the boat has been irreparably stove, or lies in danger of capsizing as the tide drops, or heavy weather is in the offing, think first of human life. You can never regret such a course.

LEAKS

If, by reason of stranding or collision with debris or another boat, you spring a leak that threatens safety, get after it at once. The first defense is to man the pump; the second, to locate and correct the leak, and as a precaution, get into port immediately. If possible, sail on the tack which will bring the leak nearest the surface of the water where lessened pressure will sometimes slow the leak rate a great deal.

In your bosun's stores should be a few strands of cotton, a putty knife or caulking iron, some patching canvas, nails, etc. I have carried such a kit over many thousand watery miles and needed it only once to repair a sudden leak in the centerboard case. Lacking such supplies you can stop a leak with rope yarns, cloth torn from clothing, chewing gum, wooden slivers, beeswax, paraffin or plain mud. Anything that will stop the leak will serve.

A real hole punched into the planking should be patched from the outside if possible. Get a canvas patch over the hole and batten down the edges with thin strips of wood. If you must patch such a rupture from the inside, plug the hole with a bundle of clothing or a wad of caulking cotton and jam a short board over it. Nail this board in well (because the pressure will be *in* and strong) or prop or wedge it against surrounding framing members.

Upon discovery of a sudden leak, always suspect through-the-hull connections. The scupper pipes of self-bailing cockpits, usually of lead, sometimes "rot" away in the vicinity of the outboard end and cause a leak. Knock such a scupper pipe out and insert a pine plug or wad of cloth. If the break is inside, cut the pipe off and peen the end over. Rubber hose connections, such as might lead from the built-in bilge pump and the pin of the centerboard, should be inspected frequently.

Leaks are alarming, of course. But they seldom mean immediate sinking unless planking has actually been ripped off. Find the cause, estimate the rate of leak, and usually a forecastle cure plus pumping will give you ample time to run to the safety of a shipyard or beach.

One of the worst leaks I ever had proved to be nothing but a joke. I was all ready to have the boat hauled but the first thing the boatyard owner did was to taste the water. "Fresh water!" he grunted, "Git yourself a new water tank." Many leaks are no more serious than that.

COLLISION

The cure for collision, like taking vitamins, is prevention.

Except in heavy fog, small boats have no reason to fear collision. Know the rules of the road and abide by them. Do not take it for granted that the skipper of the other boat knows the rules or your or his own rights. In thick weather make the proper signals and at night carry the proper lights. Under all conditions depend upon the lookout.

This personage is in all probability no one but yourself. Nevertheless, when your eyes and energies must be busy with other things, do not hesitate to delegate lookout duty to one of your crew. The duty of lookout is to *report* everything observed, not to interpret it. Interpretation is a matter for the skipper. However, you may suggest that you be told of any change in bearing of an approaching boat or request the lookout to make special reports about an object or boat already reported.

Should you be so unfortunate as to collide with another boat, your first concern should be for human life on your own and the other boat. Abandon ship without hesitation if it seems that sinking is inevitable. If possible, break out life preservers, throw buoyant cushions, boards, spars, etc., into the water as rafts and get clear of the boat. Naturally, since a light unballasted boat or a keelboat fitted with air chambers, will not sink, stay with such a boat. Confusion and lack of leadership too often convert a harmless enough collision situation into a major tragedy. Be prepared to take over responsibility—lives first, then the ship.

Since there is damage, there is blame. As soon as possible get a clear-cut picture of the situation immediately before the collision and reduce it to writing, requesting witnesses to give you their statements as well. Should the matter ever come to law, you will have prime evidence not subject to question because of lapsed memories, to assist the courts in fixing responsibility.

There are comparatively few cases of small sailboat collisions on record. It is usually possible to veer off quickly from a potentially dangerous situation and sailing boats do not often sail so fast that serious damage results when two happen to "bump." The greatest danger is from power boats and, in fog, commercial vessels. It is the show-off and the careless speedboat operator who are the chief offenders. Wave such stupid individuals off (with appropriate gestures!) and report them, by boat name and number, to the local harbor master or the Coast Guard. You will be doing yourself and the entire sport a real service. We operate our little boats without formal license only because our record over the years has been excellent. Law comes when we ourselves permit the situation to get out of hand. The great majority of boatowners are sane careful people and do not need government regulation. But, like the road hog and the drunken driver, a few individuals could bring down regulations upon us all because of their antics.

If you've ever been at the Yale-Harvard boat races in New London, you'll know what I mean. Of the dozen near collisions I've had afloat, they all occurred in that yacht-jammed few miles of river.

BROKEN GEAR

Failure of rigging, spars and gear under way may occur on even the best maintained boats.

Broken spars are the almost certain result of an accidental jibe in a strong wind. If the mast breaks there is nothing that can be done about repairing it afloat. Use the stub or the main boom and fly from it whatever sail or part of a sail that fits best. Under such a jury rig you can probably make some leeward port or haven. With what material comes to hand, brace such a rig securely. If the heel is rup-

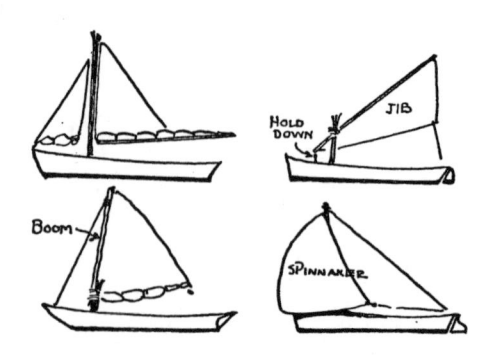

Jury Sail Rigs after Dismasting

tured or the step broken, set the mast on a cushion, lash it securely to surrounding frame members and pack ballast around it. The heel *must* rest upon the keel or some heavy frame member or it will spring planking and cause real trouble.

A broken boom (which is the most common break in jibing accidents) can be "fished" by lashing other spars, oars, boat hook, etc., alongside of the break. Always try to rig a tackle so that the broken ends are held together. Two methods of emergency fishing are shown below.

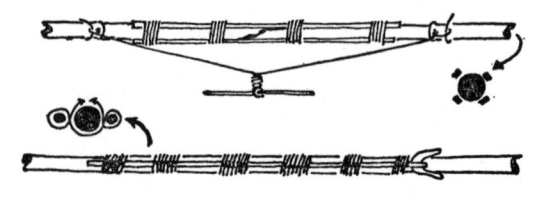

To "Fish" Broken Spars

Never carry full sail on fished spars. Reef the mainsail if the boom is broken. Change the mainsheet lead so that its strain comes forward of the break if possible. If a boom breaks close to the gooseneck, reverse it and make a rope lashing in place of the gooseneck. It is quite possible to rig the spinnaker in place of the mainsail and do a fair job of reaching.

The failure of wire rigging and turnbuckles while under the press of sails often results in the loss of the mast. Make at least weekly checks of your standing rigging. If it becomes rusted, it is weak and needs to be replaced. A broken shroud or stay can be temporarily patched by casting off the turnbuckle and joining the two ends of the wire shroud by bowlines and then bowsing down the turnbuckle end with rope. Such a lanyard arrangement can be used to replace a ruptured turnbuckle as well (see below). Set it up while luffing or when the broken shroud is to leeward and free

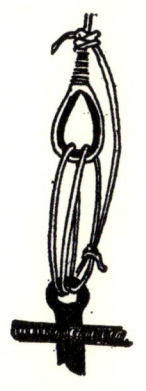

Emergency Replacement for a Broken Turnbuckle

of strain. If a shroud should part at a place which you cannot reach, douse the jib and lead the headstay to the chainplate. Shrouds are more important to staying the mast than headstays.

You can at least see the effects of wear and age on running rigging. If the outside rope yarns are worn to the breaking point, or fly apart as you untwist the rope, replace that line. It is usually possible to reverse a halyard or sheet so that different parts of it pass over the sheaves and through blocks, the greatest points of wear. If the line actually parts, you can gain some length by temporarily rerigging with one less part to a tackle. For a permanent job, put in a long splice, which will pass through a block. The long splice is made as follows (See also the sketch below).

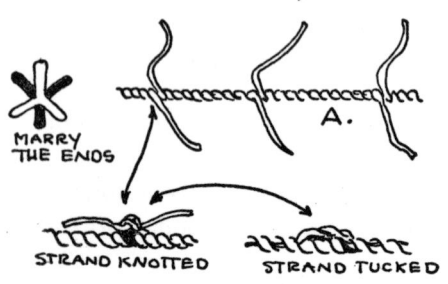

MARRY THE ENDS   A.   STRAND KNOTTED   STRAND TUCKED

The Long Splice

Unlay about 8 times the circumference of each rope end and "marry" the ends exactly as you do for the short splice. Now, unlay any strand carefully and lay in its place the matching strand from the opposite rope. Repeat with *two* strands but in the opposite direction from the first. The splice will now appear as in A. Turn an overhand knot at each set of strands, cut the strands short, tuck each once *with the lay,* halve the strand and tuck again. Roll this underfoot or pound into shape with a wooden billet so that it takes the same diameter as the original rope.

One of the most annoying things possible is to have the bitter end of a halyard go aloft. The best way to retrieve it is to go aloft and fetch it down. If you can't—and I know that I can't!—try to reach it with the spinnaker pole to which you have bent a temporary wire hook. Give consideration, too, to the possibilities of laying alongside a high wharf, or a dock with a building on it, or another boat which is equipped with rattled shrouds or a bosun's chair and tackle. The boat can be easily heeled or pulled toward you. Should this happen while at sea, reef the mainsail and hoist it by the jib or spinnaker halyard. Possibly you can throw a line over the spreaders and get the sail up at least that far. If the topping lift is fast at the after end of the boom and belays at the foot of the mast, it makes a perfect emergency main halyard.

Most of this "trouble," like the trouble of married life, is preventable. It depends a good deal on how you keep your part of the contract, "for better or for worse, until death do us part."

Sailing is pure unadulterated joy. The only thing that can ruin it is worry—worry about the condition of the boat and its gear, worry about your ability to navigate and maneuver, worry about meeting emergencies which might arise. The only way to dispel worry is to maintain your boat in top condition and prepare yourself for meeting any situation by study and experience.

A good deal of your success in sailing and making it a lasting hobby depends upon the start you make. I trust that this book has assisted you in making the start.

But your real start, the one which will personify and dramatize all that I have written, will be when you take tiller and sheet in hand and go sailing over the blue. In that, your first voyage, and all that will follow, I wish you red skies and fair winds, always.

Index

Accidents
  Broken gear, 257
  Capsizing, 243
  Collision, 256
  Leaks, 254
  Loss of rudder, 246
  Man overboard, 237
  Stranding, 247
Anchor-s
  Action of, 232
  Emergency sea, 185
  Permanent, 230
  Rules for scope, 185
  Sea, 183
  To sail from, 233
  To sail to, 232
  Trip for, 233
  Use of in docking, 236
Anchorage-s
  Cost of, 21
  Public, 21
  Sailing to, 229
Anchoring
  Discussed, 185, 229
  Under sail, 232
Areas of drive, in sails, 153

Backstay-s
  In use before the wind, 116
  In use when reaching, 111
  In use when tacking, 105
Bailing, boats, 244
Balance of a boat, 98
Ballast
  Disposal to correct helm, 166
  In heavy sea, 182
  In light airs, 190
  To balance sails, 158
  Where to place, 104, 116
Battens, 142
Bearing, navigational, 211
Before the wind, 115
  Danger of broaching to, 120
  Danger of goosewinging, 128
  Danger of jibing, 119
  Danger of rolling, 123
  Discussed, 115
  In storm, 173
  Position defined, 87
  Position of sails, 115, 118
  The intentional jibe, 127
Belaying to a cleat, 71
Bell, fog, 223
Bermuda rig, 17
Boat-s
  Defined, 27
  To bail, 244
Boatyard-s
  Normal practices, 22
  Sample bill, 23
Boat Owner's Sheet Anchor, 19
Boom
  How to rig, 72
  Jib boom, 73
  To fish, 258
Bosun stores, 63, 254
Broaching to, 121
Budgets for boats, 21
Buoyage system, described, 203

Capsizing, 105, 243
Catboat-s, 14

Index

Cat rigs, 27
Centerboard-s
  Handling of, 95, 108
  Pennants, 63
  Positions of, 90, 110, 116, 123
  Vs. keel, 14
Center of Effort, discussed, 158, 176
Center of Lateral Resistance, 159
Charts
  Discussed 201
  Tide and Current charts, 209
  Where to buy, 201
Collision, 256
Coming about, 101
Commissioning the boat, 56, 133
Compass course, 215
Covers, for sails, 148
Current
  Allowing for, 215
  In light airs, 190
  Lee bowing in current, 218
  U.S. Gov't matter on, 209
  Vagaries of, 218
Cutter rig, 28

Danger bearing, 212
Dinghies, discussed, 231
Dismasting, 258
Docking, discussed, 226
Double sheets, for jibs, 144
Drogue, 183

Eddies, in sails, 153
Eddying, 92
Equipment
  For moving boats, 57
  Needed for boat, 20
  Recommended, 76

Fending off, 227, 234
Flexible rig, 138
Flying jibe, 128

Glossary of Sea Terms
  Nautical verbs, 53
  Of boat parts, 33
  Of direction, 51
  Of orders and action, 53
  Of position and maneuvers, 47
  Of rigging parts, 41
  Of sails, 45
Goosenecks, 73
Goosewinged, 128

Hauling, 21
Hawk-s, 92, 120
Headboards, 142
Heaving down, 249
Heaving to, 180
Heavy weather, discussed, 170
Heeling, of a boat, 168
Hitches
  Clove hitch, 66
  Round turn and two half hitches, 67
  Sheet bend, 67
Horn, fog, 223
"Horse," emergency, 253
Hull
  Care of, 133
  Punctured, 255
  Windage of, 168

Insurance, marine, 21
Intentional jibe, 128
International distress signals, 241
Intracoastal Waterways, 207
"Irons," in, 102

Jib-s
  As a hawk, 120
  Balloon jib, 188
  Genoa jib, 196, 188
  How to fold, 147
  In light airs, 189
  In reefing, 176
  Overlapping, 144

Index

Proper set of, 143, 156
Steering by, 246
"Wung out," 122
Jib-headed rig-s
  Derivation of, 17
  Efficiency of, 17
Jibing, 119

Ketch rig, 30
Knockdowns, 172
Knots, for sailors
  Bowline, 65
  Figure of eight, 65
  Square knot, 64

Landing under sail, 235
Launching, 58
Laying to, 180
Leaks, in boat, 254
"Lee bowing," 218
Lee helm
  Cure for, 158, 164
Leeway
  Allowance for, 218
  As a force, 84
  Causes of, 109
  Estimating, 218
  How to note, 109
Lighted buoys, 209
Light Lists, pamphlet, 207
Lights, navigation, 222
Lightning, in storm, 185
Lines, for docking, 234
Lines of position, in navigating, 210
Lookout, the, 256

Man overboard, 237
Maneuvering
  At docks, 234
  Discussed, 129, 226
  On various sailing positions, 111, 124
Marconi rig, 137

Mast-s
  How to step, 59
  Loss of, 259
  Rake of, 134
  To fish, 258
  To foot, 60
Mast hoops, 140
Mooring, discussed, 226
Mooring gear, 230
Mooring lines, 234

Nautical language, need for, 32
Navigation
  Aids to, 203, 207
  Charts for, 201
  Discussed, 199
  Elemental navigation, 210
  In current, 215
  Lights, 222
  Local knowledge in, 213
  Rules, 219
  U.S. Gov't books on, 203, 207

Off the Wind, see Reaching
Oil, on seas, 183
On the wind
  Jib-headed vs. gaff rig, 99
  Position defined, 88
  Position discussed, 94
  Position of sails, 99
  Tacking, 101
Organized yachting, 24
Outhauls, for clew, 74

Parallelogram of Forces, 82, 85
Parbuckle, use of, 249
Permanent backstay, see Backstay
Pitch-poling, 116
Pointing, see On the Wind
Port risk, 21

Reaching
  Parrying wind puffs, 114
  Position defined, 87

Reaching (Cont.)
 Position discussed, 108
 Tacking, 112
Racing rules, 222
Range-s, 211
Reefing
 How to, 173
 In heavy weather, 171
 Order of, 177
 Shaking out a reef, 179
 To cure helm, 123
 When to, 178
Replacement-s
 Of rigging, 23
 Of turnbuckle, 259
Roller reefing gear, 176
Rolling, 123
Rope, care of, 71
Rope, parts of a, 64
Rudders, jury, 246
Rules of the road, 219
Running rigging
 Adjusting sheets, 95
 Emergency repairs to, 260
 Halyards, 62
 Sheets, 63
 To identify, 62

Safety, of a boat luffing, 98
Sail plan, design of, 163
Sailboat-s
 As an investment, 17
 Best types of, 13
 Defined, 27
 Selection of, 18
 Types of, 13, 17
Sailing
 Art of, 238
 "By the lee," 120
 From a mooring, 231
 In heavy weather, 170
 In light airs, 188
 "In reverse," 228
 On the wind, 94

Phenomenon of, 79
Positions, 86
To a dock, 234
To a mooring, 229
Sail-s
 Areas, how to calculate, 162
 Balance of, 157
 Balancing to relieve helm, 123
 Battens for, 75
 Bending, 73, 139, 148
 Centers, how to calculate, 162
 Checking balance of, 160
 Efficient use of, 152
 Emergency, 258
 Furling of, 148
 Hoisting, 95, 141
 How to fold, 146, 196
 In storm, 177, 180
 Lashing to spars, 140
 Light airs, 188, 196
 Order of making and dousing, 146, 150
 Positions, when tacking, 101
 Set for sailing on wind, 99
 Spinnakers, 188
 Storage of, 150
Sail-O, a game, 131, 224
Schooner rig, 29
Sea Anchor, 183
"Settin' pole," 190, 250
Sheet bend, 67
Sheer legs, 60
"Shoot," 102, 227
Signals
 Distress, 241
 For help, 340
 In fog, 222-3
 On whistle, 221
Sloop-s
 Becomes a cat, 115
 Rigs of, 16, 28
Skin friction, 108, 134
Spinnaker
 How to douse, 195

Index

How to set, 191
Setting in stops, 194
To fold, 196
Splices
  Eye splice, 69
  Long splice, 260
  Short splice, 68
Spreaders, 135
Standing rigging
  Emergency repairs to, 259
  To identify, 61
  To set up, 61, 135
Star boats, 17
Steering
  Before the wind, 117-8, 120, 124
  By compass, 215
  By feel of wind, 130
  By jury rudder, 246
  By the luff, 99
  By wind direction, 99
  On a course, 214
  To correct roll, 110
  When to, 97
Stranding, 247
Swedestay, see Backstay
Symbols, used on charts, 202

Tack, 91
Tacking
  Causes and cures of faulty tacking, 102
  Danger in, 102
  Defined, 90
  Discussed, 101
  Downwind, 120
  The "shoot," 102, 227

Theory of sailing, discussed, 160
Thunderstorms, 184
Tide
  In light airs, 190
  U.S. Gov't pamphlet on, 209
  When anchoring, 233
  See also Current
Track, for sails, 73
Trim, of a boat, 167
Trip, anchor, 233
Turnbuckles, 135

Used boats, 19
U.S. Gov't publications, 203

"Wallowing" out of mud, 248
Water, limitation of, 15
Waves
  Effect of, 110
  In storm, 181
  Use of oil to quiet, 183
Weather helm, cure for, 158, 165
Whipping, a rope, 71
Whisker pole, 122
Wind
  Causes roll, 110
  Feel of in steering, 130
  In thunderstorms, 184
  Parrying, 171
  Relation to sailing positions, 87
  Too little, 188
  Too much, 170
  When docking, 234
Windage, discussed, 167

Yacht clubs, 24
Yawl rig, 30

Books That Live

THE NORTON IMPRINT ON A BOOK MEANS THAT IN THE PUBLISHER'S ESTIMATION IT IS A BOOK NOT FOR A SINGLE SEASON BUT FOR THE YEARS

W · W · NORTON & COMPANY · INC ·